BROKEN SHACKLES

Old Man Henson
From Slavery to Freedom

To Dick from
Dave & Mary
Christmas 2001

D1224192

BROKEN SHACKLES

*Old Man Henson
From Slavery to Freedom*

Edited by Peter Meyler

NATURAL HERITAGE BOOKS
TORONTO

Published by Natural Heritage/Natural History Inc.
P.O. Box 95, Station O, Toronto, Ontario M4A 2M8

Frontispiece: Engraving of Old Man Henson, who was called
"Charlie Chance" in his days of slavery. From *Broken Shackles* (1889).

Edited by Jane Gibson.
Design by Blanche Hamill, Norton Hamill Design
Printed and bound in Canada by Hignell Printing Limited

Canadian Cataloguing in Publication Data

Glenelg
Broken Shackles : Old Man Henson–from slavery to freedom

Includes bibliographical references and index.
ISBN 1-896219-57-8

1. Henson, Jim, b. ca. 1798. 2. Slavery–United States–History–19th century.
3. Fugitive slaves–Ontario–Owen Sound–Biography.
4. Blacks–Ontario–Owen Sound–Biography. I. Meyler, Peter. II. Title.

E450.G53 2001   973.7'115'092   C00-933254-5

Canada

THE CANADA COUNCIL | LE CONSEIL DES ARTS
FOR THE ARTS | DU CANADA
SINCE 1957 | DEPUIS 1957

We acknowledge the financial support of the Government of Canada through the
Book Publishing Industry Development Program (BPIDP) for our publishing
activities, the support received for our publishing program from the Canada
Council Block Grant Program and the assistance of the Association for the
Export of Canadian Books, Ottawa.

Dedicated to the pioneers of African descent who were early settlers in this area of present-day Grey County.

Contents

Acknowledgements   *ix*

Why Republish an Old Book?   *x*

Editor's Introduction   *xiii*

1.   A Letter from Home   3

2.   The Long, Long Ago   8

3.   Stars and Scars   13

4.   "The Missis"   16

5.   A New Master   23

6.   Josh   29

7.   The Picket   35

8.   The Ridgelys   38

9.   John Hall   41

10. Trade in Slaves   45

11. Big Bob   49

12. Amusements   56

13. In Search of a Wife   69

14. The Cruelty and Vices of Slavery   74

15. Sophy and her Baby   81

16. A Tragedy   85

17. Still in Search of a Wife   94

18.	Emily	98
19.	Corn Husking	101
20.	Wonderful Meetings	110
21.	A Camp Meeting	115
22.	Turning Over a New Leaf	124
23.	Visiting Virginia	127
24.	Sold Again	131
25.	A Wedding	134
26.	The Star of Freedom	138
27.	The Escape	142
28.	Over the River	151
29.	Stephen Girard	162
30.	Flight to New Jersey	166
31.	The Underground Railroad	170
32.	A Discussion on Freedom	174
33.	John Brown	180
34.	The Fugitive Slave Law	183
35.	A Second Declaration of Independence	186
36.	Off for Canada	188
	Epilogue	199
	Appendix *Old Durham Road Pioneer Cemetary Committee*	201
	Notes	205
	Selected Bibliography	212
	Illustration Credits	213
	Index	214
	About the Editor	221

Acknowledgements

Many people have given generously of their time and expertise to assist in the preparation of the *Broken Shackles* manuscript for a new edition. I am grateful to the executive of the Old Durham Road Pioneer Cemetery Committee and the members of the Book Committee who provided ongoing support and encouragement and much local background information. Part of the proceeds from book sales goes to help the work of the Old Durham Road Pioneer Cemetery Committee.

Many others provided either additional material, visuals or significant research, all of which enhanced this project: Mrs. Beatrice Tillman of Owen Sound; Wilma Morrison of the Norval Johnson Heritage Library; Sally Houston and Marion Byard of the Ontario Black History Society, Joan Hyslop of the County of Grey-Owen Sound Museum; Les MacKinnon of Priceville; Rebecca Snyder of Syracuse University, New York; P. James Kurapka of the Baltimore County History Society; Paula Niall of Owen Sound; Ruth Cathcart of Wiarton; Elizabeth Thompson of Toronto; Jennifer Holness and David Sutherland of Hungry Eyes / Film Food, Toronto; Girard College of Philadelphia; and Mother Bethel African Methodist Episcopal Church of Philadelphia.

Appreciation also goes to Jane Gibson and Barry Penhale, the publishers at Natural Heritage, for their dedication to the quality production of this important manuscript of yesteryear.

I also would like to thank my family for their ongoing support.

Peter Meyler
Orangeville, Ontario

Why Republish an Old Book

THE CULTURAL links of our society are strengthened as they are passed on to us by a tradition of an oral history—the stories shared by one generation with the next. Often this process can be enhanced to achieve a broader based permanence by retaining some of the stories in a book format, such as those found in *Broken Shackles*. This book, *Broken Shackles*, is a story of struggle, starvation, stamina, and savvy, balanced with dignity, devotion, diligence, and determination. It is a story of a loving family torn apart by greed and intolerance. It is a story of the willingness to persevere and to continue in the search for freedom and peace.

This story was written in 1888, was published in 1889 and has been long out of print. That is, until now. In the pivotal year of 2000, we were given a brief moment in time and space to reflect on the past and contemplate the future, and made the decision to encourage the re-publication of this chronicle of the past. *Broken Shackles* brings names, faces and places to the struggle for freedom, and challenges more boundaries than the 49th parallel.

We get a glimpse into the past, which reveals a people victimized by imperialism, racism, avarice and intolerance. These forces were directly responsible for the forced exodus of millions of black persons from Africa between 1440–1870. Government policy and an expanding economic regime determined to make a profit on the backs of those of a different colour helped to push freedom seekers into the area now known as Grey County as early as 1820–1830.

Black skin became the dividing line between people and is still a continuing element of inequality today. Global confusion arises when we learn the thoughts of the rich and powerful. In 1562, while commenting on the slave trade, Queen Elizabeth I expressed the hope that the Negroes would not be carried off without their free consent, which "would be detestable and call down the vengeance of Heaven upon its undertakers."[1] When the Queen of a slave trading nation was this naive and seemingly ignorant of the realities of the slave trade, it is little wonder the general level of understanding about the problems created by slavery was appalling, and that this lack of awareness contributed to hatred and to the institutionalization of racism.

Here and now we take a stand that this behaviour is not acceptable, and challenge all citizens to examine their own values and decide if their vision of history needs a new window, through which a more inclusive view of history can be obtained.

We, as citizen volunteers of the Old Durham Road Pioneer Cemetery Committee, have tackled the reclamation of a desecrated local black pioneer cemetery and the destruction of the memories of the earliest non-native settlers to the southern Georgian Bay region. Those pioneers need our help now. We accepted their help without any acknowledgment; they opened up this rugged territory with axe, oxen and sweat. They built the first bridges, dams, mills, roads, schools, churches and houses, and filled the first non-native cemeteries.

We acknowledge their gift to us, and hope that in some small way the republishing of this important fact based book will help others see that history is the daily struggle of all people.

Old Durham Road Pioneer
Cemetery Committee

Editor's Introduction

I FIRST HEARD of *Broken Shackles* while doing research for a book about Richard Pierpoint, one of Ontario's earliest African settlers. Several people connected to Ontario's oldest African Canadian communities, particularly in Collingwood and in Niagara Falls, mentioned the book to me. However, *Broken Shackles'* existence seemed almost mythical, the Holy Grail of Ontario's black history. A number of people had heard of the book, but few had actually seen a copy, even though some of the original 1889 editions have survived. A copy can be accessed through the rare books section of your local library. This book is of great importance to the black community because it is one of the few books that actually documents their role in 19th century Ontario. And even more importantly, it tells their story from the perspective of a person of African descent, a resident of Owen Sound, Ontario, known as "Old Man" Henson.

Henson was a great storyteller and his imagery brings to life the realities of slavery in Maryland, refuge in Pennsylvania and New Jersey, and freedom in Canada. As you read *Broken Shackles*, you can imagine sitting on the grounds of Sheldon Place, the estate home of one of Owen Sound's prominent families, the Frosts. On a warm summer evening fireflies flit through the twilight. Just south of the house, you can see a row of cabins that are home to some of the town's African community. The water that gives the town its name glimmers in the background. Cool air from the distant harbour drifts through the valleys dispersing the heat of day.

Laughter can be heard as "Old Man" Henson regales his listeners, both black and white, with the stories of his long life. The spark of life shines through Henson's stories as he describes the horrors of slavery and his goal to escape its dreadful hold. The tales of his family, friends and enemies both amuse and shock his listeners.

John Frost, who grew up at Sheldon Place and later returned to live in Owen Sound, recorded Henson's oral history. He had to rely on phonetics to attempt to spell names of unfamiliar people and places, hence the names mentioned in *Broken Shackles* may not always agree with those in the historical records. In some cases, we have been able to correct the names published in the 1889 book, through research into historical records. An endnote is referenced whenever such a change has occurred.

Broken Shackles was not written as a history book in the strictest sense, and that is one of its strengths. It is the personal and social chronicle of "Old Man" Henson, a collection of anecdotes, some of them told more than 80 years after the events described, all set in an historical context. The stories which record one man's observations of life's struggles and triumphs are as relevant today as they were over 100 years ago.

JOHN FROST AND *BROKEN SHACKLES*

The lives of ordinary people are rarely recorded by historians. But in the mid-1800s, a prominent citizen of Owen Sound, Ontario listened to the stories of the residents of African descent. One man's stories showed that an ordinary man could lead a life that encompassed extraordinary events. This man went by the name of Jim Henson.

The anecdotes of Henson were recorded and in 1889 were published as the book *Broken Shackles*. The author of the book was listed as Glenelg, a pseudonym; his real name was John Frost, a member of one of the leading families in Owen Sound. Glenelg is the name of a nearby township; it is also a town near Baltimore, Maryland, and near the birthplace of Jim Henson, the book's subject. It is possible that Frost may have used the pen name so that he would not be harassed for his friendship with his black neighbours. At the time, there was a very strong bias against the role of Africans in society.

John Frost was the eldest of nine children born to Mary and John Frost, senior. His parents had moved the family from Bytown (now Ottawa) to Sydenham (now Owen Sound) in 1845. The elder Frost became a successful businessman as well as a magistrate. There he first opened a general store, then a brickyard, a quarry, a tannery and a flour mill. By 1868, he was also the mayor of Owen Sound.

The Frost family had at first lived on 2nd Avenue East, but by 1852 John Frost had the resources to build a house that echoed his position in the community. He walked through the woods along the escarpment that overlooked Georgian Bay and the port town that hugged the coast. There he found an exquisite site for his estate and, in February of that year, he received a crown land grant for the property. The Frosts planned the Georgian style, cut and coursed limestone mansion themselves. It was given the name of Sheldon Place. Additional dwellings, constructed later on the 51-acre estate, were home to some of the community's black residents.

John Jr. joined his parents in Sydenham in 1846, when he was eight years old. He attended Victoria College in Cobourg, graduating in 1862 after receiving the Webster prize for essay writing. On his return to the town now known as Owen Sound (a change it had undergone in 1851), he operated a store for ten years. He later went to law school and, after being called to the bar in 1876, started a practice in town.

John Frost Jr. of Owen Sound wrote *Broken Shackles* under the pseudonym of Glenelg. The book was originally published in 1889.

Sheldon Place, the family home built in Owen Sound by John Frost Sr. It was here that the young John Frost would have met and heard the stories told by the fugitive slaves who had made their way to Owen Sound. The sunroom was added in 1908.

John Frost had a penchant for public service. Before becoming a lawyer, he was a high school trustee for six years and an examiner for public school teachers in Grey County. He also served as a member of town council, as the deputy reeve and, following in his father's footsteps, as the mayor, once in 1892 and again in 1893. John also had an interest in the abolition movement. He was said to have met Harriet Beecher Stowe, the author of *Uncle Tom's Cabin*, during his travels.

It is likely that the young John Frost spent hours listening to the stories of black residents of the town. A thriving African community had existed in Sydenham since the early 1840s. Many members of this community would have been well known to the Frost family and it is said that the Frosts helped provide shelter for a number of African Americans.

The apple and pie seller, Mary Taylor, was a regular in the downtown market. John "Daddy" Hall was the town crier. Hall was a familiar sight, ringing his bell and calling out notices, with "God Save Our Gracious Queen." He was said to have been about 117 when he died in 1900. Another long time town resident, was, of course, "Old Man" Henson who could be seen chopping lumber or working on the town's roads.

As residents of a community, these people were not always well respected or acknowledged. The only mention of the black population in *A New History of Grey County* (published in 1972) describes their section of town in the mid 1880s as a place to avoid. The text reads:

> The walk uptown was hazardous, both its corduroy sections where water squirted up through the logs onto passersby, and the section through which it passed. Drunks lolled along the way. When it left 3rd Ave., at 13th St., going to 2nd Ave. the route passed a row of Negro shacks, dimly lighted by candles of a cloth stuck in oil.[1]

There is no mention of their contributions to or participation in the business or social life in Owen Sound.

Broken Shackles was John Frost's only book. He never married and died in Owen Sound on September 13, 1908.

Chapter I opens in Owen Sound, Ontario, with an ongoing conversation between Jim Henson and the author (Frost), thus setting the stage for the stories that are to follow. In the second chapter, the reader is taken to the slave state of Maryland in the late 1790s–early 1800s, to the birthplace of the young slave, his original name being Charley Chance. The same chapter takes the reader back further in time to the capture of Charley's grandmother in Africa. The succeeding chapters follow a more or less chronological sequence, documenting a series of events in the lives of slaves, the decision to escape, the impact of the Fugitive Slave Act, the role of the Underground Railroad and Henson's ultimate coming to Canada. The stories end back in Owen Sound, with Jim Henson now a well-known resident of that community.

ABOUT THIS EDITION

John Frost wrote with the social, religious, political and literary sensibilities of a well-to-do, middle-class Ontarian of the late 1880s. This value system is evident in *Broken Shackles*. The style of writing also reflects the Victorian time period in which Henson's stories were recorded. The overall style with its long sentences, the use of Biblical quotes and many references to poets popular at the time has not been altered with this new edition. As well, words that are not used today but that were common in Frost's time remain in the text. One example is the word "estray" which, according to the *American Heritage Dictionary*, when used in the context of slavery means a runaway.

Throughout the text, there are numerous references to people, places and events, especially those directly involved in the abolition of slavery and in the Underground Railroad. Wherever possible, annotations have been written and included in the Notes to inform today's reader.

In the original edition, the dialogue of every black person was written in misspelled English, presumably an attempt to imitate a type of patois. One example from the original text follows: "I heer'd my mass'r talk on dat subjec' yestidy, He said 'twuz a mighty skeerce commodity, an' dar wuz on'y one place in de hul worl' he know'd ob whar hit wuz shore to be found." In this new edition, this practice has not been followed. While the words used in conversation and in the presentation of lines from plantation songs have been spelled correctly, the integrity of the storyline has been maintained throughout.

One word that was in common use at the time, but one that will be offensive to many readers, is the word "nigger." It has been left in the conversational text, to recognize its denigrating intent in conversation and to maintain the authenticity of its usage at that time. In a few conversational instances, the word has been changed to "boy." Frost, however, throughout his narrative refrains from such usage. This republishing of the Jim Henson story (originally written in 1888) raised a number of issues regarding the use of the word "nigger" and the reference to "Sambo." Essentially, the belief that "by erasing traces of racism from our past, we are guilty of re-creating a storybook history that does not reflect the less-palatable, but more honest reality" prevailed. Furthermore, it was suggested that "the marginalization of the mistreatment that was endured by black Canadians in the past is a disservice to their memory and the fights they fought by virtue of the colour of their skin." (Rebecca Snyder, Syracuse University). Both terms remain in this new edition.

John Frost had to rely on phonetics to attempt to spell the names of unfamiliar people and places. As well, Henson may not have remembered correctly a particular name as he was recalling events that could have occurred up to more than 80 years ago. It is for this reason that the names mentioned in the original *Broken Shackles* may not always agree with those in the historical records. In some cases, I have been able to correct the names used in the 1889 book. One example of this is the name Crocksell that is actually spelled Croxall. Any such change is referenced by an endnote. Any other corrections that readers can identify would be gratefully received by the publisher and myself.

Peter Meyler
Orangeville, Ontario

BROKEN SHACKLES

*Old Man Henson
From Slavery to Freedom*

1

❧

A Letter from Home

As I passed up the main business street of the town[1] in which I live one sultry day in the month of August, in the year 1888, I noticed several men breaking stones for the roadway. Everything looked parched, brown and dusty. Not a breath of air was stirring. Pennons hung listlessly beside their topmasts on all the vessels at the neighbouring wharves. The dust itself lay motionless. Few people were to be seen about the streets. The butcher boys for once seemed willing to drive their carts slowly, and their attendant dogs followed panting heavily. Every chair about livery-stable doors and hotel fronts on the shady side of the streets held a listless occupant.

Of the men breaking stones, one was especially noticeable. He was broad-shouldered, square-built and heavy, but stood bowed low at his work, and was a coloured man, greatly advanced in years. The man was no other than my old friend Henson, the wonder of his acquaintances on account of his age, health, strength and intelligence. If you were to give him the world itself he could not straighten himself up. At work or walking his body makes with his lower limbs an angle of about forty-five degrees, the result not of age but of accident. When seated, however, he sits as straight as other men. He invariably uses the tools he works with in place of a cane, whether they happen to be the long slender-handled stone-hammer he wields in breaking stone on the street, or the bucksaw or axe, with which he cuts or splits wood for his customers, as he designates his employers—whatever that tool may happen to be, it serves him for a cane to aid him in his locomotion. Possessed of a goodly-shaped head, fairly regular features, except his lips, which are exceedingly heavy, fine physical proportions and manly countenance, he would, erect or bent, be noticeable among his fellow-labouring men anywhere. His mind is commensurate with his frame. He has a wonderful recollection of names, dates, and facts, is possessed of good reasoning powers, a full sonorous voice, and is an excellent talker. And yet he will, on being questioned, confess that he can neither read nor write. How old is he?, you ask. He is as old as this century. What, eighty-eight years of age and working for the corporation for wages breaking stones? Even so, and more. He was called "old man Henson" a quarter of a century ago, and is one of the oldest men in town, and still he is hearty and strong, and continues to work for a living, and lives well and comfortably.

Ample proof of good bodily preservation, and all the qualities physical and mental referred to, may be seen by a glance at the frontispiece. He is here seen resting from his labour on a warm summer day, when he had become thirsty, and had concluded to slake his thirst by eating a piece of watermelon. Grocer Ferguson, he had noticed, had some fine melons in his shop window, just across the street from the yard in which he was cutting wood. The grocer, however, refused to sell less than a whole melon.

"Well, I've got my expectations up for a watermelon," said Henson, "and as it appears to whole hog or none, I suppose I must buy a whole melon."

He did so, and seating himself on his wheelbarrow, commenced to partake of his highly prized refreshment, when a photographer happened to spy him and quickly set his camera for him in the yard.

"What you doing, Mr. Craig?"

"Oh, I only want to take your picture, Uncle. What have you got there?" said the photographer.

"A watermelon," said Henson; "and if I bust, you just hold Mr. Ferguson responsible."

Fortunately, neither the melon nor the grocer is responsible for any such *melon*choly event.

The old man claims, with a strongly probable showing, that his birth took place two years previous to the commencement of the present century, and entertains a lively expectation of living to the beginning of the next, and thus enjoy a privilege rarely vouchsafed to mortal man, that of seeing the light of three centuries; and, judging from his present appearance, the fulfilment of his expectation is quite possible, and even probable.

Here is a letter he brought me to read. Before looking at it, I said, "Henson, why in the world did you work on the street when it was so hot the other day?"

"Well, you see," said he, "I was just then earning a little money for Emancipation Day."

"Why, man," I said, "the first of August is past. It was, I think, the eighth day I saw you; the eighth day of the eighth month of the year eighteen hundred and eighty-eight."

"I knew that day was very warm," he said, "but landsakes, I didn't know 'twas so full of eights. Yes, sir, I'm aware the first is past, there is no doubt about that, but then it makes no difference as to the exact day. We know Great Britain freed her slaves in the West Indies, and the first day of August, 1834, was fixed as Emancipation Day and all the coloured people here love to keep up the anniversary; but, haw! haw! it's no matter about the particular day. When the first is Sunday we keep Monday. The Declaration of Independence wasn't signed on the fourth day of July, and yet the whole States keeps the glorious fourth. This year we wished to have an excursion on the Bay, and as we couldn't get a steamboat on the first, we took her on the tenth."

"Oh, that was the way of it," I replied, "all right; I hope you had a good time."

"Well, yes sir, I enjoyed myself pretty tolerable well, considering I'm only a stranger in a strange land, for you know I haven't a single relation this side of dear old Jersey."[2]

Medford, July 5, 1888

Dear Uncle James:

It is with the greatest pleasure I write informing you of the people of Medford.[3] Those that are living are well. Uncle Stephen gave us your address. I will tell you about the people of old Medford. Father is an old man now, not able to do anything much. Mother is living and is well, and both send their love to you. We live in the same place yet. A great many of the folks are dead and gone. Cousin Moses Worthington and wife are gone. Your daughters Comfort and Rose are both dead also. Uncle Isaac Shockley and his wife are dead also. Aunt Catherine, your wife, is still living. She was very low last winter; we thought she would have gone before now. Aunt Isabella is living and is well. Aunt Catherine is living with her. They live in a little village called Wrightsville. Please

5

write to them, for Aunt Catherine is nearly wild to hear from you. Her address is Cinnaminson[4] P.O., Burlington Co., N.J.

I do hope you are making preparations to make the blessed shore, so that if those who have seen you should never see you again in this world, they will see you on the other side of the River Jordan.

Please write soon, as we are anxious to hear from you, and we want you to come here and live with us. May God bless you is the desire of your niece,

Julia Truitt,

P.S.—Uncle John Truitt died last winter. His wife is dead also. I can't tell you how many of our people are gone.

J.T.

"Well, well, well, to be sure," said the old man; "silence broken after thirty years; wife still living, my two daughters dead, the old friends gone. Shall I be permitted to see the good old Jersey land, and my friends, and Kate before I die? I feel as if I must go and see them. But to do that I must have help—help from the Lord, and of His people. Yes, so many have crossed the River of Jordan. I've reason to bless the Lord sparing me so long on the earth. By and by I'll go meet them all on the shining shore."

> I'm going to ford the river of life,
> And see eternal day;
> I'm going to hear them heavenly bands,
> And feel the touch of old-time hands,
> That long have passed away.
> There's crowns of glory for all, I'm told,
> And lovely harps with strings of gold;
> And I know if there's peace beyond that sea,
> With rest for the weary, there's rest for me,
> Beyond that river,
> That river of life,
> That flows to the Jasper Sea.[5]

This letter was received just thirty-six years after he and his wife Kate parted on friendly terms at Lockport, New York, the one bound for her Jersey home, and the other for Canada. The fact that Henson can neither

6

read nor write would, of course, be no justification for this long separation and silence. The explanation lies rather in the immense distance they had put between themselves, the engrossing cares of obtaining a livelihood amid altered circumstances, and changes of location, which finally caused a loss of all trace of each other, until the time of writing the foregoing letter. The letter set him thinking and talking of his long-lost home, and of stirring incidents of former slave life, as given in the following pages.

2

☙

The Long, Long Ago

ENSON'S FATHER was named Sam, and his mother Peggy—Sam and Peggy Chance. "I suppose this will appear strange to you, child" said he, "that my name should now be Henson—old man Henson—when my parents' name was Chance, and that curious circumstance must be explained in time. My name was Charley Chance, and by this name I was known for a good many years of my life. I was born," he continued, "on old Dick Croxall's[1] plantation, Garrison Forest, near the City of Baltimore, in the very midst of slavery."

The question, "Do you know anything about your ancestry?" elicited the reply, "Certainly, I know something about my ancestry" and brought out the following feature of African life.

His mother's mother, Chandesia by name, was the daughter of Middobo, a chief of a tribe in Bagirmi,[2] a district of equatorial Africa. This Middobo's territory was located about midway between the River Niger and the headwaters of the Nile, on the River Chari.[3] One summer, long, long ago, an organized band of slavers[4] armed with swords, spears, daggers and flintlock guns, under the leadership of a Portuguese rascal named Agabeg, attacked in rapid succession the villages of this territory, for the purpose of stealing their ivory and kidnapping their inhabitants to sell as slaves.[5] The tribes of this territory were peaceable, unsuspecting, and up to that time, unaccustomed to the sound of a gun or the horrors of slave war. Generally surprised by the treachery of the murderous Agabeg, they fought at great disadvantage, and were slaughtered without mercy until overcome. Middobo fell in the first encounter by a thrust from a spear. His wife, daughter, and many of his people were taken prisoners. By fire, sword and ball, the manhunters secured their booty. By rings of iron and of brass, for neck and ankle, by chains and by ropes, the hapless victims were yoked and hampered to prevent escape. To everyone able to bear a burden was allotted a load of ivory tusks or some other commodity coveted and required by their cruel captors. Thus the murderous slave traders went from place to place for the space of four months, adding to their stores of ivory tusks and human merchandise, until enough of both were secured to form a caravan of sufficient importance to take to the seacoast. The result was that many villages had been destroyed and the country desolated throughout the area of the slave stealers' fiendish operations. Then, with a horde numbering about a thousand men, women and children, they started on their long march to the sea. On that march the same utter recklessness of human life was evinced by their cruel captors. Those sinking under the weight of their burdens, or weightier sorrows, were quickly despatched with a club and left where they fell. As many of the men had been killed or had made good their escape, women and children greatly predominated in that slave caravan.

Sorgho, cassava-tubers and bananas gathered by the elderly women, constituted their chief food. The march to the seacoast was slow, and was attended with an occasional kidnapping raid, for the purpose of supplying the places of those who had died or been killed on the way. Chandesia's mother, who had received more care than that usually given, was among those who succumbed to the fatigue of the journey. Both Chandesia and her mother had been stripped of their ornaments, worn as insignia of a chief's wife and daughter. At the end of two months, the captors and captives arrived at the coast on the Gulf of Guinea. Agabeg and his leading men here speedily disposed of their ivory tusks and other commodities to buyers, for shipment to distant markets. The human chattels were also quickly sold in round lots to slave dealers, destined for slave markets near and remote. Just then there lay in the harbour a large ship, completing a slave cargo for the American market. Nearly one-half of Agabeg's crowd was procured for this vessel. Chandesia with the rest was, by a villainous looking lot of men, quickly hustled on board ship, and thrust into the great crowd of human cattle already gathered, and bound for slave life in one of Great Britain's colonies.

After a stormy voyage, the unhappy victims, or rather those of them who survived the terrible ordeal of scanty fare, bad ventilation and confined quarters, at length reached the slave market. Many who started missed that market, because death intervened. Their bodies were cast over the side of the dhow[6] into the great deep. This was a hard fate, but not as hard as that experienced by some of those who survived, and touched the shores of Maryland, only to enter into a life of bondage under the Southern slave master.

The great slave ship, laden with *les noirs*, had come to England's America, for it was long before the time of the great war of American Independence. England's proud boast of freedom could not then be said or sung.

Shipping slaves

The captured child, Charley's grandmother, landed at Baltimore in a snowstorm, the first she ever saw and as she walked upon the snow from the wharf to the slave market, she wondered why it hurt her feet. She was quickly purchased. In the course of time, she married and had several children, two of whom were daughters and were named Peggy and Poll. The grandmother survived her husband a great many years. She was self-willed and haughty, and never lost sight of the fact that a proud chieftain's blood coursed through her veins. A presumed superiority and lofty bearing was ingrained in her very nature. She was constantly rebelling against the drudgery of female slave life. She would tell her master to his face that he had no business buying her, and that if she had not been carried off, she would then have been queen of her people, and would have been the possessor of plenty of elephants, and of more wealth by far than he had. Of course, all this was constantly getting her into trouble. Whippings without stint had been administered, but still her proud spirit had never really been broken, nor was she ever successfully reduced to the requisite degree of subserviency. Late in life she used to say she had received over two thousand lashes during her time. She used to say, too, that her master was one of the worst men in the world, and that he whipped with hickory sticks kept in the loft, where he always had an armful of them stowed away. Every Monday morning was whipping morning. This regularity in punishment, he claimed, kept the slaves in proper subjection. She declared that he used his pointer dogs better than his slaves. The former he would feed with wheat-bread, chicken and other fine food; while his slaves had to be content with hoe-cake, salt herrings, thick milk, and other coarse food. In middle life she saw her daughter Peggy married to Samuel Chance, both being slaves of Richard Croxall, then one of the leading public men of Maryland.

The colonies had greatly developed since the landing of the little slave girl, Peggy's mother, and the institution of slavery, then almost in its infancy, had made wonderful progress. Peace and prosperity had now given place to troublous times, and all eyes were turned to Boston, whose citizens had just rebelled against the motherland's taxation, and had pitched three hundred and forty-two chests of her tea into the waters of Boston harbour. Public meetings were being held in many places to discuss Great Britain's attitude toward her colonies. One of the active men in these discussions, in the colony of Maryland, was Richard Croxall, Sam and Peggy Chance's master. He was the proud owner of three thousand acres of land, a great herd of cattle, a fine stud of horses, a large flock of sheep, and one hundred and fifty slaves—men, women and children.[7] There was a beautiful double row of black walnut trees through a portion of his plantation, leading to the house, making an avenue of half a mile in length. Years before, two straight furrows had been run, into which Charley's mother, then a little slave girl, dropped the walnuts which had now grown to such beautiful trees.

The products of the plantation were tobacco, corn, rye, flax, hemp, wheat, and slaves. His slaves lived in cheap low buildings, called quarters. These consisted of a large one-story building and a number of little cabins around it. For floors they generally had the solid ground. In the main building there were board partitions, cutting it up into rooms, some of which had board floors. Two of these rooms were occupied by

Sam Chance, his wife, his wife's mother and his big family of little children. There was a huge fireplace with great cranes, upon which hung heavy pots. Two heavy pieces of pig-iron served for andirons. Here a pot of hominy was made every other day. The furniture, cooking utensils and dishes were of the simplest kind. The provision for comfort, even for those married, was of the poorest description. In this building were perhaps fifty beds. Some of these were bunks for the married slaves. The young men generally slept on benches, each with a blanket wrapped around him, with his feet pointing to the fire in winter, like an Indian in his wigwam. In summer, they generally preferred to sleep in the barn and outbuildings. There was a long dining hall, through which ran a table nearly its entire length, set with wooden plates and earthen dishes. An allowance of provisions was dealt out once a week—for a man, one peck of cornmeal, three pounds of pork, two dozen salt herrings and some vegetables; for women and children the proportions were less. The clothing was of the coarsest kind, and was carefully doled out. A hat, three shirts, two pairs of shoes and one suit of linen for summer, and one suit of cloth for winter, was the allowance for a year. Women got striped cotton or hemp ticking for their dresses in summer and linsey-woolsey in winter. The children received neither hats or shoes until they grew sufficiently large to work. Both boys and girls wore petticoats, and hence were in appearance hardly distinguishable. When a pair of trousers were given a boy, he knew his time had come for work. The women were employed in cooking, in spinning wool and hemp, and doing housework, but not often in fieldwork, except in harvest time. The men and half-grown boys and girls were employed in cultivating and saving the tobacco and other products of the great farm.

Here Charley Chance was born, and here he spent the first years of his life. Hatless and shoeless, he scampered around the quarters and great house, in the beautiful fields and amid the varied surroundings of the great Croxall plantation.

3

Stars and Scars

Two years before the Declaration of Independence, a meeting of the inhabitants of the town of Providence, after discussing the burning question of the great American Revolution, pronounced in favour of "prohibiting the importation of Negro slaves, and of setting free all Negroes born in the colony."

Jefferson, of Virginia, who subsequently drew up the Declaration of Independence, maintained one of the grievances of the country to be that King of England, George III, had vetoed all attempts to prohibit this nefarious traffic. At the great Virginia Convention, in 1774, the following resolution was passed:

After the first day of November next, we will neither ourselves import, nor purchase any slave or slaves imported by any other person, either from Africa, the West Indies, or any other place.

Shortly after, in the same year, at the first Congress held in Carpenter's Hall in Philadelphia, a similar, but more comprehensive, resolution was passed as to the importation of slaves, which concluded with: "We will neither be concerned in it ourselves, nor will we hire our vessels, nor sell our commodities or manufactures, to those who are concerned in it."

The celebrated Declaration of Independence sets out with the words: "We hold these truths to be self-evident, that all men are created equal, that they are endowed by their Creator with certain inalienable rights; that among these are life, liberty, and the pursuit of happiness." The phrase "all men" seems wide enough to include the African, but it was not so intended. There is no reference to slavery throughout this document. One was intended, but was objected to and erased. So the new nation of States was inaugurated with slavery as one of its institutions.

Never after was there such a favourable time to carry out the spirit of these resolutions. One short clause in the Declaration of Independence would have settled the question forever. An opportunity occurs but once. This opportunity was unfortunately let slip, and the new flag of stars and stripes was flung to the breeze as an emblem of national freedom, and yet it floated over hundreds of thousands of slaves, and was destined yet to float over them until increased to some millions in number. The Declaration of Independence was itself a bitter libel, and the floating emblem of liberty was itself cruel irony to the entire slave population:

> It spoke the nation's pride and shame
> In gaily bannered stripes and stars
> And to a wondering world of blame
> It flaunted Negro welts and scars.

Or, as put by Campbell, in his familiar lines:

> United States, your banner wears
> Two emblems—one of fame;
> Alas! The other that it bears,
> Reminds us of your shame.

> Your standard's constellation types
> White freedom by its stars;
> But what's the meaning of your stripes?
> They mean your Negroes' scars.[1]

Liberty poles, as if by magic, sprang up all over the land as symbols of national rejoicing and freedom; but to the slave the country was still the land of the lash, where tyranny remained the inalienable birthright of this race.

One of the four names which appear among the signatures for Maryland in that celebrated document which declares liberty to be the inalienable right of man, is that of Charles Carroll, who was the possessor of 1,000 slaves and 5,000 acres of land, and was well-known to Charley. He dressed like Captain Long and some others, in the old English style of knee-breeches, cocked hat, powdered wig and queue hanging down his back. He had a steward, who had several overseers under him to manage is estate. His slaves were required to attend the Roman Catholic Church built upon his plantation. It was his country seat, and here his family resided during the summer months only. It used to be said of him that he did not know his own slaves. When visiting his estate he generally drove a coach and four. He proudly, but inconsistently, boasted of being one of the signers of the Magna Charta of American freedom, and that he held, in his own right, one thousand slaves.

By permission of Louis XIV of France, given in 1688, a few slaves were imported into Lower Canada. Upper Canada, in 1793, when holding about four hundred slaves, passed an Act of Gradual Manumission, and, early in the present century, "Negro sale advertisements" were not uncommon in this Province. Among these is one by Governor Russell, in 1806, for the sale of Peggy, aged forty, a cook, for $150, and her son Jupiter, aged fifteen, for $200, with a promised discount for cash.

Massachusetts declared for Emancipation in 1780.

In the year 1800, when the United States began to recover from the effects of their terrible struggle for independence, the slavery question was revived. In Philadelphia, a measure favouring Abolition, introduced in the Assembly, failed to carry. The legislature of New York, the same year, passed an Emancipation Act, which recognized the right of slaves to freedom. This Act was the thin end of the wedge inserted into that national monument of iniquity which was hammered at by Abolitionists until, nearly seventy years after, it temporarily split the Union, and ultimately and forever destroyed the great institution of American slavery.

4

❧

"The Missis"

CHARLEY WAS still quite young when Richard Croxall died, and left him, with all the rest of his slaves, in care of his wife Catherine, the "Old Missis," as she was called.[1] After her husband's death there was a marked change in her bearing toward the slaves. She at once became uniformly kind, and at times even indulgent, to the slaves left in her charge. She would not go on with the cultivation of tobacco; and the tobacco-houses were, after this, used for other purposes. As she did not carry on business on as large a scale as the old master did, she had more help than she required, but instead of selling off her slaves, she hired them out generally by the year, or that part left of it, till the following Christmas. She required every slave to return home for Christmas week. The price for a year for men was $100, and for women $50. Great preparations were made at the mansion house for the return of the slaves for Christmas week. It was a reunion in plantation life, and was looked forward to with the greatest expectation. After a service of long and weary months, often of privation and cruelty, they came back to feast and rest. Brother and comrade met, and greeted brother and comrade, husband his wife, and lover his sweetheart. The "Missis" did everything she could to help the reunion; made presents and gave clothing, and hence it was a week of general rejoicing. The slaves had now learned to look upon her as a veritable queen. Christmas morning was ushered in by a band of slave singers, who sang at the quarters, and then in full force visited the great house, and made the morning air ring with their beautifully blending and rich musical voices, with banjo accompaniment, as they sang,

Hark ! the herald angels sing,
Glory to the new born King;
Peace on earth and mercy mild,
God and sinners reconciled

At which the door of the great house was thrown open, and the singers were invited in to partake of buns and hot coffee. This was greatly relished, more especially because they knew their "Missis" felt kindly towards them.

As Charley's father had long resided on this plantation and had been married many years, he was surrounded by a large number of relatives and numerous progeny. Let us take a peep into his home at the quarters on Christmas Day, when he was enjoying a Christmas dinner with his family for the first time in his own apartments. Like other slaves of the plantation, he had returned for Christmas week. The two small rooms which he occupied were whitewashed throughout, and had a low sleeping garret overhead. In one of these rooms the Chance family surrounded a long pine table, partaking of their Christmas dinner, which consisted of a huge turkey, a present from the "Missis," vegetables and other nice things prepared by Peggy. At one end, in front of the hot, well-stuffed turkey, sat Sam senior, a large, well-built, pleasant-speaking man. At the other end, presiding over the coffee pot, sat his wife, who was short, plump and tall across; sharp-featured, and had a pleasant face. Between them, on one side of the table, sat five children in a row, and on the other side, five children in a row. These were so arranged that the eldest was next to the father on the right and the next eldest was beside him on the left, and in the same order as to age they continued down to the youngest, who sat next to the mother, like steps of a stairway in a descending or ascending scale, according to the way you looked at them. The occasion bore marked evidence of being a festive one. The father lifted his hands, and in a strong, clear voice asked God to bless the Christmas feast and to give them thankful hearts for having such a kind "Missis." Twelve faces, all busy, and their owners looking contented and happy, made a sight not easily forgotten.

"You appear to be enjoying yourselves," said a visitor, who popped in to see Chance a moment to make some inquiries.

"Oh, yes, master, we're participating in the great bounteousness provided for his children by our..." "Put down that bone, Cornelius," interjected Peggy. "...Heavenly Father," concluded Sam.

"Give me a bun," said Fanny, and as she was at the small end of the human ladder and the plate of buns at the big end, it was passed down till it reached her.

"I'll take a fried cake, mammy," said Tom; and the plate bearing light, fresh doughnuts was passed up the living stairway, from the bottom to the top.

"You must have some trouble in getting all these children to bed," said the visitor.

"Not half so much as getting them up in the morning," said Peggy.

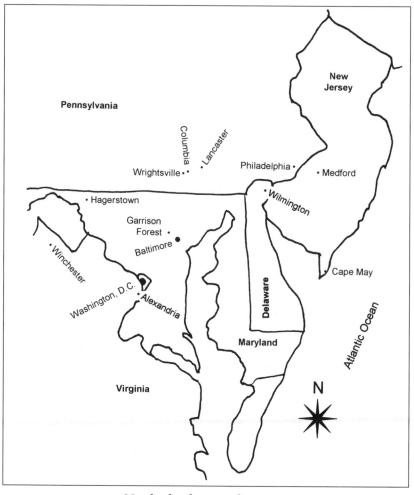

Maryland and surrounding states

"Stop you, Pete and Poll," shouted Helen, the eldest girl, "pulling that wishbone; it won't break without you drying it at the fireplace first."

A plate of gingerbread, cut in two-inch squares, passing down one side and up the other, lightening at every step in its passage, produced a temporary quiet, until Sam, who occupied a central position, made a terrible rattle that caused all eyes to turn toward him. He had taken a drumstick from Phil's plate and put it with his own and struck up a "bones" play. This was instantly stopped by the senior Sam, who had hitherto been so busy serving that he had scarcely noticed what was going on, and had only just commenced eating his dinner. Polly, who had got one of the wings, tickled Pete's nose with it, and he in turn encircled her neck with the turkey's neck, and called it her necklace.

"I never see such acting children in all my born life," said mother Peggy, as she poured out the third tin cup of coffee for Tom. Sally, a four-year-old, amused herself by balancing the Pope's nose on her own, when a poke from an adjoining elbow knocked it into her coffee, causing her to exclaim, "Now my toffee spilled; mammy, I want another cup, I does." Fanny, a two year old, produced a general titter by calling out for "more tuffin' and tater." Susy, the baby, contributed an occasional "ugh!" with great glee, the only word she could speak; and was only prevented by constant watchfulness on the part of her mother, from pulling the coffee pot over and scalding herself. The youngest but one of the boys, sitting near the middle of the left-hand row, had not joined in the pranks, but with unflagging appetite had been attending strictly to business, by helping himself to all the good things as they passed and repassed, and his name was Charley. A big dish of apples and a plate of chestnuts constituted the dessert, and now went the usual round to wind up the feast; and both apples and chestnuts disappeared with amazing rapidity. The appearance of the table had now become completely changed. It was demoralized. Disorder had taken the place of an orderly arrangement. The great turkey was now a graceless and very incomplete carcass, or pile of bones. Down the descending and up the ascending line were strewed turkey remains, potato-peelings, portions of dressing, bits of cabbage, kernels of hominy, and fragments of fried cake and gingerbread. The dishes, so recently filled with provisions, now empty, showed that scarcely two of them were alike, and that they were of commonest kind. A knife and a spoon were observable at each plate, but not always a fork.

The visitor had become interested, and had lingered to the close of the meal, talking of Christmas, and the "Missis," and good cheer. On rising to go, he said, "May you have many such a merry Christmas, Sam, with your family."

"The Lord's good to us all, and makes me feel with my children like a patriarch of old," said Sam.

The second summer after, one hot afternoon, the elder Chance, on taking a drink of cold spring water, while at work in the harvest field, fell and suddenly expired. As he was a Christian, and lived up to his light, sudden death was doubtless to him a sudden translation to the society of those he said he felt like here—the Patriarchs. The Sabbath following his death, his coffin was laid upon two poles and, with a single calla lily laid upon its lid by sorrowing Peggy, four strong men, followed by most of the slaves of the immediate neighbourhood, bore his body to its last resting place, in the slave burying ground on the Croxall plantation. That night, accompanied by the five dogs of the plantation, Charley returned to the grave, fell upon it, and found relief in crying aloud. Upon hearing him, one of the dogs, a hound, commenced to howl piteously. This started a mastiff, and soon the rest joined in a loud and mournful chorus, as if they, too mourned over the faithful slave in his grave.

Peggy fretted over the loss of her husband a great deal, but tried to conceal her sorrow from others. Attentive and painstaking, she had always looked after the interests of her children, as far as the duties imposed on her by her taskmaster would permit. After this they, however, seemed nearer and dearer to her than ever before.

"I reckon," said old man Henson, "I haven't told you yet about the Colonel. My old Missis was an aunt of President Buchanan. I remember seeing her uncle James Buchanan. He used to call my old Missis 'Kitty,' and he carried a gold-headed cane. He had a mighty bad temper, was palsied and seemed to hate black children. My Missis had a ten-acre field of currant bushes, just getting ripe, in which the old Colonel used to like to walk. On going into the garden near the house one day, he saw me and some other children among the bushes. At once we heard him call 'Kitty, Kitty, these niggers is here eating up the currants. I saw their woolly heads dodging among the currants bushes.' He threw his gold-headed cane at me and said 'Bring that here to me quick, you little black rascal.' But I was just then too busy eating currants. I knew very well if I brought it to him, it would be putting a stick in his hand to beat me with, and I knew I could run the fastest. So I felt safe. Then he said in a soft voice, 'Come to me, my little man, bring my cane, and I will tell you something.' I thought it wasn't necessary for me to know any more just then and I stayed quiet among the bushes. Then he got very vexed, and indulged in abusive language, and I indulged in the currants. I was young and still in petticoats, about five years of age, and the Colonel was about five and seventy years of age. The contest lasted perhaps fifteen minutes. Volley after volley of cuss words was fired among the bushes. To these we replied in silent glances. At last, the old Colonel, who had hobbled for his cane himself, retired, stamping it on the ground. The enemy, as soldiers say, was defeated, and we remained in possession of the field."

Charley's Master and Missis had no children, and when his Master died he left all the chattels to his wife, but he gave the plantation, subject to her life interest, to his two nephews, Dick Croxall and James Croxall. After the troubles of 1776, Dick went to England, and wrote back to his brother James that he might have his share, as he would never return to America, and he did not. This subsequently made James a very wealthy man.

The Missis, after a few years of careful management of the plantation, went the way of all the earth, and Dr. George Buchanan, who was her executor, proceeded to wind up the business of the plantation. At the end of a month, at which time it was understood by the whole country round that the will would be read, the chattels were advertised to be sold. Not one sentence of that will had, in the meantime, been made known to the public, and it was fully expected, both by the slave traders and the slaves themselves, that the sale, which they called the great "wandoo," (vendue), would include the slaves.

On the morning of the day named, the grain, stock, agricultural implements and household stuff were arranged for the sale. All the slaves were marshalled in front of the homestead, in families and in groups. The old people stood in a circle. Charley's mother was encircled by her eleven children, weeping bitterly, as all the mothers were, at the prospect of immediate separation. Hovering around were many slave traders, on the alert for bargains. Tubs of cider and vessels of peach brandy were conveniently placed about, but remained untouched by the slaves. The slave dealers, however, partook of copious draughts. Heedless of the sorrows of the assembled slaves, they indulged in coarse jests at their expense, and before the executor and his auctioneer had come to offer the chattels for sale, they had walked around and among the slaves, and had made personal inspections, with a view of making good selections and profitable purchases.

Suddenly the buzz of undertone conversation ceased, and the sobs were suppressed, as the executor mounted a table, and commenced to read the will, which to everybody's surprise, soon proclaimed every man and woman over thirty-five years of age free. A shout of delight and tremendous cheering stopped further reading for a time. The slave dealers were noticed coming together in a group, and falling back from the crowd of slaves, who for a long time kept indulging in shouting, leaping, handshaking and embracing, in a frenzy of delight. At length quiet was restored, and the executor proceeded to read the next clause, which stated that all slaves under thirty-five years should be absolutely free at that age. Then the scene of rejoicing just witnessed was again enacted, and during the excitement, the slave traders were seen slinking away. As soon as order could be restored, the executor went on reading the will, which further provided that Fanny and Susy, Peggy Chance's two youngest children, should be freed at once, and that all the slaves of which the testatrix died possessed, who were not freed, should go to her nephew James Croxall and other relatives. The will also provided that every man then made free should have $100, and every woman $50, with which to begin the world. The sale of the household goods and other personal property was then proceeded with by the auctioneer.

This freedom at once became the exciting topic of the neighbourhood. Some of the freed men and women were compelled to remain in the vicinity, and some, indeed, on the same plantation, on account of their children, whom they could not leave, wishing rather to impart to them such parental care as they could. These arranged a hiring, while others were divided and scattered.

Charley's brother Sam was willed to Dr. Buchanan by the old Missis, in payment of his services for managing and winding up her estate. Charley himself, fell with the great bulk of her slaves, to her nephew James Croxall.

5

A New Master

FIVE YEARS of Charley's boyhood were spent with James Croxall Sr., a nephew of the great Richard Croxall, to whom he had been bequeathed with the plantation and other property, by the will of his aunt, the "ole Missis," and thus he resided still at the old plantation. In passing the quarters one day, the new master who was a merchant at Baltimore, noticed Charley and some other boys playing and rolling on the ground.

"Mr. Ross," said he to his overseer, who had been overseer under the elder Croxall, "these boys are fit to work. Let Nellie make them some trousers and jackets, and put them at work pulling grass from the corn. If they don't work, whip them."

Soon after coming into the possession of this master, a curious event took place, in which Charley was the principal actor. The account of it may be designated a "Pig and Puppy Story."

James Croxall Sr. was a parishioner of Parson Brown. When the Parson came, James Sr. was always very attentive, and showed him around his farm. If there was anything of especial interest, he was sure to show it to Parson Brown. On his last visit, there was something of this character in the pigpen.

"They will be ready to wean next week," said he, "and if you would like one of them, I'll send you over one."

The Parson, on going home, announced the coming gift to his boys, who went to work and got a pen ready for his pigship. The boys asked the Parson a good many questions about the expected pig, so that the matter was in no way lost sight of until Charley came one day in the following week, with a linen bag on his shoulder and something alive within, a present from his master. The boys saw Charley coming, and telling their father, ran to meet him and commenced to ply him with questions. "How old is he?" "Is he heavy?" "Was he hard to catch?" and other boyish questions were asked, which Charley good-naturedly answered. The prisoner within, hearing the voices with out, moved about restlessly. One of the little fellows commenced to stroke him, saying "Poor piggy, piggy." The Parson had, in the meantime, come out, and all had now gone to the new-made pen. Charley carefully dumped him out, and immediately threw up his arms. One of the little boys shouted, "It's a little puppy!" and the other clapped his hands with delight, and said "Let me have him."

"What does that mean?" said Charley, with a most puzzled expression of countenance.

The pup growled, and the Parson alone remained silent. At length, after gazing a moment at the ugly, chunky little pup, the Parson, addressing himself to Charley, said: "I won't thank your master for doing this."

"He didn't do nothing," cried Charley. "That was a handsome white pig when I left home. Master put him in himself. Black puppy now," he added, in a sort of meditative voice.

The Parson's indignation was not so easily appeased, and he at once picked up the bag which had fallen to the ground at Charley's feet in the midst of his surprise, thrust the pup inside and said, "Take back the pup to your master, and tell him it is not needed."

The Parson's sons would gladly have kept the pup, but their father's anger rendered this impossible; so away went Charley full of wonder at what had occurred at the Parson's. On his road home, at about halfway, there stood a tavern at which Charley had rested and had a glass of water to drink on his way to the Parson's. So dropping the bag containing the pup just at the end of the steps of the bar room door, he went in to relieve his mind and tell the proprietor of the place, whom he knew, what had happened. The hotel-keeper came out with him and looked at the pup, and then both went inside to talk the matter over. While doing so, the hosteler, who was a waggish fellow, was busily engaged in opening the bag, taking out his pup and putting in the pig he had taken out when Charley had called earlier in the day. Attracted by the movement of the pig, it had occurred to him that it would be a good joke to play on Charley, although he knew nothing of his errand. The hotel-keeper had been let into the secret by the hosteler, and instead of getting any explanation from him, Charley's wonder was, if anything, on the increase. He soon returned to his charge, threw the bag over his shoulder, and started for home in a perplexed frame of mind. When he arrived there, his master noticed the bag on his shoulder, and as it appeared to have its occupant just as he had left with it in the forenoon, said to him: "Why have you brought the pig back?"

"Cause it isn't a pig at all," said he, in a half-crying tone, as he proceeded toward the dog kennel.

"It isn't a pig!" repeated his master, who now followed over to the dog kennel. "What do you mean?"

The string was soon untied, and Charley gave the bag a shake at the door of the dog kennel, saying : "I mean it ain't a pip-pip pig."

The bag flew up high in the air, and so would Charley's arms if they had not been well fastened to his shoulders.

"That beats the old fellow himself. It was a pig when I left home, a pup at Parson Brown's and now it's a pig again."

Charley looked on the pig in profound astonishment, until his master said: "Why would not the Parson accept the pig as a present?"

"He wouldn't. I mean he wouldn't have the puppy."

"What puppy?"

"This one, er-ah, the one I took to them."

"Didn't you take the pig to him I gave you?"

"Certain, I did, master. It was a white pig when I started, and it was a black pup when I got to Parson Brown. Doggone, this nigger don't understand it no how. It changes from a piggy to a puppy to a piggy as I never see before. That is the devil trick for sure."

Up to this point Croxall had been out of patience, and inclined to be cross, but at this last sally of Charley, attributing his mishap to satanic influence, he burst out into a loud haw! haw! haw! and turning away said "Go and put the pig in the pen."

"Pig?" said Charley, in a tone of inquiry.

"Yes, certainly; what else is it?"

"It's bewitched, master, sure," said Charley, as he caught it. When he got to the pigpen, he placed it between his knees and commenced to slap it, first on one side of the head and then on the other side, interjecting between slaps such exclamations as, "Yes, piggy here (slap), and puppy at Parson Brown's, piggy here (slap), puppy there, devil's pig here, and (slap) devil's puppy yonder."

"Charley," shouted his master, who noticed him linger, without knowing the reason, "you are wanted to hoe in the cornfield." This was just in time to save the poor pig's life, as Charley's anger burned furiously. Piggy was hastily thrust into the pen and was soon lost to view among the litter.

This master's wife and sister, about four years after the occurrence just related, wished Charley to become a waiter in the house. The former procured him a stylish velvet suit for that purpose, and then ushered him into the parlour to make his bow in them, for the purpose of getting Miss Croxall's approval of the outfit.

If one of the ladies let fall her handkerchief or a fan, it was Charley's duty to pick it up, and return it with a pleasant smile and graceful bow. He was, of course, not always so well-dressed, as he had rough work to do, as well as that of waiting on the ladies.

James Croxall Sr. managed the plantation pretty much on the same lines as his aunt, except that he had no conscientious scruples about the cultivation of tobacco, and used his slaves fairly well, without the indulgence which she was so fond of granting. The time for work was from sunrise to sunset, with the usual allowance for meals as on other plantations.

Five years after the death of old Missis, James Croxall Sr. died also. Then one-half of the great plantation was broken up. The land was sold in five-hundred-acre blocks to three different purchasers, who were George Rhynaker, Christopher Canahan and Charles Cockey,[1] all of whom were well know to Charley. Cornelius Howard was the senior James Croxall's executor, and was required to manage the estate until the testator's son, James Croxall, junior became twenty-one years of age.

The sheep, cattle and horses, and products of the farm were all sold, and the slaves that had not yet attained thirty-five years of age had now to be scattered. Some of them were sold, but the sale was only for the balance of the time until they became thirty-five, for at that age, no matter where they were, or under what circumstances placed, they were, by the terms of the will of the old Missis, to become instantly and absolutely free; terms which were, however, in some cases violated, as will be subsequently seen.

One of the master's last acts, while suffering from an attack of asthma, was an attack on Charley for carelessness. "Charley," said he, "why did you leave that wheelbarrow out in the sun to get warped? I told you to keep it in the shed; I shall give you a whipping when I get better." But neither the one nor the other of those events happened, as this master shortly after closed his earthly career. At his death, Charley was taken in charge by Cornelius Howard, Croxall's executor, who took him home and put him at work in his flour mill at Owing's Falls.[2] At this, the miller

Charley as waiter.

Jack Owens, rebelled, and declared, "He would never teach a nigger a trade, and take the bread out of a white man's mouth;" as if a black man had not as much right to earn a living and eat the fruit of his labour as a white man. Charley was still but a boy, and notwithstanding the miller's feeling of opposition to him, he was determined to learn the business. On the most trivial provocation the miller would scold, pull his ears, cuff or kick him according to the humour he happened to be in. If he found Charley closely watching anything he did, this was considered a sufficient excuse to indulge in the sort of abuse mentioned. He, however, needed assistance, and in time the boy learned the art of milling, from picking the millstones to making the finest bolted flour. With his head and face all powdered white with flour, the young miller was quite a sight at times. Although only about sixteen years of age, he could take three 56 pound weights in each hand and lift the whole from the floor.

It was now near the close of the War of 1812–14. And as his tormentor, Owens, was drafted into the American Army, the mill-slave boy thereafter had peace at the mill. On Owens' compulsory retirement, Mr. Howard secured a new miller and put him in charge. He was of Hibernian origin, sympathetic disposition and inclined to be superstitious. On learning of Charley's bad usage by the old miller, he at once attributed his cruelty to the fact that Owens was a Methodist, and declared that in the part of Ireland where he had lived, no Methodist would be allowed to give evidence in "coort." He evidently had a bad opinion of Methodists, but was kind to Charley.

6

❦

Josh

ONE OF the oldest boys in the group with whom Charley played in those early days was Josh, who was his first cousin. He had been given to Betsey Croxall, afterwards Mrs. John Wilmore,[1] and was a waiter in her house. He was called Josh for a short name, but his real name was Josiah, and no name was better known, both on account of the boy's outlandish pranks and the custom of his mother, then a little, dried-up woman who used to come out of her quarters in the evening and, putting her hand over her forehead to shield her eyes from the level rays of the setting sun, would send with her shrill voice far over the playground in a rising accent the call, "Josi-ah! Josi-ah! Josi-ah!" And before the echo had died away in the distance, Josh, in obedience, could be seen rapidly scampering away from his play to his mother.

Charley and Josh one day talked over a whipping that Joe Ross, Croxall's overseer, had given Charley's sister, and it was agreed that if he did it any more they would hit him on the head and bury him deep in the field. Strange to say, Ross was walking right behind them and heard all that was said, and told their parents about it. The boys were soundly punished by them; and that ended their scheme to knock the overseer on the head.

Once when slapped by his master, in the parlour, Josh turned and attempted to fight. His master said he would either subdue or kill him. Josh was then little and easily mastered, but nothing could break the buoyancy of his spirits or rid him of his fanciful notions.

Shortly after he had got over the fighting escapade, he fell sick with a cold. His master called in a doctor, who, after a slight examination, told the attendant to make up a quart of catnip tea and give it to him good

29

and hot. It appears that Josh had always been a great milk-drinker, and on one occasion after some little talk between him and the woman who milked the cows, he undertook to drink a quart of milk fresh from the cow. Josh had just eaten a hearty breakfast, and got stuck[2] when about half the milk had been turned down. One of the milk-woman's girls, taking in the situation, offered to shake him in order that he might be able to finish his task. He declined, and abandoned it. Clem, a companion, asked Charley to come and see Josh as he had got low-spirited and believed he was going to die. Charley at once went to the quarters where he was, and found Josh down sure enough, but pretending not to notice it, said in a cheering voice:

"Well, Josh, how does you feel this morning?"

"Bad enough, I can't live", he replied, "and nobody cares."

"Why, Josh, you'll be up in a few days."

"Yes, up in the graveyard," replied Josh.

"What makes you feel so bad?" asked Charley

"Well, Charley," said Josh, "the doctor has just done gone out, and he told me I must take a quart of catnip tea."

"Well, so you can."

"Well, so I can't, and I have to die."

"Why can't you drink a quart of catnip tea?" inquired Charley.

"Cause you see I only hold a pint," said Josh.

"Haw, haw! haw!" laughed Charley, and said, "Josh, you can take it in two doses, and so save your life."

"Oh," said Josh, "thanks to goodness, I never thought of that before." His mind had been running on his failure to drink the quart of milk. He brightened up at once and afterwards recovered rapidly.

When about twenty years of age, Josh became desperately in love with a young slave girl on Caldicott's plantation, and never was satisfied unless he got off every second Saturday evening to see her. The story had been told around that the girl he went to see was only fooling him and she had, in fact, a more favoured lover. Josh, however, thought very differently, and continued his fortnightly visits.

One summer Saturday evening it threatened rain, and Josh's master advised him not to go. This did not dampen his ardour, however, and he replied in effect that he thought it was only going to be a slight shower, and Lucy would be expecting him. Consent was obtained and away he went, but did not reach his destination before a sharp thunderstorm came up. Overhead were thick black clouds accompanied with a high wind, and a dense darkness, unequalled in his experience, settled about him. Chain lightning shot hither and thither, making an imposing display on the dark background. A rumbling sound, faint at first, increased in volume as it rolled along the sky, until it seemed to fill and shake the whole heavens. Then it gradually died away, after the manner so fondly imitated in the production of a thunderstorm on the stage; this was followed in rapid succession by others, until it seemed as if heaven's artillery had indeed got into full play. A vivid flash lit up for an instant the whole surrounding country, and was quickly succeeded by a loud clap of thunder, which made him fairly jump from the ground, and this was followed by alternate flashes of lightning and short periods of Egyptian darkness. Great balls of hail, such as he had never before seen, fell; and as they rolled along the ground, driven by the fury of the wind which had now increased to a tornado, they looked like balls of fire. Their weight on his head and body had, however, convinced him that they were fire in appearance only. In the glare of the lightning he saw, close by, a short, stout tree. He ran and crouched behind it. Each successive peal seemed louder than its predecessor. Many trees within hearing were twisted by the wind from their roots and fell with a crash to the ground. Then came a short downpour of rain. Josh was terribly frightened. He could not cry, and tried to pray; but even this he could hardly do as the elements warred about him with such intensity and uproar that his own mind fell into a similar tumult. His agony was, however, of short duration as the pelting hailstones did not fall for more than a couple of minutes. The whole storm, which was at the first wild, weird and awe-inspiring, next grand in its pyrotechnical display, and then fearful in its exhibition of destructive power, lasted scarcely half an hour and disappeared as suddenly as it came. The black clouds carried away by the tornado, left a mild, full-orbed moon and a bountiful supply of twinkling stars overhead. The elements so recently at war were hushed into silence and rest, and but for the scene of havoc about him, Josh could hardly have realized the wonderful transformation of nature from war to peace possible. The change assuaged his fears and confidence returned to him.

At first, Josh purposed retracing his steps homeward, but as he was fully three-fourths of the way on his journey, he finally concluded, although drenched to the skin, that he would go on. The night was clear with an occasional drifting cloud, the air balmy, and the vegetable kingdom gave forth a fine fragrant freshness. All these instilled a new buoyancy of spirits, which cheered almost to elation the sole traveller of the locality. As he passed along, he noticed more particularly the havoc caused by the tornado. The grain, now in full ear, was completely cut off and shelled, fences were levelled, and on the side of houses from which the storm came, every pane of glass in the windows was broken.

In due time Josh reached the house in which Lucy lived. He rapped at the door, but there was no response. The fact was that Lucy's favourite was there, and she was determined she would not see Josh that night. As there was a light in the house, and he had walked all the way over and got wet to boot, Josh thought he would talk with her, even if he could not get in. He went around to her chamber window, which was on the ground floor of the kitchen and shaded side of the house, and tapping lightly, called "Lucy, Lucy." Lucy answered and intimated that she was very sorry, but it was impossible for her to see him that night. "Well," said he speaking in a lower tone, "lift the window, my lovely Lucy and put your head out, and just give your Josh a kiss." Unfortunately, he was heard by the favourite beau within who stood at her chamber door. He beckoned for Lucy to come to him, and when she did so, he whispered that she was to go to the window and say that he would have to wait a minute for it. This she did, without having any idea of what he intended. When she returned, he said, "Leave the rest to me." Beckoning her to the other side of the room, he immediately ran on tiptoe to the kitchen. On entering a half-hour before, he had noticed a cleaned pig's head lying on the kitchen table. Wrapping the head in a towel to conceal his intentions from Lucy, he again tiptoed back in, and went straight to the window, outside of which Josh stood impatiently, waiting for it to be raised. A chance cloud had wrapped Josh in a temporary shade, and as the precaution of closing the chamber door had been taken, it was moderately dark within and without. Quietly raising the sash, the practical joker placed the pig's head on the windowsill and, holding it with his hand, said softly, "Now, Josh." He at once felt the nose of the head come in contact with Josh's mouth, and immediately there was a smack of lips, upon which the head was quickly pulled in and the sash closed down, lest there might be an embrace as well. Josh at once started for home, quite satisfied and the favourite returned to the kitchen table and dumped down the head, and then tumbled and rolled about the floor with a chuckling laugh that quickly brought Lucy to the spot. What this all meant, she could not tell, and for a while he wouldn't. She, however, at length worried it out of him, and, in consequence, felt dumbfounded. As soon as she could gather her senses, she implored him not to tell. He did, however, and the story soon reached Josh, whose affections were thereby effectually chilled forever. He had loved her, and would have gone through fire and water for her; he indeed did literally pass through these very elements to see

Josh in peril.

her on the luckless Saturday night. He never saw her afterwards.

Soon after, Josh was sold to Reed, a fisherman, on the Patapsco River, and matters went from bad to worse with the poor fellow; for on being discovered abstracting pullets one dark night, the owner of the roost determined to give him a good frightening, and at the same time have some fun at his expense. So a day or two after, he arranged with a few of his friends to give Josh a toss in a blanket. Josh, seeing what they were up to, ran to a cluster of trees and, being hard pressed, climbed one of them and in his eagerness went so high that his weight bent the tree over and placed him in peril, which did not appear to be lessened when his pursuers reached him. One of them threatened with an axe to chop the tree down if he did not let go his hold. The leader gravely informed him as they opened the blanket, that they were a newly formed "Local Society for the Prevention of the Apprehension of Hens," and they wished to initiate him into the Society, and were ready. Josh did not quite understand him, but let go. Subsequently, he obtained a reputation which was more than a local one as a wrestler and boxer.

His master did a good deal of weir pocket-fishing in the winter season on the Back, Middle, Bird and other rivers, and used to buy his weir splits from Charley. Josh accompanied his master for years, until at last as if one

> Whom unmerciful disaster
> Followed fast and followed faster,[3]

while plying his vocation on the Patapsco River, he fell in and was drowned.

7

The Picket

URING THE military troubles of 1812 to 1814, there was considerable excitement at times among the black population. In several places freed men were enrolled and organized for service. Shortly after Owens, the man in whose charge Charley was in the mill, had left for active service, a company was formed in the vicinity of the mill. It was Charley's boyish delight to watch the men drill. Slaves were not allowed to join. A sort of exception was made in just one instance. Charley's master, Orrick Ridgely,[1] was friendly with the captain who had command of this company, and was very enthusiastic in the cause. In order to make their drilling and training prepare them as much as possible for active service, they had to camp out on certain nights. Pickets were posted, and everything arranged just as if an enemy were in the vicinity and might at any time attack. Charley was employed about the camp in lightening the duties generally of the men. One night, one of the pickets was feeling poorly, and instead of making application to be relieved from duty, he asked Charley to take his place for him. Charley consented and was duly instructed as to his duties. He buckled on the regulation belt containing half a dozen rounds of ammunition and shouldered a somewhat dilapidated musket, and never felt prouder in his life. Conscious of newly attained power, he walked his beat with an unusually erect bearing, and was fired with all the enthusiasm which could be begotten by war stories. Nothing would please him better than to be enrolled in the company. As that could not be, he congratulated himself on one night's military service in his country's cause. Throughout the night, a very dark one, his mind ran over all the thrilling stories he had heard of the great War of Independence. In consequence he became much excited and, at about two o'clock in the morning when thus all aglow, he heard a crackling sound and saw something apparently approaching him. Remembering his instructions, he shouted at the top of his voice, "Who comes there, three times?" levelled his musket and fired. Bang! resounded the musket with a terrible report, which aroused the whole company. "Whew!" shouted Charley, as he heard something fall heavily to the ground and give a deep moan. Concluding to make sure work, he loaded again, and fired in the same direction. Bang! bang! in all, three reports.

By this time the regular soldiers, in different stages of dress, began to arrive. They found Charley where the picket should have been, and so much excited that it was only after much anxious questioning and uneasy delay that they could get anything like an intelligent understanding of the cause of the disturbance at that dead hour of the night. Finally, they ascertained that the picket had told him to ask, in case of any approach, "Who comes there?" three times, and if there was no response, he was to shoot.

"Where's the picket?" shouted the corporal, who was now in charge in the captain's absence.

"I left him in the tent in camp fast asleep," said one of his comrades.

"Where did you shoot?" was the next question put to Charley; and on his pointing in a certain direction, there was a general rush that way. They did not run very far, however, until the foremost runner tripped on something and fell headlong over it. The next did the same, and such was the impetuous force of those behind, that at least a dozen crowded over in the same way.

The corporal shouted "Halt!" but, except as to lessening the speed a little of those bringing up the rear, the command had no effect. The dozen men who had fallen in a heap were struggling to rise, and a hundred at least were crowding around the corporal who was standing erect on some object at a slight elevation, shouting "Halt! halt!" in a thundering tone, interspersed with numerous cries by the soldiers, of "What's the matter?", "Who's killed?"

"Keep back," said the corporal. "I can explain it all."

So the restless, surging crowd quieted down, and the corporal explained that the picket had deserted his post, appointing a substitute who misunderstood his instructions. Instead of asking, "Who comes there?" three different times before firing, he had just said, "Who comes there, three times?" and then fired. "A very different thing," remarked the corporal, "as it did not give the unfortunate individual trespasser time to answer, or retreat and thus save his life. A fatal mistake has been made, and I'm now, in consequence, standing on the dead body of neighbour Jones—"

"Oh! O-o-o-h!" groaned half a dozen soldiers.

"Who?" shouted others.

"Of neighbour Jones' cow," concluded the corporal.

They all joined in a hearty laugh. After duly inspecting the prostrate cow, the soldiers returned to camp. In the morning the captain, on hearing what had occurred, ordered the delinquent picket to be tried by court martial.

"There is no other way," he remarked, "that we can legalize the death of that cow, and squarely meet neighbour Jones' loss."

The trial was duly held, and the picket was convicted of disobeying orders. He was therefore degraded and drummed out of the ranks of the company. If Charley appeared in sight of one of those soldiers after that terrible night, the greeting he was sure to get was, "Who comes there three times, fire! bang! whew!" the last three words being repeated in an increasingly elevated and explosive tone. Charley, in consequence, was troubled over the affair and lost all relish for military life.

Just about this time a number of blacks, male and female, who were prisoners [of war] passed by Owings Mills on their way to the city of Washington. The prisoners created no little interest, on account of having been brought from Canada. Charley, watching his opportunity, had a short conversation with one of the young prisoners whose name was John Hall.[2] From him he learned that the whole party, which included nearly all of Hall's relatives, had been taken in a battle fought at Canard River near Amherstburg, a village on the Detroit River, in Canada.

8

❦

The Ridgelys

ONE OF the oldest and greatest families of the State of Maryland was the Ridgelys. Charles Ridgely,[1] who was elected Governor of Maryland in 1815, was one of the most extensive slave owners of the State, holding 450 men, women and children. The measure of his Government which produced the greatest commotion among the slave population, as remembered by Charley, was the enactment that a black man should take off his hat and place it under his arm as he passed a white man. The slave owners would not permit their slaves to obey the enactment.[2] General Swan informed his slaves that he would whip any one who did it. The idea of one of his slaves making obeisance to one of the "white trash," as the extremely poor were called, was something abhorrent to the haughty mind of the General.

In after years when the old ex-Governor was on his deathbed, his daughter, Mrs. Dorsey who came home to see him in his last illness, after great urging, got him to alter his will so that all his slaves over twenty-five years old should be set free, and that those younger should be set free on attaining that age. After the old Governor's burial, his will was read at a gathering of all his relatives. At the close of the reading, young David Ridgely blamed his late father openly, on account of the clause about the slaves. His slaves formed, however, but a small part of his wealth, as he had extensive iron works and several thousand acres of land.

Nicholas Orrick Ridgely was a first cousin of Governor Ridgely, and was married to a niece of the great Richard Croxall on whose plantation, as we have seen, Charley was born. It was on a Friday in the same year that Charles Ridgely became Governor of that State, and nearly a year after his master's death,[3] that a slave broke sad news to Charley thus:

"Boy, you're to leave here; you're sold to Orrick Ridgely."

This was as unexpected as lightning in a clear sky, and filled him with great sorrow. Already he had passed from the old master, in whose quarters he had been born, to the old Missis, and from her to her nephew, and from her nephew to his executor, during the minority of that nephew's son. But now, for the first time, he had been sold outright, like a bullock in the market, or a horse at the sale-stables. And, although there was some consolation in the fact that he was falling into the hands of a great man who was connected with his first old master's family, yet he knew not what kind of treatment he would receive. Hope and fear alternated in his breast. He had enjoyed a short respite at the mill, and greatly desired to remain where he was. He was not long in suspense, for on the following Monday morning, he was ordered to go with a team to the house of young James Croxall at Baltimore, and from him learned that he had been sold to his uncle Ridgely. Charley was soon sent over to the new master and, on arrival, was put on his horse behind him, and both rode out to the rear end of the farm. Here Ridgely's men were picking up stones, with which they were making a stone fence. The men and the work were both strange to Charley, but he at once dismounted and was soon at work with his new comrade slaves. From them he learned that Ridgely had bought the farm unseen, and had been deceived by the representation that "there was not a stone on it that a man could throw at a bird"—a statement which proved literally true, as the hard heads were all too big to be used for such a purpose. The slaves cracked many a joke as they rolled a particularly heavy boulder into the fence, about "the safety of the birds from boys throwing stones in master's fields."

Ridgely kept his farm for three years, and then traded it off for a timber lot of three hundred and thirty-three acres at Middle River Neck, and soon set about clearing up the latter farm. The timber consisted of hickory, oak, chestnut, black walnut, mulberry and locust. The bark was allowed to remain on the black walnut a year after being cut down, and this gave the wood a dark, rich colour, making it more valuable for commerce. Charley was soon after taken to Baltimore, to thresh grain. This was done in a house that was formerly used for storing tobacco and, while he was at this work, a night school was started in the city for blacks. Charley went, and the first night thought there was no sense in it. He could not remember a single one of the letters. The teacher used Dilworth's spelling book. On the third night, however, he had mastered the seeming impossibility, knew his letters, began to spell ba, be, bi, bo, bu, boy, and got on rapidly. But just then his master spoke to him about the school.

"What good will this schooling do you?" said he.

"Master," said Charley, "I want to learn to read the hymn book." This is what he said, but he thought more. He thought he would like to learn to read the New Testament also, to see what right his master had to hold him as his slave. Further attendance at school was forbidden. The interest of pro-slavery men was in keeping slaves in the densest ignorance, except as to their daily work, and hence they wished no education, save in that direction.

After this, a white lady asked him if he would not like to go to another evening school. He told her he had been at one a short time, and would like to go again. She said she would have to get his master's permission, as it was against the law to teach blacks without this. She asked for it, but his master refused, saying: "That boy had enough learning now." On hearing of his master's second refusal, Charley's heart sank within him and, although then almost grown, he cried bitterly as he saw this fine opportunity of learning to read, the last he ever had, disappear.

On learning that a Sunday school had been started in the neighbourhood, he went with a companion to see if he could gain admission. He was met at the door of the school room by Mr. Buck, the originator of the school, who was a hotel-keeper.

"I hear you've started a Sunday school," said Charley to the superintendent.

"Not for you," said the Sunday school officer coldly, eying his interrogator from head to foot; "it's only for white children."

Charley turned sorrowfully away, wondering if God cared for black people and if after death whether the soul of the black man would appear different from the soul of the white man. He had heard a white preacher once say that God was no respecter of persons. If souls all appear alike in the next world, there should not, he thought, be such a terrible gulf between their bodies here, and there should be Sunday schools to teach the black child as well as the white child the way to the heavenly land.

9

✂

John Hall

S HORTLY AFTER Charley was sent to Baltimore, Mr. Ridgely had occasion to go into the northern part of Kentucky, and took Charley along to assist him. After crossing the Ohio River, about twenty-five miles along as they approached Flemingsburg in Fleming County, they chanced to meet a young man on the road whom Charley concluded he had seen in Maryland.

"Hi," said Charley, "ain't you the person I saw in Maryland with the prisoners from Canada?"

"I came a prisoner from Canada," said the young man addressed, "but I don't know you."

"Why, I saw you with the rest of the prisoners," said Charley, "when you camped at Owings Falls, and you told me your name was John Hall."

"Oh, yes! I remember you now," said Hall.

"Where do you live?" asked Charley.

"Over there on the next plantation," was the reply. "I'm Haskill's slave. Perhaps your master would let you come with me to my master's quarters for a little while?"

On receiving this invitation, Charley asked and obtained permission to go with him, first promising to meet Mr. Ridgely next morning in Flemingsburg at an appointed time and place. The two young slaves were delighted to have an opportunity to talk together.

Charley at once asked Hall how he came to be there, as when he saw him before he was on his way to Washington, and thereupon learned from him the following particulars. His mother, sisters and brothers and an uncle, numbering with himself twelve, were all in the crowd of prisoners he saw at Owings Mills. They had been taken near enough to Washington to see that its capitol and other buildings had been fired by the British, and there learned that the prisoners were ordered to the interior of the country by President Madison, who was then fleeing from the city. They were all taken to the County of Frederick, near Winchester in Virginia, and kept as prisoners until the end of the troubles between England and the United States, early in 1815. Then, instead of being delivered up or exchanged, they had all been made slaves, except a few who effected their escape, among whom was one of Hall's sisters.

Hall, who was himself part Indian, had been a scout with the Indians under Tecumseh, and had skirmished all along the way between the Detroit and Niagara rivers. At Stoney Creek, near the last named river, he had been bayonetted in the leg, and although he did not think it very serious at the time, the wound was still troubling him. He never dreamed of being made a slave, but a slave he had become, and was owned by one of the most cruel and passionate slave owners of Kentucky.

"But how did you get from Winchester here?" inquired Charley.

"Well," continued Hall, "Captain Catlett,[1] the man that took me prisoner first, still kept me and my mother and some of my brothers and sisters as his slaves, for about three years; then he lost all his property and we were all scattered, and I've never seen any of my relations since. Dan Morgan brought me down here, and delivered me to my master Haskill."

The two young slaves, in their wanderings about the quarters, continued to relate their personal history to each other, until they brought up at the whipping-house, a solid, square, dingy-looking building, which they entered.

"Here," said Hall, as he sat down and pointed to a seat for his comrade, "I saw a terrible whipping."

"Just after the husking last year, two women, a big one and a little one, fought in the field; and the big one bit the little one's lip, and the little one came in and told master. Then he sent for the big woman, and put them both in the Spanish stoop."

"What's that?" asked Charley.

"Why, don't you know? The woman's hands were tied together and she was stooped down and her arms put round her knees and a stick was put through under her knees and over her arms, making her look like a ball. Both women were fixed that way. And master he gave a cowhide to his son and told him to whip. Each gave nine-and-thirty lashes, and then he cussed his son because he didn't half whip, and ordered all of us here to this whipping-house, and told me to bring a pan of salt. Oh, my God! I never did see such a sight. See that rope and pulley? The largest woman, with very little clothes on, was hoisted by her hands until she was on tiptoe, and then he laid on the whip, and the poor woman kept on a-screaming. Mistress and her son were here, and the little woman was crouched in that corner shaking with fear. I stood just where your sitting, holding the pan of salt in my hands. Master appeared crazy mad. He whipped and he whipped. Mistress begged him for God's sake to stop, and young master said 'You'll kill her, you'll kill her!' but he was boiling with rage, and kept on whipping and cussing. At last her screams grew very weak. Sudden, when I thought she was just gone, she flung her knees round master's neck. Then he jumped, and the rope broke, and the woman fell writhing in a fit on the ground.

" 'There now,' said young master, 'I told you you'd kill her, and it's not the first one either.'

" 'You brute!' screamed Mistress, 'she's dying.' And then the little woman let a great screech.

" 'You had no business hoisting her any way after putting her in the Spanish stoop,' said Mistress, crying and wringing her hands. 'You've killed her and her soul's lost. This will go all over Kentucky.'

"Master, he sat down and cussed himself for a cruel wretch, and cried like a baby.

"It was dreadful. In all my scrimmages from Detroit to Niagara, in the war, I wasn't half so frightened."

"Did she come out of the fit?" inquired Charley.

"Twasn't any fault of his that she didn't die. After a long time she got better, but never was exactly like herself again."

The two young slaves then hastened away from the scene they had been contemplating, and strolled about the plantation again.

"What's that young fellow got the ball chained to his ankle for?" inquired Charley, as he saw a chained slave weeding and hoeing in the tobacco.

"Oh, that's Jim," said Hall. "Master's just having the greatest time you'd ever see with Jim. He ran away, and master got all the gentlemen round, and all the hounds. Why, it was like a fox hunt; over the field of crops and over the fences they went. 'Twas like a holiday, with a great party bent on lots of fun. I reckon it wasn't any fun for poor Jim, running with clothes torn and eyes most out of their sockets with fear. He had a pretty good start, and the hunt party rode seven miles, and then they caught poor Jim. I reckon he won't try running away again. 'Tain't no use trying to get away from here, because they can bring you back from Ohio, although it's a free state. And when you're caught, there's no end of the misery, and next you're sold down to the cotton fields."

Hall, at the close, took his companion through the oil-cake factory, where he worked the greater part of his time, and then over other parts of the premises.

"Awh!" said Charley, as his eye caught sight of the face of a beautiful white girl working in the kitchen; "what does it mean having a white gal working in the kitchen yonder?"

"White gal!" exclaimed Hall. "She ain't no white gal. That's Mabel; she's a slave."

"A white slave sure," said Charley.

"Well," continued Hall, "there was a great discourse about her once, as to whether she was really white or not. Some Abolitionists claimed there was no Negro blood in her; but the slave holder that Master bought her from showed the dark stripe down the centre of her back, and the mark behind her ear, and so proved his point conclusively. If it hadn't been for the marks she'd have been set free then, on account of the interference about her. There's lots of children of mixed blood born as white as the whitest and grow dark afterwards, but Mabel stayed white."

"I expect there isn't much of the Negro blood in her anyhow," added Charley.

He subsequently remained all night at the quarters with Hall, and in the morning bade him goodbye, and arrived at the place appointed by his master in good time. Charley at once related Hall's story of his capture, detention and master's cruelty. Whereupon Mr. Ridgely expressed great indignation against Haskill, and said he would see before he left if Haskill would be allowed to hold Hall as his slave.

10

❦

Trade in Slaves

MARYLAND HAD now become a great slave-breeding state. Every city of this state of importance had its slave market. Slaves were here raised for the great cotton lands of the South; and slave traders visited these markets and drove through the country on the lookout for purchases, as cattle drovers do in Ontario. There was money in the business. Money to the producers, as well as to the trader, who bought in the cheapest and sold in the dearest market. Hence the institution was dearly cherished, and the Marylanders, like slave owners everywhere, became very sensitive on the subject and were easily irritated by anti-slavery sentiments. That slavery was an evil they would grant, but, as they viewed it, a necessary evil. There was, however, always enough of the abolition leaven to start an agitation when a new territory was to be admitted to the Union and the question had to be decided as to whether the new state should be a slave state or not. During the Missouri Compromise Debate[1] in Congress, in the year 1850, Calhoun[2] "boldly avowed his intention to carry slavery into the territories under the wing of the Constitution, and denounced as enemies to the South all who opposed it."

On these occasions the question became a burning one, and a source of great national agitation and irritation, and the subject of lengthy debates in Congress. The line of reasoning taken in these debates in defence of slavery was in some respects closely analogous to the arguments used in defence of the liquor traffic at the present day.

Lawrence Silverthorn, of Shoal Creek, used to raise slaves on the eastern shore of Maryland for the market. He sold them to Woodhawke[3] and other buyers, for Georgia, South Carolina and for New Orleans. He usually sold the young people at from eighteen to twenty-five years of age. One day he said, "I think I'll go down to Centerville and sell thirty head or so." He went, and made a bargain with Woodhawke for thirty young men and women. He shipped them next day on his own vessel, and was to go down for his money on the day following. That night he was called away to give an account of his stewardship and never received the price of his slaves.

It was then a very common sight to see twenty or thirty chained together, going from Baltimore to the Ohio River, there to take the flat-bottomed boats for New Orleans. They were driven through free states in chained gangs, like herds of cattle, to some great city market; sleeping at night on board floors in bar rooms and outhouses, under guard.

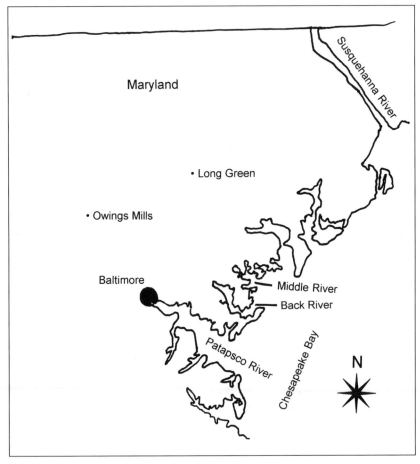

Northern Maryland

On one of these tramps, a slave owner, who was on his way to a southern market, was taken sick at a place called Brownsville in the state of Ohio. A physician was sent for, but without avail; for, after a severe illness lasting three days, he died. His gang of slaves consisted of about twenty men. The hotel-keeper and some neighbours held a meeting as to what should be done. The slave owner had a small amount of money, and a good horse and rig, with which he had been pursuing his journey. A committee was appointed by the meeting to sell the horse and rig, and take the proceeds along with the money found on the slave owner's person, and pay the bills owing to the hotel-keeper, the doctor and the undertaker. It was resolved that the slaves should be at once set at liberty, and instructed to shift for themselves. They were informed in what direction they should go; and they hurried off lest some relative or agent of the slave owner should come and claim them. It did not take them long to disappear; and doubtless most of them reached places of safety. It was one of these escaped slaves, named Elijah Smiley, who gave Charley the particulars of this case, as they worked together some years after the occurrence.

Jake Ramsay, who had been bought on the eastern shore of Maryland by John Stansbury, of Back River Neck, told his master that he would do his work, but would not be whipped. Stansbury informed him he must submit to be whipped, or he would sell him down South. Shortly after, Austin Woodhawke, the slave dealer, came along and bought him; but the bill of sale was to be executed and the price, $500, was to be paid on his return in a few days.

At the time appointed, Woodhawke drove up with his carriage to Stansbury's house, just as Jake had come in from his tobacco weeding. "Jake," said the slave dealer, "you are to go with me to New Orleans; I've bought you." Upon hearing this, Jake walked directly to the woodpile, where stood an axe which he caught up, and with one blow, cut off his left hand. Dr. Davis was summoned, and said he believed he could save Jake's life. The slave dealer declined to take him and went away. The doctor asked Stansbury what he would take for the injured slave and, on his saying he would now take $50, the doctor at once accepted the offer. When the arm healed, the doctor got him a hook for a hand. Jake was a smart, active fellow, and became so expert with his hook that he could do about as much as other men with both hands.

The importation of slaves having been effectually cut off, and the demand for slaves for the cotton fields of the sunny South having become great, Maryland largely gave herself to an effort to meet the demand. The article of slaves, therefore, became her chief product of commerce—and what a trade that was. The power of gold had aroused the avarice of the people, and a traffic in human beings, of appalling dimensions, resulted. Marital rights, along with social and family ties, were set at naught among the people thus raised and bartered. Owners conscious "whose passion gave life, and whose blood ran in the veins" of fair-looking young slaves born on their own plantations, conforming to the absorbing custom of the country, exchanged even such with dealers for money. It often happened that husband and wife were owned by different masters. The form of marriage among slaves was sanctioned by slave holders, not only from mercenary motives, but because experience had shown it to be preventative of frequent quarrels among the male slaves. The tide of greed rose high, and, like the rushing waters of the Johnstown disaster,[4] bore everything down with it, and nothing, or next to nothing, could be done to ameliorate the condition of the hapless victims of that nefarious and villainous trade.

> Within earth's wide domains,
> Are markets for men's lives;
> Their necks are galled with chains,
> Their wrists are cramped with gyves.[5]

11

❦

Big Bob

NELSON DEDRICK, a minister of the Baptist Church, residing at Hagerstown, owned a slave named Big Bob who was an excellent mechanic, and earned a great deal of money for his master by ironing off carriages.[1] Bob's great ambition was to obtain the freedom of himself and his good little wife Cassie. After considerable effort he effected an arrangement with his master, by which, on payment of a certain amount over and above ordinary earnings, the freedom of himself and wife was to be granted. He had no children. The amount fixed upon was the large sum of $2000; $1,250 for himself, and the balance for his wife, which was to be paid in from time to time as the slave blacksmith could save it. Bob worked unlike a slave, for he worked with a will for years, until at last he could see, as he supposed, the beginning of the end. As he made each successive payment to his master, his hopes rose higher. And at length, as the amount at his credit began to come near the total sum required, he conversed freely with his slave companions and with his customers, of his prospective freedom and future plans, which included leasing a blacksmith shop for himself. He was in the act of hammering out an axle, and mentally consoling himself with the hope that at the end of another three months, if business kept as good as it had been for some time past, he would be able to pay the balance, and obtain the freedom papers for himself. Unfortunately for him, just at this crisis a Georgia slave trader, in passing through Hagerstown, happened to see him at work as he made the sparks fly briskly by the rapid blows of his hammer on the anvil. The name over the door gave a clue to the ownership, and he soon obtained an interview.

"No," said Dedrick, "I can't sell him. I have promised him his freedom, and he has very nearly paid for himself now."

"Oh that's nothing," said the trader. "I buy lots of 'em just that way. Don't you see, the price is all clear profit to the owner?"

"I know, but it isn't right," said the owner.

"Well, I have no time to discuss that question; but you know he's your property, and the law allows you to sell him, and Bob can't help himself, he has no papers. See here, I'll give you fifteen hundred dollars cash for a bill of sale of that nigger. Here is the paper; I'll fill it out, and you can sign it. He is going to leave you anyway."

Dedrick hesitated, and while he hesitated greed was getting the mastery; and while greed was getting the mastery, the trader was busily writing. "There, sign that," said he, with a flourish, pushing the document toward him and, yielding to the temptation, Big Bob's master took the pen and signed "Nelson Dedrick." Thus was this man, endowed with brain enough to be an excellent mechanic, and with a soul fired by ambition and energy which had brought him to the verge of freedom, by a stroke of the pen in the hand of an unscrupulous and selfish owner, thrust back into slavery for the rest of his life,

Bartered as the brute for gold.[2]

The money was immediately counted down. The trader noticed that Dedrick did not touch it, and that he looked nervously at the paper just signed. Seeing this, the trader hastily seized the bill of sale and thrust it into his pocket, walked out of the house and into the blacksmith's shop, and said:

"Bob, you may put down your hammer, I want you to come with me."

"Where you'd wish me to go, Master?" said Bob.

"I'm your new master, Bob and I'm going to take you down to Georgia."

"No that can't be," said Bob; "I bought my freedom, and I'se nearly paid for."

"See here, boy, no nonsense. Look here, that's the bill of sale. I have bought you, now be quick."

At this, Bob flew out of the shop and into Dedrick's house, demanding an explanation. Dedrick had shut himself up in a room, and would not see Bob.

"I couldn't help it, I couldn't help it, Bob," was the sickening whine of his treacherous master, which came from the next room. Bob then ran home and told Cassie, his wife, what had happened. She at once became almost frantic and ran screaming to Dedrick's house, but she could not find him. Then, following her husband into the blacksmith's shop where both husband and trader were,—the scene for a time beggars any description that could be given of it. Bob was allowed a few minutes to change his clothes at his cabin, where he lovingly embraced his wife and gave her a parting, sad farewell. Then he was chained with the rest of the gang, and hurried off for Georgia.

After this Cassie was never the same at her work; and so to get rid of the unpleasantness, as he termed it, Dedrick sold her to the next trader that came along.

A year after, Big Bob was heard from. He was working at black-smithing, and was well used by his new master, who resided in the southern part of Georgia. His master fully appreciated his skill, but never would listen to any proposal from him for the purchase of his freedom. Failing in this, Bob meditated on an attempt to escape, which he well knew would be attended with great risk and difficulty. But while so meditating, he accidentally heard that his wife had been sold away South, too, to become a cotton picker; he then lost heart and, crushed to earth, continued to toil as a slave without hope.

One morning, nearly two years after he had been so heartlessly sold, while he was blowing the bellows and raking the hot coals on his iron in the forge, a mulatto slave led a horse into his shop to be shod. While shoeing the horse, the mulatto made himself as agreeable as possible to the shoer, whom he noticed was very quiet, and talked but little. The mulatto was Sol, from a plantation about three miles distant, owned by a Mr. Dunwaddy.

"Master's pushing work very lively this season," said Sol, after a little talk about the horse; "and he's just bought a new batch of hands."

"Yes," said Bob, who knew Sol's master; "how many?"

"Three; two men and one woman," replied Sol; "but Lord me, those men don't know nothin' about picking cotton seed."

"Where did they come from?" asked Bob carelessly, as he singed the horse's forefoot with a trial shoe, while he held the foot between his leg.

"I don't know about the men, except that one comes from old Virginia, and Cynthey told me the woman comes from South Carolina and before that she lived in Maryland."

"Maryland!" shouted Bob, in a voice that startled Sol. "What part of Maryland?"

"Why, why," stammered Sol, "I think it was near Baltimore."

Bob let the horse foot fall to the ground and sat down. "What kind of a woman is she? What's her name? How old is she?" And other questions were rapidly put by Bob to Sol as the latter sat in dumb silence, wondering what was the matter with Bob, that he had got so suddenly excited, and acted so differently from what he did before he mentioned about the woman. He proceeded to answer Bob's questions as well as he could, but could not give her name or age. He, however, had seen her, and knew that she was small and good-looking. It had flashed across Bob's mind that the newcomer might be his Cassie; and while Sol's description was like her, yet there was something he said which let him to suppose that it must be another woman. After a moment's silence, he rose to his feet and proceeded with his work, and as he worked he told Sol the story of his wrongs. The silent tongue had become loosened, the "fountains of the great deep" in his heart were broken up and, for the first time to human ears, with hot tears coursing down his manly cheeks, he poured forth the sorrows of his soul to listening Sol, whose rattling tongue had been awed into silence in the presence of a heart-burdened man.

"My old master," said he, in conclusion, "was an ungrateful wretch. I worked very hard for him for years, and he took all my earnings from me, and sold me away from my poor little Cassie. There was no gratitude whatsoever in that man."

"That so," exclaimed Sol; "I heard my master talk on that subject yesterday. He said 'twas a mighty scarce commodity, and there was only one place in the whole world he knew of where it was sure to be found."

"Where's that place?" queried Bob.

"In the bookshunary," said Sol, all unconscious of his master's incisive criticism on human nature.

"You mean dictionary," said Bob, correcting him.

"I expect so," continued Sol. "Anyhow, Master's fairly boiling over with book learning."

"Now," said Bob, as he rasped the last nail of the horse's hoof, "I want you to go straight to that woman and ask her if she ever lived with Dedrick, at Hagerstown in Maryland, and lived with her husband Bob, Big Bob the blacksmith, and see if she is my Cassie. Go force haste to her and come again, quick as this horse can carry you. Is she my Cassie? Bring me good tidings. I'll watch for your coming."

Sol quickly mounted his steed and dashed off with high speed, for he was now almost as excited as Bob, who had wonderfully quieted down as he had talked of his great troubles. Sol, on arriving home, gave his master an account of what had happened at the blacksmith shop. His master could not tell anything about the woman, except that she had come from South Carolina and her name was Cassie.

"It's Cassie, is it?" said Sol. "That is Bob's wife's name."

Mr. Dunwaddy, having become greatly interested in the account Sol had given of the matter, immediately summoned Cassie into his presence, and asked a few questions, which at once identified her as Bob's lost wife. Without the slightest intimation to her of what he had in hand, he despatched another slave, who knew nothing of what had taken place, for Bob, having first cautioned Sol not to utter a word.

While this was going on, Bob was pacing up and down the shop, every other minute looking up the road to see if a horseman was coming. Once two horsemen came down and galloped past. Having asked permission, he concluded he would walk over to Dunwaddy's plantation where Sol was, as he could not rest until he knew more about the matter. He had not gone far until he saw a cloud of dust in the distance, then a horse and rider. He strained his eyes to see if it was Sol. It was a bay horse like Sol's; but as he came nearer he saw it was not Sol, and so his excitement lessened, and he walked on. To his surprise, the rider reined up his horse when they met, and said:

"My master's sent me to ask you to come over to his place." The messenger, whose name was Zeke, knew Bob.

"What for?" quickly asked Bob.

"I don't know," said Zeke, "he didn't tell me. He only said 'Tell him I want to see him.'"

The rider then dismounted, and asked Bob to ride.

"If you let me have the horse," said Bob, "I must leave you and go quick."

"All right," said the messenger, and away went Bob at a full gallop.

In the meantime, Cynthey had been ordered to get Cassie fixed up in her best clothes and sent to Mrs. Dunwaddy. The latter took her into the parlour and asked her to dust the room carefully, as she expected a visitor in shortly and wanted everything to look nice.

When Bob rode up, he was disappointed in not meeting Sol, who was nowhere to be seen. Throwing the bridle rein over the gatepost, he walked up to the front door with his heart thumping terribly in his breast, and a ringing noise in his ears. "The master has sent for me, so I've a right to call and ask for him," said he to himself, as he lifted the knocker at the door. Mrs. Dunwaddy herself answered the knock.

"Does Master Dunwaddy want me?" asked Bob.

"Yes; come in," said Mrs. Dunwaddy.

Bob stepped in, hat in hand, and was shown into the parlour, and told to be seated. The door was closed after him, and he supposed he was alone in the room, when he heard a little knock on a piece of furniture at the other end of the parlour. Looking in that direction, just as the little woman dusting turned to see the visitor, the eyes of Bob and Cassie met.

"Cassie!" "Bob!" were exchanged words which flew across the room, as lost husband and wife rushed into each other's arms, and embraced each other with all the impassioned ardour that would be expected under such extraordinary circumstances. Cassie immediately went into hysterics, laughing and crying alternately, as Bob supported her with his strong arms; while he, almost bursting with emotion, wept like a child. Mrs. Dunwaddy soon entered the room, and summoned Cynthey to assist her in getting poor Cassie's nerves quieted down. A little after, in came Mr. Dunwaddy himself, followed by Sol, who now wept with Bob. Soon Cassie recovered, and all were rejoicing together. Bob and Cassie received hearty congratulations from Mr. Dunwaddy and his wife. Sol said he never felt so happy in all his life; and as for Cynthey, she was fairly wild with excitement and delight. Then they learned of Cassie's efforts to get her master in South Carolina to sell her, so that she might get to Georgia and search for Bob. She expected it would take years to find him, as she had been sold away by Dedrick before word came from Bob as to where he was. At this point Zeke returned, perspiring freely on account of his walk, which had been quickened by curiosity to know what Bob's anxious face meant. At the click of the gate, Bob went out to meet him. No sooner had he done so, than Zeke stood, as if transfixed, gazing upon a wondrous change in Bob. The face with the anxious look was now wreathed in smiles, and beaming with exultant joy; the dim eye now fairly sparkled; the head which drooped was tossed high, and the bending body now bounded with irrepressible animation. Zeke's eyes extended more and more in astonishment at Bob's transformation. His lips parted to inquire its cause, when Bob anticipated him by saying:

"Old fellow, my wife's come, my own Cassie. She's found me, and Sol brought me the news, and didn't know it. Come and see her, Zeke. She is one of the best little women on the top of this earth."

"So that's what it was?" said Zeke, as he went in with Bob to make Cassie's acquaintance.

The news of Bob's good fortune quickly spread, and they soon had plenty of friends. An arrangement was immediately made whereby Cassie was to live with Bob in the house of his master, and so they were again united, and lived together as in the days of yore, as happy as slaves could possibly be.

> God moves in many a way,
> So the good old Bible say,
> He counts the drops and all the grains of sand,
> And when the darkness falls
> Upon these here cabin walls,
> It is just the break of day in other lands
>
> The great black clouds on the fly
> Cover up the lovely sky,
> And gives many and many a rainy day,
> But the gloomering will pass,
> And the sun shines out at last,
> And the darkest days of sorrow pass away.

12

⁂

Amusements

ON THE RIDGELY farm Charley had much hard work, but after all, as he was of a buoyant and cheerful disposition, ever making the most of surrounding circumstances, he had much sport and enjoyment. With the exception of the period he worked in the flour mill, he had never been ill-used, in fact, never once whipped since he had grown up.

One of the most pleasant features of slave life on one of these great plantations, was the dinner hour. When the slaves were called upon to labour far from the quarters, in the tobacco or cornfields, just at noon a pair of oxen, or horses, with a cart would bring the dinner. The cart was well loaded with provisions, as follows: a tub of bonny-clabber,[1] great loaves of cornbread baked in kettles and cut into thick slices, trays of boiled herrings and potatoes. The herrings were caught in the Chesapeake Bay, by slaves sent to fish at the fishing grounds there. "The shad was for the great house; they wouldn't allow us shad no how, unless we stole them," was information contributed in a half-soliloquizing manner by Charley, as if he were again in imagination feasting on thick milk, brown bread, "a pone of corn-cake," and salt herrings, beside the horse cart in the field of some great plantation in Maryland, as in the days of yore. Many a prank, and lots of merriments, were now and again indulged in at the noon spell. The young slaves agreed well together, and it was rare indeed that play degenerated into a quarrel.

Patrolling was very much in vogue in those early days. The slave owners, in order to put a stop to the very general custom of night-visiting between the slaves of different plantations, then prevailing, instituted a system of mounted night patrol. If a slave was found at large in the daytime, and

56

could not show his permit paper, any white man could treat him as an estray.[2] He could arrest, and then advertise for the owner to prove property, pay charges and take his slave away. At night, however, it was quite different. The proceedings were of a more summary character, the slave caught out could be tied up and whipped on the spot. This was looked upon by the slaves as an innovation, and there was a very general and organized resistance on the part of the young men. The patrollers, too, had trouble. At the head of a road they would hear shouting, and putting spur to their horses, would gallop forward, and the first thing they knew they would be swept from their horses to the ground by a rope of grapevine stretched across the road, just a little higher than a horse's head. Again, they would rush toward a bonfire elsewhere, only to meet a similar fate. At other times, a stirrup or girth, almost cut through, would give way, and let the rider turn halfway round and down suddenly. Nothing worked more effectually than the fox-grape vine and, for a change, they sometimes stretched one across the road, about a foot from the ground. This would trip up the horse, and send the rider over his head, frequently considerably hurt. One of the patrols got his arm broken. So persistently were these pranks kept up, that it became impossible to procure men who would undertake the duty of patrolling. It was, therefore, soon abandoned, and then plantation visiting resumed the even tenor of its way. Charley took a hand in the amusement while it lasted and, although he experienced hairbreadth escapes, never once fell into the clutches of the patrollers, a good fortune for which he even now expresses great satisfaction.

One of the privileges permitted slaves was Sunday shooting. They were, however, not allowed to go off their master's plantation. Indeed, it was a general law of the State, that if any slave was found off his master's estate with a gun, his gun, powder-horn, shot and other material could be summarily taken from him, and his case reported to his master; and the person detecting was entitled to a fee. The hunting consisted mostly of squirrel, opossum, rabbits, raccoon, pheasants and, when the plantation was on a river, of duck also. There was a great temptation to roam over other plantations.

On Middle River, at Frogmore Landing, large quantities of wood, mostly oak and pine, were got out and shipped down to Baltimore. It was here that old Mose, a well-known character in those days, on account of his bibulistic propensities, eccentric actions, and stuttering speech, lived. He was the general butt and subject of raillery at that time, and received many a gibe, just to see what he would say; and when drinking, he had plenty to say. It was here, too, that Harry Barr started a little grocery and, as his place was the slaves' great Sunday resort, did a thriving business in New England rum and gingerbread. Of course, he kept other supplies besides these. Mose called at his little shop one day, to get a darning needle for his wife, who had sent as an exchange a hen's egg. In due course, the egg, a large one, was tendered and accepted as payment in full for the needle, and the needle was safely thrust into the lapel of the purchaser's coat.

"S-see here" said Mose to the shopkeeper, "isn't this here a tr-trade atwixt us both?"

"Yes. Certainly," said Barr.

"Well, what's you going to stand?" continued his customer.

"Nothing", said Barr

"Nothing?" repeated Mose, in a well-affected tone of surprise. "Come now, a tr-trade's a trade, and who ever heard of a trade without a tre-tre-treat?"

Barr was at first staggered with the largeness of the demand compared with the smallness of the deal, but in a moment recovered his equilibrium, and yielding to the fellow's whim, just for the fun of it, got one of his largest and best tumblers, poured in some excellent brandy, and handed it in good style to the seeker of his patronage.

"Master, B-B-Barr, not exactly that way," said Mose, as he put the glass down on the counter, "I always t-take an egg in it."

"An egg?" demanded Barr, in real astonishment, but immediately recovering himself, concluded he would again humour his curious customer, went to the egg-basket, and picked out the identical egg he had a moment before exchanged for the needle, and broke it into the brandy; when, lo! it proved to be one with a double yolk. Mose immediately tossed the treat down, and as he replaced the glass on the counter, said, with a shrug of his shoulders, "Master, B-Barr, that was a double yolk egg." I sold it to you for a s-single yolk, so you may give me another darning needle." And Mose brought two darning needles home instead of one. His great success on this occasion was soon clouded by a misfortune which befell him on his way home. Mose was so constantly attended by a companion, in the shape of a large, yellow dog named Tiger, that everybody was familiar with the expression, "Mose and his yellow dog." Tiger was not only company, but protection, and sat with his master many an hour in the evening and sometimes half the night, as he fished from a log or a stump on the bank of Middle River. Mose was a great fisherman, and nothing pleased him like fishing in the river, attended by Tiger. A strong affection had grown between the dog and his master. Mose had his doubts as to whether any person in the world cared for him, but he knew he had Tiger's affection, and loved him on that account. He knew of nothing he would exchange for his dog, which had but one failing. He was cross to strangers, and it was this that let to the misfortune referred to. On the road home, as a burly slave crossed the road from one field to another, Tiger attacked him with great fury. Unfortunately for the dog, the fellow happened to be carrying a pitchfork on his shoulder, and immediately lowered it therefrom, as if about to give the dog a warm reception. Mose seeing this, threw up his hands and said "Sis-sis-sis." In an instant a dull, heavy thud was heard. The fatal thrust had been given. The tines of the fork had pierced Tiger's body through and through, and the poor dog fell dead at this slayer's feet.

"Stop!" shouted Mose, in a voice almost explosive.

"Stop what?" asked the big, burly slave, in a somewhat regretful tone, as if already sorry for his act.

"Why you k-k-killed my dog," said Mose, half crying.

"Well," retorted the stranger, "you soot him onto me."

"I never done so," said Mose, indignantly denying the charge.

"Yes, you said sis-sic-'im," continued the slave, "and I wasn't going to stand here and let your dog tear me to pieces."

"No, I only told you to s-s-stop," stuttered Mose, as he strove to repeat the word which had been so unfortunately misunderstood.

Mose then began to expostulate with his antagonist on account of his cruelty. "Why, doggone it," said he reprovingly and in anger, "why didn't you took the other end of the fork f-first and beat the dog off you."

"The other end first?"

"Yes, undoubtedly."

"Well, I suppose-er-ah," stammered the man with the pitchfork, "I would have took the other end first if your dog had come at me with his other end first," hardly conscious of the humour concealed in the idea of the dog running backward at him extended tail-end first.

The loss of his "yellow dog" was keenly felt by Mose for a very long time, but he did not, in consequence, give up his rod and line. The very next time he went fishing after the death of Tiger, he had a surprising catch. At the first bite he hauled up a mud-turtle.

"Ah! that's a queer fish," said Mose, as with broken pole he landed it safely on the pier. He took his captive home, and tried to make a pet of it. The slaves called it his "funny fish," and tried to tease him about it. Mose did not mind this, as he knew they did not know that he was playing with the mud-turtle only to divert his mind from sadness on account of Tiger's death.

In the course of a couple of years after these occurrences, a brick tavern

A queer fish

was built a little farther up the river, at the forks of the roads, and ever after the "Bull's Head" was the great centre of attraction, and headquarters for sport. It was the custom of sporting slaves of the gun, of the fishing-rod, and other amusement lovers, to assemble here. Shooting matches were frequently held. Some huntsmen would bring in a lot of wild duck shot on some of the many marshes of Back River Neck, Bush

River Neck, and Middle River Neck, the home of a great variety of wild duck. The ducks were generally bought from their owners, and put up at five cents a shot, at a pretty long range, and ten cents for a shorter one.

Not only on Sunday afternoon, but on Saturday evening, the Bull's Head was well patronized. Here were held and witnessed raffles, dice throwing, card playing, quoit pitching, wrestling, boxing, dog fighting, cockfighting and other amusements. Among them were many good singers and instrumental players, and frequently the evening was largely devoted to melody. All other amusements stopped at once when singing began. Old Mose was here often called on to contribute one of his favourite songs. He always readily responded with great gusto, except when compelled to excuse himself on account of an affliction which he had contracted during some of his protracted night vigils, fishing in the chilly damps of Middle River, and which he designated his catarrh, invariably placing great emphasis on the first syllable of the work, so that it sounded like two distinct words, "cat" and "tar." The last time he said his "cat-tar" wouldn't allow him to sing, Charley replied, "That's nothing; dog-tar is far worse." At this someone laughed, and while someone laughed, old Mose nearly cried, for the sound of the words used by Charley had suggested to his mind his poor, long-lost, trusted dog Tiger. After a little coaxing, however, he commenced to sing, and exhibited what may be truly termed an open countenance, since his mouth opened so wide that his eyes shut, and besides this there was little else of his face to be seen; but there was no stuttering as he sang:

> I've been to Tennessee,
>   I've sailed the Mississippi,
>   'fore master set me free;
>   I've seen the lovely Creole gal,
>   On Louisiana's shore,
>   But never seen a gal like
>   My pretty gal of Baltimore.

CHORUS

> Ho! the gal of my choice
>   Has a melancholy voice,
>   But her figure and her face
>   Make the Venus of her race.

Charley was fond of singing:

> Now, don't be foolish, Joe.

And all would join in its charming chorus:

> U-li-a-li, O-la-ee,
>   Courtin' down in Tennessee,
> U-li-a-li, O-la-ee,
>   'Neath the wild banana tree.

This stirred the crowd, and "Dandy Jim from Caroline," "Lucy Long," "Uncle Ned," "Mary Blane," "Ole Dan Tucker," "Boatman Dance," and other songs followed in quick succession, until it grew late, and the impromptu concert closed with:

> Touch light the banjo-string,
>   And rattle the old jawbone,
> Oh! merrily sound the tambourine,
>   And make that fiddle ring."

CHORUS

> Then commence, ye darkies all,
>   As loud as ye can bawl,
> Commence, commence, ye darkies all, to-night.

Thus many and varied were the songs sung at the Bull's Head.

Christmas was always a great day for shooting matches, cockfighting and wrestling. The last named was a popular amusement, but sometimes degenerated into a fight. Charley worked hard in spare time making splints for weir fishing, for which he got thirty-three cents per hundred, and so did others, to get money to spend at these gatherings at the Bull's Head.

A yellow man,[3] who had not previously taken part in sports at the Bull's Head, one day entered the tavern, and threw down a dollar on the counter, saying, "I'll wrestle any man in the crowd if he'll put down his dollar."

Bully Bill happened to be present, and accepted the challenge in the following impromptu:

I'll bet him a dollar,
    I'll catch him by the toe,
Should it make him holler,
    Why then I'll let him go.

The crowd laughed heartily and, as soon as the preliminaries were arranged, went out to witness the wrestling match.

A short distance from the main crowd, beneath a clump of trees, were seven Irishmen, recently arrived from the Emerald Isle, who had obtained a quart of whiskey and were drinking it together, and appeared to be enjoying themselves very much. Charley felt pretty good that day and, just for the fun of it, went over to them, and demanded some of their whiskey.

"Go way, nayger," said one of them; "go back to your crowd of black naygers beyond."

Charley got vexed at this, and called them "a sassy lot," and told them he could thrash any Irishman that ever crossed the Atlantic Ocean. In a twinkling they drew their sticks and, surrounding him, commenced to belabour him around the head, shoulders and sides. Whack, whack, went their sticks as fast as they could fly. Charley wanted to shout fair play; and that he did not undertake to fight them all, but he had no chance to say anything. His great anxiety was to break their ring, and get away. After a tremendous effort, he succeeded and started for the crowd, who were so intently watching the wrestling match that they had not noticed what was going on at the trees. Charley was hard-pressed, and the Irishmen followed close after, but at little different distances. Whack came a stick on his shoulder again. When he turned and struck the holder between the eyes, he fell back, but number two was then right on him when he partially warded off his blow, and hit him in the pit of the stomach, which doubled him up in short order. By this time the crowd had found out what was going on, and came running down to the affray. At this the Irishmen all turned and ran away, one of them saying, "The nayger was as bad as any Old Country bull." Charley was badly beaten, bruised and bleeding from the free use of the shillelaghs, and immediately started for home; but his troubles were not over yet. In his anxiety to get home, for he was suffering greatly, he took a short cut through a field of tall rye, just in blossom. He hoped to escape notice, but did not; for, when about halfway through the field, he saw the owner on the fence, pointing at him, and heard his vicious dog coming tearing down toward him. He thought for a moment this might be worse than the Irishmen. He would have to use some tact, or be torn to pieces.

Directly the dog came up panting, with gleaming eyes and open mouth. Charley spread his legs far apart and swayed his body as much as possible and, as the dog jumped at him, he struck it just behind the left shoulder and it fell as if dead. The owner then came running up in great anger, but as soon as he saw Charley's battered condition and bloody face, his countenance changed. He at once asked what was the matter. Charley, of course, explained his recent encounter with the seven Irishmen. In the meantime, the dog recovered its breath and stood by quietly. The man wanted to take Charley to his house and have his wounds dressed, but he thanked him and pushed on toward home. This he reached in an exhausted condition, wearing a very large lump on the back of his head and a bad cut on his cheek. One shoulder felt as if it was dislocated, and his ribs hurt when he breathed. In fact, so badly had he been used that he was unable to do any work for nearly three months. Charley wound up his account of this adventure by saying, "I was so thankful to escape with my life! The Lord was good; if it hadn't been for Him, the Irishmen would have killed me sure, with their shillelaghs; and I can take my qualification I never afterwards so far forgot myself as to say I could whip any Irishman that ever crossed the Atlantic Ocean."

Nothing, however, created such intense interest at the Bull's Head as a cockfight. It would draw the largest crowd and produce the greatest excitement. The Christmas following the encounter with the Irishmen, arrangements were made for the largest gathering of the season, and no less than fifty birds had been promised for the main. When the appointed time came, a motley crowd, of all ages, sizes and colours, assembled in the driving shed of the Bull's Head for the great fight. Charley was among the number, and had a prize winning chicken of former occasions under his arm. There had been several fights, some of them keenly contested, before Charley's turn came. The excitement by this time was intense. Already many plugs of tobacco, jackknives and bits of silver had exchanged hands at the close of the successive fights. As Charley's bird had already won a great reputation, three of the best birds at command had been reserved to match him in successive fights. Great was the excitement when it and one much heavier were placed in the pit for battle. As they stood for an instant, each glaring at his antagonist with fierce eyes and ruffled neck, the larger bird had much the preponderance of favour. The cocks at once dashed at each other and, as each gained a temporary success, his backers cheered to the echo. The betting for a time kept pace with the fight. All the tobacco, jackknives, pocketbooks and bits of silver in the crowd were put up again and, when these were all up, some very enthusiastic ones put up fairly good hats against inferior ones. A more excited, noisier and wilder lot, perhaps, never attended a main. Suddenly, an extra thrust of spurs into the side of its opponent by Charley's bird, became the turning point. The heavy bird wilted and its wings drooped. It was evident the cock was vanquished, and immediately his owner snatched it from the pit and thus rescued his bird from premature death. There were two others reserved to fight Charley's bird; but the unanimous voice of the crowd was that the cock had fought so nobly it would be unfair to put it in another fight. Charley was very proud as he held the bird in his arm, surrounded by the crowd, who were lavish with their praises of its great fighting qualities. The two birds held in reserve, some- one suggested, should be placed in the pit to fight each other. This was done, and a somewhat guarded and tedious battle took place. It, however, served to let the highly wrought feelings of the crowd down gradually to their natural condition. At the close it was declared a drawn game. As it was now dusk, the crowd was about to repair to their respective homes when two powerful dogs, one a mastiff and the other a bull, rose on their hind feet with an angry half-growl and half-bark and faced each other in a savage fight. To the crowd, who immediately formed a dense ring about the fighting dogs, this was an unexpected and highly appreciated sport. Such was the eagerness with which they pressed around the dogs, that they swayed hither and thither as the combatants rolled about in the dust and changed their positions in their fierce contest. "Let 'em have it out." "Stand back." "Give 'em room." "Don't they fight well?" and such-like expressions were of frequent occurrence. As well, many words of encouragement, which appeared to be neither needed nor heeded, were directed to the dogs themselves. So well-matched were they, that neither had gained the mastery when their owners, concluding they had fought long enough, asked and obtained assistance to separate them. This was accomplished with some difficulty, as the bulldog could not be persuaded to let go until his jaws were pried open. The dog fight, being an extra piece of sport, put everybody in the best of humour, and all were highly pleased with the day's proceedings.

There were many minor amusements, such as swooping down on an outlying and unguarded melon patch.

> Of all that's found beneath the moon—
> Ham-bone, pigeon, possum, pullet, coon,

> Pineapple, cherry, sweet potato,
> Orange, banana, fig, tomato,
> Berry, prune, coconut and peach—
> That can be in the darkies' reach,
> This is the best of every kind:
> The watermelon smiling on the vine.

It took Sambo[4] but a short time to give a melon a whack across his knee, and, when it naturally fell into two or three parts, to scoop its delicious contents with his fingers, exclaiming only "er-um-yum-yum."

There was also the risky amusement of the hen coop, when the pullets were fine and fat. At a certain season of the year, skirmishing parties were frequent.

"Josephine," said old Mose to his wife, "have you got them chickens shut up in the smokehouse, like I told you?"

"No, I ain't, but what makes you so mighty particular about them chickens?" inquired Josephine.

"Never you mind, I know what's the matter, and that's enough said till them chickens is carefully penned. When I heard yesterday that the folks over near the huddle are going to have a birthday party at their house tomorrow night, I want to be sure that my chickens don't attend that party, d'you hear?" shouted Mose.

"O-ho, old man, I see the drift of your discourse now," replied Josephine, as she started to lock up the chickens in the smokehouse.

Another amusement which may be mentioned was black serenades which were of common occurrence in those days. They consisted of the solitary lover with his banjo and of groups of all sizes with great varieties of vocal and instrumental music. Many a Dulcinea's heart beat quicker as she heard the voice of her lover in song, accompanied with the sweet strains of the banjo or guitar, float upon the balmy zephyrs of a summer evening. It was a form of amusement which involved more than a mere pastime, as it developed Cupid's archery and contributed to the ever-widening domain of love by affording opportunities for susceptible and seeking hearts to come together. The following are given as specimens of the serenading customs:

> Come, come, darkies sing,
> Listen how the banjo ring, ring, ring;
> Hark! Negroes, hark! the echo wake,

Another banjo in the brake,
His answer to the strain we pour
Comes from the skiff by the shore.

———

Old master gave me holiday,
    I would that they were more,
With happy heart I push away,
    My boat from off the shore,
    And paddle down the river,
        With spirits light and free,
    To the cabin of my darling May,
        I burn so much to see.

CHORUS

Oh! dearest May, more lovely than the day,
Your eyes are bright as stars at night,
When the moon is gone away.

———

Down in the cane-brake, close by the mill,
There lived a yellow gal, her name was Nancy Till;
She knew that I loved her, she knew it long,
I'm going to serenade her, and I'll sing this song

CHORUS

    Come love, come, I've a boat to row,
    She lies high and dry on the Ohio;
    Come love, come, come along with me,
    I'll take you down to Tennessee.

Heigh! Nellie, ho! Nellie, listen, love, to me,
I'll sing for you, play for you a dulcem melody.

———

Oh! dear Lucy Neal,
    Oh! good Lucy Neal,
If I had you by my side,
    How happy I would feel.

Oh! Susannah, don't you cry for me,
I'm going to Alabama with my banjo on my knee.[5]

During the eleven years of his slave life with Ridgely, Charley saw much of the great slave system of the country in respect to its amusements as well as its vices and cruelties. He had the satisfaction of knowing that he was appreciated by his master, and thus he enjoyed many privileges denied the ordinary slave. With this master he grew from boyhood to manhood. While with him, he became noted as a leader among the young slaves of that section of the country in the various sports of slave life, and surpassed all his associates in strength and agility.

It was Ridgely's practice to hire his slaves out as they were required by his neighbours on their farms and plantations. Thomas Raven, whose fine wheat farm was nearly ten miles away, for several seasons in succession hired Charley and other slaves from Ridgely, to cut his golden grain with the sickle, for neither cradle nor reaper had yet come into existence. Charley was appointed leader of one of the gangs, and this was deemed a great honour. Out of a gang of forty-four, the great heat of a harvest day had prostrated all but fourteen, who still followed Charley's lead. The thirty exhausted ones were stretched out beneath the shade of a large black walnut tree. The big tree was at once named the hospital. A waggish fellow still at work, looking wistfully toward the thirty beneath the sheltering tree as Mr. Raven happened to come up, said, "If I had my big duck gun, couldn't I kill a crow?" "The crows are almost dead now," said Raven.

Charley, for his first ten days' work, carried home ten dollars to his master, who said "Good boy, Charley." This was his only reward on that or any other occasion when he brought home his earnings. Mr. Raven was more generous, and paid him for his leadership, and for his own use a York shilling a day. This he was glad to get to spend at the Bull's Head.

13

In Search of a Wife

OLD CASKEY, whose plantation was about fifteen miles distant, had some business with Ridgely, and spent a good part of the day on his premises. Charley was working in the garden that morning and had a conversation with him. He commenced by asking some questions about his master's plantation and Charley's personal history, and then talked quite freely about his own. The interest he appeared to take in Charley was unusual and made him wonder what was coming. Perhaps, thought Charley, as he left him, "He's preparing the way to buy me."

On passing the garden an hour later, Caskey spoke to him again, and broached a very delicate subject. Said he, "You're a fine powerful-looking man and I would like you to see my cook, Lucinda; she and you would make a fine team." He mentioned several nice things about Lucinda, and closed by giving him a warm invitation to come down to his place and see her. Charley felt greatly flattered, and assured him that as soon as he could get through with the hurry in his work in the garden, he would ask his master's leave to go down.

About ten days after on a fine Saturday afternoon, after putting on his best clothes, which included a white cotton shirt and stand-up collar with large, black neck stock, and stuffing in his pocket a bright bandana handkerchief, the latter well-perfumed, he started down the road to make his visit to Caskey's plantation. He was naturally anxious to make a favourable impression and thought over what he was going to talk about. His plan was first to go straight to Caskey and report his arrival. He had not the slightest doubt he would receive a warm reception. As he mused on these things, his fancy was pretty active as to Lucinda. She was large he knew, because Caskey had said they would make a good team. To her person, he added good disposition, engaging manners and beauty of face; and as Caskey had said nothing as to these matters, his imagination had full play. While full of these thoughts, a man drove up with a wagon and a pair of mules. He was returning from market empty, and invited him to take a ride. Charley gladly accepted and his walk was thus shortened, so that in about three hours and a half from the time of starting he arrived at Caskey's front gate.

He had just put his hand on the latch when, aroused by the noise of the wagon he had just left, a great mastiff came bounding toward him. He concluded to wait just where he was and keep the gate between himself and the dog. This was a reception he had not counted on. The dog stopped inside, and contented himself with a deep growl and by indulging in a heavy, coarse bark, which was somewhat grating on Charley's nerves and discouraging to his undertaking. At the back part of the mansion, which seemed old and out of repair, in what appeared to be the kitchen, a head encircled in a greasy paper cap popped out of the window to see what caused the racket at the gate. The head as quickly disappeared. Whether it was the head of a man or woman, Charley could not tell; but whichever it was, he expected its owner to see that he would be quickly relieved from his embarrassing position. "The course of true love never runs smoothly," and Charley was considering whether he should advance or retreat, when the front door opened and Caskey appeared on the verandah. He shouted at the dog, using language which was, to say the least of it, more vigorous than polite. It had, however, the effect of calling off the dog. Charley's way, which for a time had been seriously interrupted, was now clear, and he opened the gate and walked down the path toward the house. As he passed along, he noticed that the lawn was badly kept, that there were a variety of flowering shrubs, such as lilac, snowball, oleander and others, but they bore a neglected appearance. Both house and lawn seemed to speak of better days. There was, however, one redeeming feature; on either side of the path was a row of rose bushes now in full bloom and, being in great variety, the sight was pretty, and made Charley feel somewhat reassured. As he walked up the steps to meet Caskey, he received the following salute: "Hello, nigger! It's you, is it? Take a seat," he said, pointing to a wooden chair from which the back had disappeared. He then went on to speak of his dog. "Captain," said he, "is very cross, especially with niggers, and it was lucky that I happened to be in when you came, or you would probably have fared badly."

70

Charley began to think he was faring pretty badly as it was, but he thought of the "true love" adage and said to himself, "This will appear as nothing when I meet the vision of loveliness within."

Caskey scarcely appeared to be the same man. When Charley saw him before, he was dressed in a good black cloth suit with a broad-brimmed felt hat, and had with him a fine horse and buggy. His language was then smooth and pleasing. Now he wore rough clothing, a dirty old hat and his shoes were run down at the heel, and altogether his *tout ensemble* was decidedly tacky. His language, too, was as repulsive as his garb. As he commenced talking about his dog Captain, Charley's eyes began to wander over the plantation. He could see both to the north and to the west. There were corn fields and tobacco fields. In these were perhaps a dozen slaves, all told, hoeing and doing other agricultural work. Among them he noticed a few women and girls, but knew that the object of his search was not without, as her occupation would, of course, confine her to the kitchen.

"I got Cap from a Virginian when he was about half-grown," said Caskey, who seemed proud of the immense size and good qualities of the dog. "You see," he continued, "I used to be a great dog fancier, but my wife was opposed to dogs. I had two pups; one was a mastiff and the other was a bloodhound. They used to fight and make great rackets, and my wife used to grumble about those pups. I knew there was money in those pups and hated to part with them unless I could get a good price. This Virginian took a great notion to my mastiff pup and wanted to buy him. I refused, unless I sold both. I valued the pups at fifty dollars apiece. 'Well, stranger,' said the Virginian, 'I can't give such prices as that, but I'll tell you what I'll do. I'll make an even trade. You take my bulldog, he's cheap at a hundred dollars, and I'll take the pups.' We traded on the spot. I had to send the pups to the Dew Drop Inn, a tavern in which he put up at Baltimore, and on doing this I was to get the bulldog.

"After he left, I went into the house, and told my wife I had sold the pups. 'Both of them?' she asked. 'Yes, both of them,' I said. 'How much did you get for them?' 'Fifty dollars apiece,' I replied. 'Fifty dollars,' she repeated, and seemed greatly surprised. She, however, recovered at once and asked another question. It was, 'Where's the money?' I then, of course, had to explain that I had first to deliver the pups at the 'Dew Drop.' 'Good deliverance, good riddance to bad rubbish,' said she, rather tartly; 'and the money?' 'Oh, I don't get any money,' I had to say. 'No money? What to you get, then?' she asked. 'Why, I'm going to get one of the finest bulldogs you ever set eyes on. He's worth a hundred dollars, at the least.' At this, my wife gave me a very strange kind of look.

"Well, I've never been sorry for my bargain. For aught I know, the Virginian had just the same kind of experience with his wife, only in his case he got a hundred dollars for his bulldog, and took his pay in two pups, at fifty dollars each. Cap is a fine dog."

"Cap"

Charley wondered when this dog tale was going to end and he was to be ushered into some sitting room to meet Lucinda. Caskey, however, went on and gave the dog's history, from the time he became the lucky owner down to the dog's attack on Charley. It had gone through a number of wonderful exploits; had rescued a child from drowning in the river, had beaten all the dogs in the country round fighting—there was nothing to match this dog. It had played a very important part in the capture of runaway slaves on more than one occasion. Just then, Charley saw a white man coming from the tobacco field. Caskey said he was his overseer.

"What shall I do now?" thought Charley. "I didn't come here to see these men; I came to see Lucinda."

"I reckon," said Caskey, "the overseer wants to see me. I suppose you came to see Lucinda."

Charley was about to make some remark about their former conversation, when he stopped him by saying, "That's the way," pointing to a path that led round to the kitchen door, and started off to meet the overseer.

It must have been full three-quarters of an hour since Charley arrived at the gate, and now it seemed that he was no nearer than ever to Lucinda. In fact, he felt farther off, because he had counted on Caskey's assistance. And now, just on the threshold, when he could have paved his way with ease and broken the barrier which he felt still existed between him and the object of his visit, he had suddenly left Charley to work out his own salvation, it might be added, "with fear and trembling." His first look was for that wonderful dog Cap, and there he lay, stretched his full length on the lawn beside a camp stool, apparently fast asleep. Charley wanted him to remain asleep, at all events until he had reached safe quarters in Lucinda's presence. Not to arouse the dog, he stepped softly on the pebbled walk pointed out to him and proceeded around the house toward the kitchen door. If ever he felt like a fool it was then. He had been talking with Lucinda's master a long time, indeed, to him it seemed an age; and yet, while he had learned much about Cap he had not gleaned a single bit of information about Lucinda. He did not know whether she was expecting him, or even if she knew there was such a man in existence. Would she be alone? What should he say? And a great many other questions harassed him exceedingly. But he had got to the door and the next thing was to rap, in doing which he turned half round, in order that he might keep an eye on the sleeping dog. But Cap did not stir; this he considered a favourable sign that his mission would after all be successful. The door was opened by a large, heavy-boned woman, whose bullet shaped head he immediately recognized as the one he had seen three-quarters of an hour before, when he stood facing the furious dog at the gate, but the greasy paper cap had disappeared. The woman invited him in, and he saw at a glance that he was in the kitchen and that preparations were going on for supper.

14

❦

The Cruelty and Vices of Slavery

IN HIS time, knocked about as he was from pillar to post, Charley became acquainted with a great many slave owners and their overseers. Some of the former were genial, splendid men; others of them were like their overseers—coarse, cruel and profligate. Some of them, Charley claims, acted as if they had the world in a sling and could do what they pleased with it, and as if they were unaccountable either to God or man. A few samples may be given by way of illustration.

His old slave master, Richard Croxall, was rich, haughty, cruel and passionate. His wife was naturally of kindly heart, but sometimes excessively severe with her female slaves. Both were Episcopalians and attended the little Episcopal church which stood on a corner of their own plantation.

One summer Sunday morning, Mrs. Croxall wished to wear a particular muslin dress to church, but it was not done up and not fit to wear as it was. She became angry at this, threw the dress on the brick floor of the kitchen, spit and stamped upon it, then ordered Charley's mother and her sister Poll to have it washed and ironed by ten o'clock, so that she could wear it to church. The women knew it was an impossible task, but they went at it and, although they did their best, it could not be got sufficiently dry to iron in time. On account of this their master was called in, and he gave orders to two male slaves for their punishment. The two women were marched to the whipping house. Here they were made to stand on the floor, and were bound with a small cord by the wrists. Their hands were then drawn up toward a beam in the ceiling by a pulley, until they stood on tiptoe. In that position the rope was tied, and then their master and mistress stepped into their carriage and drove away to church to worship(?) God. Taking revenge on two helpless female slaves, and at the same time praying the blessing of heaven to rest upon themselves and expecting forgiveness without forgiving, was inconsistency in itself. Oppressing the creatures of His hands, in forgetfulness of the fact that it is beyond mortal's power to do anything for God, except by benefiting his fellows, and that it is impossible for man to injure Him, except by injuring his fellow creatures, betrayed ignorance of the first principles of Christianity.

What a weary waiting by the two women for two long hours—and then relief? Oh, no! but instead, their bodies were stripped to the waist. The lash was vigorously applied to their backs, which were cut through the skin in many places, and were then hastily washed with salt and water. The two slave women feebly walked away to their quarters. Their owners had been their own avengers and were satisfied. To their mistress all the difference was she had been compelled to wear a striped gown instead of a checked one, which was no better, although made of lighter material. To the slave women the difference was stripes, indeed, and almost death—the cruelty of slavery!

Not quite two miles from Croxall's plantation there lived a slave holder named John Leester, who was very old, exceedingly distrustful, and as wicked as he was old. One day, when drawing near the end of life, he requested his overseer to get Nellie, the cook, to prepare some soup for him to eat. The man ordered the soup and went out to his work. Half an hour after, the cook sent him word that the soup was ready. On hearing this, he came to the kitchen, obtained the plate of soup, and took it to the old master.

"Did you stand over the cook while she prepared it?" he asked.

The overseer admitted that he had not.

"There is poison in it," said Leester, "and I won't take it. Tie her up and whip her."

The overseer tried to calm his fears and reason the old man out of his delusion, but failed. Leester reminded him that he was his overseer.

"Whip her, as I tell you."

"I will not," the man replied with firmness; "and now I tell you more. From henceforth I cease to be your overseer."

At this Leester became more enraged than ever and said he would whip her himself, and suiting the action to the word, took up the overseer's whip and tottered into the kitchen. There he used his remaining strength in whipping Nellie, who was taken by surprise and soon fell in a fainting fit. Before she recovered, a child was born. The whipping was equally disastrous to Leester, for the overexertion produced a nervous prostration and paralysis, and he passed away the same night. Nellie lived, but the child died. Soon after, the Leester plantation was broken up and the slaves were all sold off by public auction, and scattered far and wide. This occurred in the adjoining county of Hartford, and the circumstances, as here related, came direct from a lady who lived on the farm adjoining the one on which Leester lived. The lady was much affected, and wept as she told the story of Leester's suspicious rage and Nellie's unjust punishment.

Old Ben Pickle, who lived five miles away on the opposite side of the river from Leester's plantation, owned a great number of slaves, kept two bloodhounds and, for devilish cruelty to his slaves, outstripped Leester. He seemed to delight in torture, and if a slave died under his process of punishment, he would become enraged and still more hardened. Owing to the vast marshes and swamps of the locality, mosquitoes and gallinippers of enormous size swarmed in abundance.

A slave of his, named Pompey, endowed with great stubbornness, had now fallen under his master's displeasure for a petty theft that had been committed. Ben said he was tired of whipping him, and he would resort to severer measures. So he had Pompey taken to that part of the marsh at Back River Neck most lonely and most infested with bloodsucking gallinippers. Here he ordered poor Pompey to be stripped to the waist; then the usual order, "nine-and-thirty well laid on," left many bleeding cuts on his back. His hands were tied behind his back and he was further stripped of all clothing, except for a loin cloth. Two stakes were driven into the white sands of the marsh ten feet apart. Pompey was stretched on the ground between the stakes with ropes. His head was tied to one and his feet to the other so that he could not move, and thus he was left by his fiendish owner for torture by the ravenous gallinippers. In the morning at break of day, he sent two slaves to release and bring him home. These, on coming to the place of torture, found poor Pompey dead. Through the night, so great was the agony inflicted by the relentless bloodsucking gallinippers that it became more than the beaten slave could endure, so appealing to God to establish his innocence of the charge laid against him, and offering up a prayer to receive his soul unto Himself, he drew heavily with his feet and produced strangulation.

> And his lifeless body lay,
> A worn out fetter that the soul
> Had broken and thrown away.

Round and about that lifeless body was a thin, bright red line made by his lifeblood as it trickled down upon the white sand, so that when his body was removed there was a perfect outline of its form. The two slaves returned to their master and reported what they had seen. On learning the news, Ben cursed terribly at his loss, and ordered them back to bury the body. This they did in the spot which witnessed his death and was outlined by his life's blood. They removed the stakes to which he had been tied to the head and feet, to mark the lonely grave, and then fell upon their knees and wept over poor Pompey.

"Thank the Lord," said one of them as they turned to leave, "Master can beat Pompey no more; he's free from the lash and the gallinippers."

"Yes," said the other, "Pompey was very good and religious, and I'm sure his spirit is now at rest in the bright world on high."

The news of Pompey's death created a great sensation, not only on that plantation but on neighbouring ones. And three days had not passed over before the discovery came that Pompey was entirely innocent of the paltry theft with which he was charged. Ben Pickle was ever after both hated and despised by the whole slave population of that section of the country.

On Back River Neck there was a small plantation owned by Oscar Raymond. He had no quarters and his few slaves lived in his kitchen. His youngest son Horseth, a boy of about nine years of age, was accustomed to play with a child slave of his father's house, a boy of nearly the same age named Pete. Pete was one of Charley's cousins, and is well remembered by him as shoeless and hatless and scantily clad. With a bright, laughing face he played on the home lawn, or ran an errand when required. His natural sprightliness and activity made him the leader of the slave children of his own age. These qualities endeared him to his parents, and made him a general favourite on the Raymond plantation. One pleasant summer afternoon Horseth and he were amusing themselves beneath the shade of a large walnut tree. They were gathering the walnuts which grew on the branches above them. Horseth suggested that they should see who could first get a kernel out whole from the shell. After a few moments, Pete called out that he had got one. Horseth at once came over to where Pete stood and ordered him to give the nut to him. Horseth's tone offended Pete and he refused. Then Pete received a blow, and quickly returned it. A rough-and-tumble scuffle ensued in which Horseth got the worst of it, and he went into the house crying and bleeding at the nose. His mother, looking out of the window, saw the fight and, on seeing the plight of Horseth, became enraged. She took down her husband's gun, cocked it and gave it to Horseth, and said, "Go right out and shoot Pete." The boy immediately ran out, fired, and shot him in the breast. Little Pete dropped dead. The dead child's parents lived in the woman's own house and dared not make any outcry, but were compelled to stifle and hide their convulsed feelings.

Hundreds of slaves from adjoining plantations came to see the murdered boy. So did a good many white people; among others were Mrs. Ashton, Raymond's daughter and her husband. They had come from their home, several miles on the other side of the Back River. Everyone seemed sorry for what had happened, but no one dared to sympathize with the heart-stricken parents. This was strictly watched and forbidden by the Raymonds. Preparations were made for the funeral. A platform was built under the trees near the house. The preacher, a freed black, preached a sermon to suit the slave holders. He said a great deal about obedience. He enforced the scriptural exhortation, "Servants, be obedient to your masters according to the flesh." Slaves should be obedient to their owners, and children should be obedient. The sermon over, Pete was carried to his little grave, given him in a corner of the plantation on which he had lived a sunny, happy life. There was no investigation of any kind in connection with the matter. Horseth, however, never prospered. As he grew up, he became very wild, took to drinking hard, and finally became insane. His parents sent him to the insane asylum, where he died some two years after. Mrs. Raymond was never quite herself, nor free from trouble after the day she had ordered the fatal shooting, and died within a year of Horseth's death. At her death it was whispered about that it was all a judgement upon them on account of little Pete, over whose little grassy grave the wild daisies were then in full bloom.

In the earlier times Charley's mother used to say to him, "A heap of barbarity's gone out of slavery, child; you're born free to what I was." And yet he saw for himself enough of its working to show him it was the field for bad men's avarice, lust, cruelty, and that it was prolific in toil, torture and premature death. It was, by many slave holders, deemed as necessary to provide whippings as it was clothing and food, and they easily fell into the habit of being more lavish with the former than the latter.

Acts of cruelty may have been the exception in slave life, as is contended; but the number of cruelties perpetrated within a radius of ten miles of his several different homes, as he was hustled from plantation to plantation, and from master to master, would of themselves fill a book. He knew slave masters who thought nothing of giving one hundred and fifty lashes, and would then have their victim's back washed with salt and water. What wonder that these victims occasionally sank beneath such fiendish torture. Often had his mother told him the cruel murder of her sister Polly by her drunken master, Walter Quigley, to whom she had been sold. It was after the Methodist meetings had been started among the salves. Polly was a strong, sweet singer and was fond of singing at all times. While busily engaged over the washtub in the laundry one day, and singing as hard as she was working, the old, well worn hymn:

> Come, sinners, to the Gospel feast,
> Let every soul be Jesus' guest;
> Ye need not one be left behind,
> For God hath bidden all mankind

Her master, fired up with peach brandy, happened to be passing, and ordered her to stop singing. Returning shortly after, he heard her singing another verse of the same beautiful hymn.

"Poor woman," sighed Charley, "I expect she forgot herself."

Her master rushed in and struck her across the back with his heavy ivory-headed cane. She was within a few days of her confinement and fell down in convulsions, and died in a few minutes. What did this dealer in human flesh and blood say and do? He went away whining, that by an unlucky blow he had lost $1,000 worth of property. Was he arrested? No. Not a bit more was said or done than if it had been one of his horses he had hit on the head and, by an unlucky blow, killed. It was slavery, and no white man would, and no black man, in those days, dare, say one word in condemnation. This was then one of the darkest places of the earth, and the land was "full of habitations of cruelty." How the blood boiled in the veins of her brothers and sisters at this terrible murder, and yet they dare not condemn it. The laws of God and nature had been brutally violated, but the law of man had nothing to say against it. So there was no help for it. He was but one, a brute man, so why did not the slaves combine and slay him on the spot, you say? Why? What then? The whole power of the state would immediately have been brought to bear on them. Although there was no law to help them—for their evidence against a white man was inadmissible in court—they would soon have found law enough against them. And death by that law and the power of the state would have been the sure fate of every one who had yielded to the impulse of revenging poor Poll's untimely death.

By Walter Quigley's death, his two sons, Philip and Charles, became wealthy. Both freely spent their father's accumulation of money in the common vices of the day. They were particularly addicted to horse racing and gambling. Shortly after his father's passing, Philip got into trouble in connection with some of the chattel property which fell to his lot in the division under the will, from which he extricated himself with difficulty, by the payment of a large sum as hush money, and setting his female slave Josey free.

Charles, in addition to Philip's failings, had a great weakness for peach brandy. This liquor made him irritable. One day in the field one of his slaves was guilty of an act of disobedience and, when ordered to strip for the lash, fled. Charles had driven out to the field in his gig and immediately gave chase with a drawn pistol. The culprit ran across a ploughed field, whose uneven surface somewhat impeded the speed of the horse, and made it difficult for the slave's master to keep his seat. The horse was whipped on, regardless of the uneven surface, when directly a wheel struck a stone and upset the rig. Charles, in falling off, got his leg broken. The slave, looking round to see what distance there was between him and his pursuer, saw the horse running in another direction with a part of the gig, and his master lying helpless on the ground. At this he stopped and looked for a few seconds. Then this man, whom his master wished to shoot, returned and, ascertaining the misfortune which had befallen him, caught the horse which was taking a circular course round him, temporarily repaired the broken gig, lifted his now penitent master into it, and took him home.

When Bill Black went into the employ of Quigley as slave overseer, he was quite a young man, probably not more than twenty-two years of age. Bill was not a hard driver, but managed to get as much done by the slaves as many a one more harsh. He would rank probably as an average man on the point of whip service. He never lost sight of his master's interest, and this quality caused him to be greatly appreciated by the Quigleys, who paid him a salary of $1,000 a year. He was addicted to no great vice, save one. The very first year he ruled over the Quigley plantation, he formed an alliance with one of the young female slaves under his charge, named Bell White, a full blooded black. The names of Bill Black, a white man, and Bell White, a black woman, were associated together for years by the slaves.

15

৩

Sophy and Her Baby

A BOUT THIRTY miles away from Ridgely's farm there lived a slave owner named Mallory, who tolerated a very passionate overseer called Dan Hunter. His cowhide whip, which was looked upon as a weapon of defence as well as offence, was heavily loaded at the butt-end with lead. Many a poor slave had writhed beneath the lash of this terrible whip. One of the slaves under his control at the time now referred to, was a mulatto woman of about twenty-one years of age, named Sophy who had a babe about a month old.

There was considerable excitement just then among the slaves on account of a recent occurrence. That section had become recently infested with baldheaded eagles. And one day, when a slave mother had left her little infant beneath the shade of a black elderberry bush as she worked binding in the field, a very large eagle swooped down and took the infant in its great talons, spread its wings and bore its precious burden away. If there ever was excitement, it was then. The distracted mother screamed and ran in the direction of the bird, but too late to rescue her child. Up went the eagle with its prey to the top of a very tall pine tree. The slaves quickly ran shouting in the wildest manner and gathered around the tree. Every face was then intently upturned to see what would happen. Every moment seemed a day. Will the bird let it fall? was the anxious inquiry. It seemed to be holding the child with one of its great claws, while resting with the other foot on a limb of the treetop. Someone suggested running for a gun and shooting the eagle; others said, "No that will never do; the bird will let go, and the fall will kill the child." Up to that time the baby had not cried, and the bird had remained quiet on the limb. Now, however, the eagle began to move, its feathers ruffled, the wings began to outstretch and, raising up, it seized the little infant with the great foot which had rested on the limb and, drawing the babe close to its breast, soared away in an easterly direction. Intently they watched the flight of the immense eagle. It was evidently heading for the great swamp about four miles distant. Permission was at once obtained to follow and all the slaves of this plantation, along with many from those between Mallory's and the swamp, joined in the search for the eagle and the baby, but no trace of either was ever found. From that time forth, slave mothers had the greatest fear that their young children might be carried off by baldheaded eagles, and many were the commands given by their mothers to those in whose care the small children were left, as they went to the fields to hoe or bind, to look out for the baldheaded eagle.

It was nearly a year after that in which the baby had been carried off, that Sophy was ordered to the harvest field for the first time since her child was born. She would not take it to the field, a distant one, on account of her fear of baldheaded eagles; so she left it in the charge of her grandmother at the quarters, and started with the rest for the field. She was in a bad humour, on account of having to be separated from her baby. Owing to the distance of the field, dinner was brought for the slaves. Sophy would not eat. She complained of a pain in her breast and she said she must go to the quarters to see her baby. The overseer said she should not. At about two o'clock in the afternoon, when in great distress, finding the overseer in another part of the field, she took the opportunity of slipping off. It was noticed that before going she put a carving knife, used at the slaves' dinner, under her apron. When Dan returned he missed her, and at once he asked what had become of her. He was told that she complained of pain in her breast and that she had gone to the quarters to her baby. At this Dan grew savagely angry.

"I'll teach the huzzy," said he, "to disobey me. I'll knock the stubbornness out of her before I'm done with her." Then, mounting his horse, he started at a gallop for the quarters. On the road near the quarters, he passed two men who were at work with a whipsaw, cutting lumber.

"Did you see a yellow nigger gal pass here? he inquired.

"Yes," they answered, "she passed nearly an hour ago and went into the quarters."

He swore some great oath, and dismounting, rushed into the quarters. No sooner had he entered, than they heard blows of a whip and the peculiar whistling sound a lash makes as it flies rapidly through the air. They stopped work and listened, and heard Dan's voice saying, "Quit,

Sophy." Then the whipping ceased, and all was quiet. An instant later, Sophy's grandmother rushed out of the door, screaming: "Tell Master to come." In her hand was the carving knife Sophy had brought from the field, now covered with Dan's lifeblood. "Dan and Sophy were fighting, and she's killed him," she screamed. "Oh! tell Master to come."

The two men ran in and found it even as she had said. Dan lay on the floor covered with stabs, weltering in his blood, dead. Sophy was wringing her hands and crying in a corner of the room. Mallory came shortly after, and was appalled at the sight which met his gaze. Dan's body was borne away by four male slaves, and Sophy was shortly afterwards arrested and conducted to jail. The tragedy was the talk of the whole country round.

When the time drew near for trial, Lawyer Hickey announced that he would defend the woman without fee or reward. The prosecuting counsel put the old grandmother and a couple of girls of about sixteen or seventeen years of age (all of whom were present at the time) in the witness box. The story told by all three varied very little in the main points. From what they said, as the result of the examination by both lawyers, it was clear the deceased had brutally attacked the prisoner with his great whip, first laying on the lash, and then, as if this did not satisfy him, he closed in to strike her with the butt-end of his whip; and it was at this crisis of the attack that one of the witnesses first saw Sophy grasp a long knife from a table close by. The other two did not see the knife until Dan was bringing down the butt-end of his whip on Sophy's shoulder; then they saw the gleam of the blade, which in an instant was buried in his side. He fell, but she did not stay her hand until her grandmother got to her and caught her arm. The two men at the whipsaw were also put in the witness box, and gave the information they had already stated. It was clear from what one of the young female witnesses said, it was when Sophy first caught up the knife that Dan said, "Don't, Sophy!"

Lawyer Hickey pleaded earnestly before the jury for the life of the prisoner. He pointed out that "she was untutored and improperly cared for, that the unnatural treatment in separating her from her offspring for so long a time was harsh and uncalled for, and that the instincts of her nature and love for her babe swayed her as powerfully as nature would influence the most refined lady of the land. Her whole soul on that fatal day cried, 'Give me my child! I will have my child, come what may!'" Then, on the other hand, he pictured to the jury "the brutal nature of the man who sought to stay the long pent up yearnings of her soul, and

83

dared to treat her as he would not a brute beast under the same circumstances; and then, because she disobeyed his cruel and unlawful—yes, in the sight of God, unlawful—command, like a savage let loose, to bear down, trample upon and perhaps kill, as he supposed his helpless victim. Then, and only then, in self-defence did she draw the weapon which cut short his hellish rage. Without father, without brother, without husband or natural protector, shall she now suffer death, because she slew her oppressor to save her life? She had been brutally beaten for her offspring; and now, in turn, she struck a blow for the same offspring. It always was, it is now, and ever shall be, the law of nature and the law of the land that an antagonist may be killed in self-defence. Gentlemen of the jury, I ask you, in the name of humanity, nature and justice, that you let this captive young woman go free."

These were but some of the closing sentences of his powerful appeal, of an hour's duration, to that attentive jury. When he took his seat there were not many dry eyes in the courtroom.

The prosecuting counsel even seemed visibly affected. His words appeared to be powerless and, after talking about fifteen minutes, he sat down. The judge then went carefully over the evidence, and finally left it for the jury to find whether the prisoner had given those fatal stabs in self-defence; if not, it was murder. If done in self-defence, then it was justifiable. The jury retired, and in less that ten minutes filed into court again.

"Gentlemen, have you agreed upon your verdict?" asked the clerk.

"We have," said the foreman, amidst a profound and painful silence in the courtroom. "Not guilty!" Then everyone seemed to draw a long breath, at the same time the judge said, "Prisoner, you are discharged."

Mallory, hard-fisted man as he was, had been greatly moved by the painful case, and immediately announced, in the presence of the whole court, that "as the jury had acquitted Sophy, he would now set her and her child free." The whole courtroom of people cheered his magnanimity to the echo, and it was all in vain for the crier to cry, "Silence! silence!" The enthusiasm of the crowd was too strong to be easily suppressed. Many now gathered round Sophy, and congratulated her upon her double escape, from death and from slavery. Mallory was as good as his word, for he immediately took her to Lawyer Hickey's office, and had freedom papers made out for herself and child.

16

A Tragedy

J OE EAST was one of the worst slave holders of the Ridgely neighbourhood. He had a great many slaves and wished to get a more severe
overseer for them than available in the locality. He heard of a hard
man in Virginia he thought would suit him, and wrote for him. In the
course of a few weeks, Ted Eastman, for such was his name, arrived and
was duly installed as knight of the slave whip over his half-namesake's
herd of slaves. East's slaves had been somewhat troublesome and difficult to manage, and hence this new policy. The commission he gave Ted
was "Take charge of 'em. They're a bad lot, and have got ahead of me. If
they want flogging, flog 'em. Take all the work out of them you can get."

"That's just what I like," said Ted. "I know just what to do with a
nigger." And, suiting his action to his words, he gave his lead-loaded whip
a swing and a terrible crack, as if finally to convince the slave master that
he would carry out his wishes to the letter.

The slaves in their quarters, who had before heard of their master's
intentions, now learned of the new driver's arrival, and knew there was
trouble in store for them. The crowd of slaves and Ted met next morning. His appearance was coarse, his voice harsh, and his words threaten-
ing. He was a large, loose-built man, and held in his hand, as a symbol
of his power, the whip he had so significantly cracked in the slave holder's
presence the day before. He made a short speech to the slaves, in which
he told them of what he had heard of their laziness and insubordina-
tion, and closed by telling them, in coarse language, that he was fond of
flogging niggers, and he would take care that they should get plenty of
it. "I was fetched here," said he, "to whip, and I will whip, and make lots
of raw backs;" and, claiming that one of the quailing crowd before him

was inattentive, he called him out and proceeded to strip him. He lashed him cruelly and sent him, in charge of two others, to have his back washed off in brine. Then the slaves were put to work and every day, on some pretext or other, a slave was whipped; and when the whipping was severe, as it usually was, there was the customary accompaniment of pickle-wash.

This brutal man, in the faded likeness of God's image, went on from day to day, and from week to week, and from month to month, with his inhuman treatment, until every field working slave had felt the sting of his lash except two. These two were mulatto men, who were brothers, Jack Bain and Sam Bain. They were tall, lithe men and fine workers, and were supposed to be the sons of Joe East by their slave mother. They had been eyewitnesses of a terrible flogging given to their mother by this monster Ted, and their hearts craved revenge. After six months, during which time his reputation for harsh treatment had travelled over many surrounding plantations, Overseer Ted and his half-namesake, the slave holder, held a conversation. The latter was much pleased at the increased volume of work by his slaves, and the former was elated that he had been so successful.

"I've done it with this whip. I told you I knew what to do with a nigger. The fact is," said he, with a coarse laugh, "I've flogged every one of 'em, except Jack and Sam." These were the two brothers.

"Why didn't you flog them?" said the slave holder.

"Why, they never gave me any chance. They are splendid workers, and I never could find fault with the way they worked. They always mind me promptly. I could not wish for better niggers."

Just at that moment Jack happened to be passing.

"Look here, Jack," said Overseer Ted. "Get down on your hands and feet."

The slave did so.

"Now trot around the yard in that position," was the second command.

They slave obeyed.

"Now gallop," said Overseer Ted, at the same time giving the great whip a crack, as if he were a horse master in a circus ring, and away Jack scampered around the yard, in a circle about the slave owner and his overseer, as if he were a veritable horse. By sundry cracks of his whip, he urged the slave horse to his utmost speed. It was great sport for the two, East and Eastman, but it was hard work for Jack. The latter began to get out of breath, when "Whoa!" was called, and he was allowed to go on his way.

"Yes," said Overseer Ted, after he had gone, "these two niggers are the only ones I haven't whipped, and I'll catch them yet."

Unfortunately, he had not long to wait for an opportunity. Close to the quarters, on a neighbouring plantation, lived their Uncle Steve. He had been superannuated, as the clergymen term it, for he and his wife Dora had grown too old to work and were allowed to live by themselves in their own little whitewashed cabin. This cabin was crowned with a moss-covered chimney and mantled with a Virginia creeper which left little of the front to be seen save the door and a couple of windows. Within everything was kept scrupulously clean by Aunt Dora. They were both of industrious and economical habits. Steve made and sold wood-split brooms, and was a great lover of fowls. His wife attended to the fowls and raised chickens, and marketed eggs, chickens, and the fruit and other produce of their little garden. As their home was neat and comfort-able, it was not strange that their children, nephews, nieces and other young folk, were often found visiting old Uncle Steve's cabin. Sam, know-ing his uncle's admiration for bred fowl, had formerly left with him a fine game cock. There was a great deal of cockfighting in this neigh-bourhood. On Sunday afternoon, just as at the Bull's Head, it was a favourite pastime for the young men to gather in some tobacco or other out building and have a cockfight. Sam and Jack were as fond of it as others, and one fine summer's morning in the month of June, when their Uncle Steve was away to meeting, Sam went over to his cabin and carried the game bird away, intending to have him fight elsewhere that after-noon. When Uncle Steve returned and found what had happened, his righteous soul was vexed. He was what the slaves termed "a locus preachah."

"In the first place," said he to his wife. "It was wrong for Sam to come and take the bird unbeknownst to me. Secondly, it was wrong for him to do that on the Sabbath day; and in the next place, it was very wrong his going a cockfighting, 'specially on the Lord's day; and lastly, Sam must be punished for the sin."

Sam, all unconscious of his act being divided up into so many different heads by his uncle, was enjoying himself immensely at Nicholson's great tobacco house. Sam's bird had been very successful and had won in two engagements, on account of which Sam was in high spirits. On his way home, he called at his Uncle Steve's to return the bird. He was surprised at his reception. Uncle Steve, always so kind and good heretofore, was angry, and scolded, threatened, and even accused Sam of stealing the bird.

"Why, unc', how could I steal my own bird? He's mine. I never gave him to you, I only left him with you!"

"Don't talk, shut your mouth, child; look at that bird's head, see the blood and these cuts; he's been fighting, fighting on the Sabbath day. Afore the Lord it's a great sin, and you must be punished. Do you hear? I'll tell Overseer Ted, and he'll flog you for it. Go away and leave my door."

Sam saw that his uncle was angry and that it was useless to argue with him in his present frame of mind. So he turned and left him, simply saying, "I don't care if you do;" never once thinking that his uncle's threat to tell Overseer Ted would ever be heard of again.

On Monday afternoon the overseer rode out to the fields as usual. After staying with the slaves in the tobacco field about an hour, he rode over to where Jack and Sam were putting in two large posts for a gate. Sam noticed that he looked strangely at him, but never suspected the cause.

"Sam, I've got a crow to pick with you; have you got a bag to put the feathers in?"

"I reckon", said Sam.

"I hear that you stole your uncle's chicken and went fighting on Sunday. Ha! ha! ha!" laughed Ted, gloating over the chance that had come at last.

Then Sam knew his uncle had carried out his threat and, after the coarse laugh had ceased, replied: "I didn't steal that chicken. It's mine; I only left it with my unc'."

"Sam," said he, "there must be a stop put to this chicken fighting on Sunday," and jumping down off his horse, said, "Off with your shirt!" Sam did not move or speak. "Off with that shirt, nigger, I say, quick!"

"No, my shirt won't come off."

"Nigger!" howled Overseer Ted as he rushed forward and struck at him with his whip.

In an instant, the whip was jerked out of his hand and the two men were in holds. Both were powerful men, and in fierce anger, dealt heavy blows against one another. The mulatto was the most lithe of the two, and put his antagonist down.

"Reach me the broadaxe," said Sam to Jack; "this is the villain that whipped Mother."

Jack, fired by the same spirit of revenge, lifted the broadaxe from the spot where Sam had let it fall when the overseer first ran at him, and handed it to Sam, who, with one hand holding his antagonist down, with the other drew and struck him on the head with the pole of the axe. The overseer, fell back as if dead. They both thought that he was dead. But while they were deliberating as to what to do with his body, to their amazement, he came to, got up, and sat upon the log intended for one of the gate posts.

"Here," said Sam, "let's finish him and take his head off, and make it better for the rest. He'll never whip Mother again."

The overseer begged piteously for his life, but all in vain, for the men were furious. All the wrong things and injuries that had been heaped upon them and their fellow slaves, appeared to cry for vengeance, and it seemed as though the whole hatred of the past six months was concentrated in the passing seconds. They quickly laid his head on the log and, with one blow of the great broadaxe, Sam severed his head from his body. The head fell to the ground, and Ted the slave driver was dead. Instantly their feeling of anger and revenge gave place to an intense desire to conceal their crime and hide the beheaded body. For though they justified themselves for becoming self-constituted executioners, they knew they were amenable to the law. And almost as quickly they were aroused to a sense of peril by the shrill scream of the little boy Tommy, who had brought out their dinner and had remained playing around, but who, in their excitement, had been entirely forgotten by them. The little lad had, from a short distance, all unknown to them, been a silent witness throughout the enactment of the terrible tragedy, until he saw the overseer's head fall and his lifeblood flow. Up to that time the brothers fully supposed that they were alone. The spot being hid by a ridge of hill on one side, and the old tobacco house on the other, they never dreamed that any one witnessed the execution of their terrible deed. They were, therefore, startled beyond measure at the boy's outcry. They well knew, however, that they were too far away for any one to hear him. They, therefore, first directed their attention to the boy and succeeded in getting him quieted. They at once told him that he must never tell what he saw, and that if he did, they would surely kill him. The boy promised he would never tell. They then set about disposing of the body. Close by, as intimated, there stood a tobacco house and press, and they concluded to put the body beneath the tobacco press. The press rested upon a couple of short, heavy pieces of timber, beneath, which, after some hard work, they succeeded in placing the body. They carefully littered the spot where they had been digging with tobacco leaves, leaving it very much in appearance as they found it. They next hewed the blood off the log, where the fatal blow was given, and then gathered the chips and set them on fire, and kicked the pile of ashes about. It was now growing dark. The lad had been sent home. The overseer's horse had now to be disposed of. They knew it was the practice of their victim to ride over to the post office in the evening for his mail. So, under cover of darkness, they took the horse over near the post office, on the opposite side of the road, in the bush, and tied him to a tree. They then went to their quarters, made some reasonable excuse for being late, and thought they had fixed the job beyond power of detection, if the little boy did not tell.

That night the overseer's wife wondered why her husband did not return. The next morning she sent word to East, the plantation owner, that Ted had not been home all night, and she feared there was something wrong. Inquiry was made, and the slaves in the tobacco field said the last they saw of him was when he went toward the back fields, where Sam and Jack were building the big gate; and Jack and Sam said the last they saw of him was when he rode over to the post office for his mail. Inquiry at the post office revealed the fact that he had not reached it. The alarm was given, and a searching party was formed. They searched the first and second days without result, but upon the third day they found the horse in an almost famished condition opposite the post office, tied to a tree in the bush. The ground was all pawed up about him; he had evidently been there all the time the overseer had been missing.

The search was continued day after day the first week, without further results; but, in the second week, a singular circumstance was noticed. On all hands the conclusion was that Ted had been murdered; but, if so, where was the body? The strange circumstance noticed was, that every day after Friendship, the overseer's little dog, was fed, he quickly disappeared, returning in the evening. In the excitement of the search, it was not until the second week that this had been noticed. Mrs. Eastman concluded to watch Friendship and see where he went. She had noticed that he had howled a great deal at nights during the time of the search. This she attributed to the unusual bustle and excitement then existing. She found, when she followed him, he would return to her and go wherever she went. So she returned home, and arranged with a young man who was one of the searchers, that he should watch the dog the next day, after he was fed at the usual time. This was done, the young man keeping a long distance behind, so as not to attract the dog's attention. The little dog went straight to the back field and into the old tobacco house, which had not been used since the preceding season. There it was found that he had been busily occupied, from day to day, scraping up the earth from under the tobacco press. He already had a large hole excavated in the light, sandy soil. The young man, concluding that he had now discovered the place in which the body had been hid, returned to the house and reported what he had seen. Word was immediately sent in every direction to the searchers; shovels were obtained and all hastened to the old tobacco house. Here they soon found the body, with the severed head. It was clear the deed had been perpetrated with some broad and sharp instrument, and the broadaxe Jack and Sam had been working with at the gate was immediately recollected, and suspicion at once fell upon these men. They, however, stoutly denied all knowledge of how he had come to his untimely end. Again, it was remembered, too, that Friendship had gone with his master on the last day he was seen alive, as was his custom and, hence, had seen the terrible fate of his master, and knew all about what the searchers so long sought for in vain. Jack and Sam both thought the boy was the sole witness, and never dreamed that the little dumb brute which trotted along behind his master's horse, could tell the tale of blood.

If great criminals could always completely cover up their tracks, they would, of course, never be found out. Some little slip or mistake gives a clue, and one clue leads to another, until the "murder is out." Some one remembered that little Tommy took their dinner to the two brothers on the day the overseer was missed.

A lady loved by the child was selected to see him, and ascertain if he knew anything about the mystery. She saw him alone, and began a long way from the terrible deed all were anxious to learn about. The child had taken out the men's dinners several times before the terrible occurrence. She commenced talking about little Friendship, and then spoke of Billy, the overseer's horse, and asked if Mr. Eastman had tied up the horse the last day he went to the back field. His answers, without divulging the secret, soon gave evidence that he was present when the overseer rode over to these two men. By skilfully questioning, shreds of information came one after another, until it became clear that he was present when the overseer met his death. Then, with tears and feeling she begged him to tell his Aunty all about it, when he burst out crying, saying,

"They will kill me."

"Who will kill Tommy?" was the next question.

"Sam."

"Why?"

"He said he would if I told," said Tommy, faintly.

She assured him "that was not true, and if he told her all, Sam would not hurt him." Then he told her all. Shortly after, these two men were arrested for this murder, and not they only, but Tommy as well.

Owing to the long suspense and search for the missing overseer, and the excitement following the astonishing discoveries made in connection with the murder, the matter was known far and wide. When the day of the trial came, the courtroom was crowded to its utmost capacity. The prisoners, who were now sitting in the dock, had obtained a clever and rising young lawyer to defend them.

All eyes had scanned the prisoners, and a loud hum of conversation was heard in all parts of the courtroom. Directly the door opened and the judge entered, the counsellors-at-law stood up, and the crier shouted, "Order!" The judge took his seat, the counsellors then sat down again, and a profound silence reigned in the courtroom, as the crier proceeded to call "Oyez! Oyez! Oyez!" and open the court. After a little time, a jury was selected and the trial commenced. It lasted all day, as many witnesses were called, and counsel for the prosecution and defence, each addressed the jury in a speech of about an hour's length. Then came the charge of the judge to the jury. In the evidence, addresses and Friendship, the overseer's little dog were frequently referred to. At the close of the judge's charge, the jury retired. The courtroom was, if anything, more closely packed than in the morning when the trial began. The jury's return was anxiously awaited, and when they filed in there was a painful silence. The evidence pointed clearly to the adult prisoners, and the opinion prevailed that they would be found guilty and the lad Tommy allowed to go free. The main interest throughout the whole trial had centred about the boy Tommy. All were in breathless suspense when the clerk of the court asked the foreman of the jury if they had agreed upon a verdict.

"We have," was the reply. "We find all three guilty of murder in the first degree."

A murmur of dissent immediately ran throughout the courtroom. The contention of the State prosecutor, that Tommy, in withholding the information so long as to how the overseer met his death, was an accessory to the murder and equally guilty with the other two, had prevailed with the jury, but was surely a perversion of justice.

The judge at once asked the prisoners if they had anything to say why sentence of death should not be pronounced against them. They did not speak. He then wrote on the margin of his Record, opposite the name of each prisoner, the significant *sus. per col.,** put a black cap on his head, and sentenced them to be hanged on the twenty-second day of the following month. And at the time appointed, the two men were hanged, but Tommy had been previously pardoned by the Governor of the State.

Suspendatur per colum—"Let him be hanged by the neck." This marginal note was formerly the only warrant the sheriff had for so material and terrible a task as taking away the life of another—*Blackstone.*

17

Still in Search of a Wife

CHARLEY, AS we have seen in chapter thirteen, had arrived safely in Caskey's kitchen, but felt ill at ease. As well as he could, he stammered out that Master Caskey had invited him to call and that he would like to see Lucinda. The woman first handed him a seat, saying as she did so: "Yes, Master told me he seen a man at Master Ridgely's that he took a great fancy to, and he expected him down, and when I told him there was a man at the gate, he said, 'Lucinda, that's the fellow I spoke to you about.'"

"Is your name Lucinda?" Charley managed to gasp, while his courage was falling rapidly to zero.

"That's what they call me," she replied, with half-and-half a grin and smile.

With that answer, hope died in his bosom. The contrast between the vision of beauty he had pictured for himself and the great, muscular, thick-skinned, high-cheeked, wide-mouthed, heavy-voiced woman standing before him, was distressing in the extreme. For a few seconds he had to struggle against a sudden outburst of disgust; but he conquered his feelings, concealed to the utmost his chagrin, and entered into general conversation with her. Although two or three young girls, who appeared to be also engaged in getting supper ready, were flitting in and out, for the most part of the time he was alone with Lucinda, and felt, perhaps, less embarrassed on this account. He had now time to look about him. There was a long meal table set with wooden dishes and laden with abundance of coarse food. The kettle was boiling at the hearth fire, and it was evident that his stay must be short, if he was to get away before the slaves came in for supper. He began to scan Lucinda more closely as she walked to and fro, busied about her evening meal. Her walk was awkward and her step heavy. Her hands were like a man's hands, her features decidedly coarse, her nose flat, lips thick, teeth good, but coarse and irregular, and her ears were disproportionately small, while her eyes were excessively large. She was ugly. As she talked on, however, of her duties as cook, and of the slaves on the plantation and of her master and missis, the latter being away just then on a visit, her voice seemed to grow less harsh and more pleasing. And he found himself taking more interest in her than he thought possible a few minutes before. She had evidently fixed up subsequently to the time of seeing her head in the window, and he now suspected the reason of his being detained by the dog talk.

Although perhaps a year or two older than himself, there could be no great objection on that ground, and he had no fault to find with her dress; but when he compared her with a dozen of his acquaintances, any one of whom was probably within his reach, his whole nature rose in rebellion against Caskey's proposition. While he kept up a running conversation with the woman, he was also philosophizing on the situation. He saw that his trial was a purely mental one. He had been building a castle in the air, had built high, and when it fell, great indeed "was the fall thereof." Already he found reason coming to the rescue. No harm had been done. No one, as far as he was aware, knew anything about the object of his visit at Caskey's. He would get away as soon as he could reasonably, and that would be the end of the matter.

Lucinda evidently wanted him to stay for supper, and when she gave him a pressing invitation to do so he consented, although it was not without fear that some of the slaves might soon get an inkling of the object of his visit. Soon Lucinda tooted the long dinner horn and the slaves came flocking in. There were, perhaps, of men, women and children, in all about a score. Washing of hands and faces was soon over, and they arranged themselves at either side of the table to pour out the coffee. Tea was reserved for sickness in those days. A rather good-looking, gray-headed man, nearly full black, sat at the other end of the table. On his right hand sat a middle-aged mulatto woman, who was evidently his wife and, opposite her on his left hand, sat a brown-skinned girl of about seventeen years of age and who, from the likeness to both the man and the woman, Charley concluded must be a daughter. She was of medium size, good figure and was somewhat darker than her mother, but her features were clear cut and exceedingly regular. She had a broad, high forehead, beautiful eyes with long, dark lashes, graceful neck and a splendid set of pearly teeth. She was pretty.

As she sat on the opposite side of the table from him, although at the other end, he had a good chance to scan her features. He was as pleased with her appearance as he had been displeased with Lucinda's. She and her mother came from the laundry to the supper table, and returned after supper. The father appeared to be much respected by the slaves generally. After supper, he had a few words of conversation with him and learned his name was Johnson. He would have given all he possessed to have had the same chance to talk with his pretty daughter, whose name, he afterwards ascertained, was Emily, but he had the fear of Lucinda in his mind's eye and dare not do such a thing. In fact, when looking at her across the table, he was very careful that Lucinda did not catch him at it.

After supper, the slaves soon scattered and, as he had a walk of fifteen miles before him, he concluded to start at once. So he said goodbye to Emily's father and to Lucinda, who said, "You must come again," and of course he promised to do so. That was easy to do, for he wanted to return and make Emily's acquaintance. He took the same pebbled path round to the front door, glancing around to see if Cap was about, and was glad to find him absent. On reaching the front door, he found Caskey on the verandah, enjoying his evening pipe with Cap stretched at his feet. "Well," said he, in a low, confidential tone, "how do you like the gal?"

Charley was not exactly prepared for the question, and at the same time thinking how much better Emily was, said, "Well, she's a bouncing, big woman, healthy, and appears to be a grand cook."

Caskey then commenced to give him her history, praising her cooking ability greatly. Doubtless he would have continued for a long time on the subject, had not Charley, who had lost interest in that quarter, fearing as long a delay as had occurred over the tale of the wonderful dog Cap, and knowing that he dare not even suggest a word as to Emily, cut his conversation short by saying that he had to get home that night. It was necessary for him to go at once. In leaving, he, however, did not forget to say that he would probably be back again.

"All right, old fellow," said Caskey in a kind voice, which sounded in strange contrast to his greeting on his arrival, "I've no objection to your courting Lucinda."

Charley turned and walked up the same pathway between the lovely tinted roses, now partially hidden from sight by the dusk of evening, but loading the air with their sweet scented perfume. On reaching the gate, and turning to shut it, he saw Lucinda's head in the same window as at first, that Caskey had disappeared from the verandah, and that Cap was bounding up to the gate. If he had any disposition to linger a moment at the gate, it instantly vanished at sight of that massive bulldog's rapid pace. The gate shut with a click, and he started off on a sharp run. Looking over his shoulder, he found Cap drew the line at the gate, and so he ventured to slow down to a brisk walk. On the way, he thought over his strange adventure. His expectations had been raised, and his affection had been drawn out after the creature of his imagination, only to receive a rude shock when he came into contact with the original. He had, however, gathered up the shattered remains of his broken hopes and wrecked affections, and transferred them all to another real flesh and blood, fair to look upon, and her name was—Emily. His thoughts ran on Caskey's conduct from beginning to end, and it all seemed a puzzle. Was he in earnest, or was he playing a practical joke? And with this doubt he was harassed many a day.

He arrived home about two o'clock in the morning, glad to get back and be free from Caskey's rough reception, Lucinda's watchful eye, and Cap's evil intentions. He had promised to return, but there were two great obstacles in the way—Lucinda and Cap.

18

ᚙ

Emily

WEEKS HAD rolled by, and still Charley had not mustered up courage to visit Caskey's plantation and face such an experience again. And yet the longing to get acquainted with Emily had only increased. At length, a lucky idea came into his mind. She would surely be at some of the corn huskings in the coming season, and this would be his opportunity. He then began to lay his plans to bring about the desired acquaintance. Patience and perseverance, he had heard, accomplished great things, and he was willing to try what these would do for him. He resolved to visit, if possible, every husking in Caskey's neighbourhood, commencing at once and continuing up to the last husking, or until he should meet his idol face to face. She lived fifteen miles away. He was pretty well acquainted about half the distance toward Caskey's plantation, but beyond that, with the exception of those he had met at Caskey's, he knew as little of the slave population as he did of the people of Africa. He saw at once that it would be necessary for him to extend his field of acquaintances farther, at least in the direction in which Caskey lived, when possibly, good fortune would enable him to meet Emily.

After this, he always made it a point to talk with any one he met with who came from the vicinity in which he was interested. In a short time he got pretty well posted as to all the intermediate plantations.

About a month after, when down in that direction about four miles, he fell in with a man who lived quite close to Caskey's, and who would shortly return home. He was a slave and appeared to have good sense, and to him he confided his secret. This man promised to render what assistance he could. He said he would keep a lookout, and would try and get him word when Caskey's slaves were invited out to a husking match.

He sometimes got his master's little girl to write for him, and he would get him word in that way, if no other. They parted, and Charley's hopes were brighter and higher than they had been since the time he presented himself at Caskey's gate, just before he had caught sight of Cap.

In about two weeks the expected letter came. It was short, but significant, and read as follows:

Chales Chance:

> I've Bin aat Mass'r caskey's—he's Bad enuff.
> Cap was chain'd and i manag'd it Aall Right with my BanJo and a little singin. Bee at Mass'r rutleges husskin—Be toosday weak. The Girls will Bee there, so will i. No more at present from your frend,
>
> Henery DeBBs.
>
> P.S.—I'd have sent word Befour only i coodent get LiBBy to rite for me till now."

Rutledge's plantation was only about two miles from Caskey's, this side, fortunately, so that he had a tramp of thirteen miles before him. There was, however, the difficulty of getting permission to be away so early in the week. He, in consequence, became especially industrious for the few intervening days, and fortunately, he was able to secure the necessary leave of absence without divulging his secret. At the time indicated in the letter, he reached the Rutledge plantation. The first person he met was his friend Debbs, who had arranged for his attendance, and was on the lookout for him. As he had the opportunity, he at once told Charley of those who were present from Caskey's. He was disappointed; Emily had not come. More than that, Lucinda had. In the midst of this gloom, there was a ray of hope, which shot across his mental horizon, when he learned that Emily's father was among those present. Already the husking was in full play; all hands were busily engaged except Debbs who asked Charley to go with him and join the rest. They started and, just as they turned the corner of the great barn, who should they meet but Lucinda herself. Her look of surprise surprised Debbs. The bushel-basket of corn she carried before her fell heavily at her feet. Up went her arms, and back went the top of her head, something like the upper half of a hinged snuffbox, as she exclaimed, "Why, Charley, is this you?"

She then slipped off the red bandana handkerchief, which formed a band around her head, and wiped off the perspiration from her face.

"I didn't expect to see you here," said she.

"Neither did I expect to see you," was Charley's rather crestfallen answer.

Debbs picked up her basket and carried it to its destination. Lucinda, after recovering from her surprise, seemed pleased and grew very chatty. All three kept pretty close together throughout the husking. At supper time, as Lucinda waited on the table, Charley noticed that Debbs' eyes followed her. Subsequently he got a chance to see Emily's father for a few minutes, and learned from him that Caskey, who was a heavy drinker, was in financial trouble; that his lands were heavily mortgaged, and that some proceedings were going on against him in the courts.

Shortly after supper he rose to go home, when some one commenced to sing, and the whole company burst forth in a grand melody:

> Way down upon de Swanee river,
>> Far, far away,
> There's where my heart is turning ever,
> There's where the ol' folks stay
> All up an' down de whole creation,
>> Sadly I roam,
> Still longing for the ol' plantation,
>> And for the ol' folks at home
>
> CHORUS
>
> All the world is sad and dreary
>> Everywhere I roam
> Oh! darkeys, how my heart grows weary
> Far from the ol' folks at home.[1]

Gladly would he have remained and enjoyed himself with that musical and jovial crowd, but knew he must get home in time for the following day's work. So, after lingering half an hour, he started, arriving, after a weary tramp, at daylight in the morning. He had not succeeded, and yet he felt that he had made a long step in the direction of his idol, and so his hopes beat higher, for he now fully believed he would yet win the beautiful brown-skinned girl Emily.

19

Corn Husking

I N THE MONTH of November, soon after the corn was harvested, the great corn huskings began. Every plantation that grew corn to any extent had its annual corn husking. A corn husking match was a sort of night bee, for which the owner made great preparation. For some days before the husking, there was an unusual bustle in getting ready for the event. If anything had been left unfinished at the harvesting, this was now attended to and the granaries were got ready. A large quantity of sweet cider was prepared, or obtained ready for use. An unusual supply of provisions was laid in and the kitchen slaves were busily employed in preparing the husking supper. In the midst of all this bustle, a trusty slave was mounted on a fleet horse and dispatched to the neighbouring plantations with invitations for the husking match, and was required to ascertain the quota of slaves that each plantation would contribute.

At the time appointed, the slaves could be seen coming from all directions toward the great centre of attraction, the husking match. These events were looked upon by the slaves as high days and holidays, or rather, high nights. Two captains were chosen, who alternately called their assistants for the contest which consisted in an effort on the part of each side to husk its half first. The corn had been previously gathered into a long pile, which in the distance looked like an extended haystack. Across its centre a rail was laid to divide the pile equally. The huskers were then arranged at each end of the pile. Sometimes there were two tiers and then, of course, each gang took a tier. Work commenced, the husks fell rapidly from the golden ears, which the attendants gathered and carried in baskets to the corn bins. While their hands were thus busily employed, so were their tongues. Stories were told, local news retailed, plantation songs were sung—exercises not always free from obscenity, but frequently exceedingly humorous and grotesque. An attendant passed round with a great pitcher of sweet cider for the thirsty.

For a variation, a good singer would mount the corn pile and start some such plantation song as the following. A hundred or more voices would join in the chorus, which in the instance here given consisted of the single word "buglelo," of which, though short, did duty for a great variety of sweet chords.

> I will start the holler! Buglelo!
> I will start the holler! Buglelo!
> Oh, don't you hear me holler? Buglelo?
> Massa's got a bugle! Buglelo!
> A ten cent bugle! Buglelo![1]

No one ever called encore, for the same song was kept up until the crowd got tired of it, and the leader was persuaded to stop by a volley of corn in the husk being hurled at him. The corn throwers invariably brought their man down hastily, only to be succeeded by others in succession, who would ring the changes on:

> Who's that knockin' at the door?

> Oh! O-ho! the ol' jawbone.

> Possum up a gum tree, 'coon in the hollow.

> Hey, get along, get along Josey,
> Hey, get along Jim, get along Joe.

> My Aunt Sal she dreamed a dream
> That she was a floatin' down the stream.

> In ol' Kentuck in the afternoon
> We sweep the kitchen with a brand new broom;
> And after that we form a ring,
> And this am the song that we do sing.

CHORUS

Clear the kitchen, old folks, young folks;
Clear the kitchen, old folks, young folks;
   Ol' Virginny never tire.

The leader frequently improvised words for the song, all the rest crashing
in on the refrain. Verses were multiplied *ad infinitum* to suit the occasion.

Walkin' in the light of the moon,
   I spied a lovely coon,
Sittin' on a rail, sittin' on a rail
   A sleepin' very sound.

I jumped across his back
   He started on his track
An' galloped round the fields,
   The dust flyin' at his heels

REFRAIN

   I spied a lovely coon,
Sittin' on a rail, sittin' on a rail
   A sleepin' very sound

The dog, he give us chase,
An' make a mighty race
All the darkies come to see
The lovely coon an' me

At last he reached a knoll
Then he popped in his hole
Left me an' went down below
To put a stop to the show

As stupid as a log
The darkies an' the dog
Stood lookin' at the mound
De lovely coon had found

Impromptu efforts were numerous, and heartily enjoyed. They naturally frequently pointed at peculiarities of the great institution of slavery itself, as in the following:

> Missis an' massa's mad at me
> 'Cause I wouldn't eat the black-eyed pea
>   Missis give me one
>   Massa give me two
> An' broke my jawbone
>   Very short in two
> Heigh ho! the ol' cowhide
> Wilts the nigger's pride
> Missis an' massa's mad at me
> 'Cause I wouldn't eat the black-eyed pea.

As the pile began to grow small and "beautifully less" the night would fairly echo with:

> Lookin' for the last ear!
>   Ring a ding, a ling, ling
> Round up the corn pile
>   Ring a ding, a ling, ling
> Lookin' for the last ear! etc.

Precisely at midnight the owner announced supper and, if popular, would probably be seized, lifted up and borne away by strong arms. The whole crowd of huskers would follow, singing as they went to the great house, some well-known song as:

> Now I am growin' faint an' old
>   I cannot work much more
> Oh! carry me back, before I die
>   To Ole Virginny shore

CHORUS

> Oh! carry me back to Ole Virginny
>   To Ole Virginny shore

Or,

Round the meadows is a ringin'
  The darkey's mournful song;
While the mockingbird is singin'
  Happy as the day is long
Where the ivy is a creepin'
  O'er the grassy mound
There ol' mas'er is a sleepin'
  Sleepin' in the cold, cold ground

CHORUS

Down in de cornfield,
  Hear that mournful sound
All the darkies are a weepin'
  Mas'er's in the cold, cold ground.

At the end of the march they came to the supper tables spread in the yard, convenient to the kitchen of the great house. After the feast, and indeed often during the feast, the fun and frolic commenced in accordance with the humour of the crowd. This feature of the corn husking was as heartily enjoyed as the rest. An hour was allowed for supper and, then, if the harvest was a heavy one, another hour or two would be given before the last ear would be found. The breakup would then take place, which was generally preceded by a "breakdown," or general dance in which old and young would participate amid the enlivening strains of fiddle, banjo, bones, tambourine and other instruments. Except in case of a press of work as mentioned, the music and dancing commenced immediately after supper. This dance was generally held in the large kitchen or yard of the great house, and was often witnessed by the slave holder and his family. Dancing in the olden times was of the jig type, performed heartily, and accompanied with many gyrations of the body and comicalities in word and facial expression.

In later times there came an innovation in the shape of round dances, slower movements and calls. The dance calls partook of the same hearty, round and ready style as the dance itself, and seemed to make the entertainment more generally enjoyable.

These calls were at least expressive, as many be seen in the following specimen:

Salute your partners!
Opposite the same!
Swing your honey!
All cut away!
Right hand to your partner and grand right and left!
Cheat er swing!
First boy skips to the right!
Gal follow after!
Hoe er down!
Gal in the centre and three hands round!
Lead to the next!
Swing your duckies!
Cage the queen!
Cheat 'em if you can!
Break down the floor!
All shake your feet!
Each gal grab a boy!
First team pull to the right!
Grab hands and cut away to the next!
Six hands round!
Doe, se does, and a doe, doe, doe!
Fourth couple sashay down the centre!
Sashay back!
Whoop 'em up!
Get away gal; get away fast!
Boys in the centre and four hands round!
There you go. Whoop la!

The hilarious shouting and song singing might at times be heard a mile away.

At some of these great husking matches as much as two thousand bushels of corn in the cob would be husked. It sometimes happened that there would be two or three husking matches in a week and, as the slaves were not expected to lose any time on account of attending them, it became very trying to work all day after enjoying the husking all night, especially when the huskings had been attended two or three nights in the same week. After such an experience, Charley felt dreadfully fatigued one Saturday morning, because he could not get a chance to sleep.

"Charles, ain't it time to pull the cabbage?" said Nicholas Ridgely, his master.

"Yes, master," he replied.

"Very well; you may pull them today," said Mr. Ridgely.

There were over four hundred heads and, what was worse, they grew in front of the house, plainly in sight. Eliza, the cook, knew how he felt and sympathized with him. At the work he went, and cabbage after cabbage came up by the roots and was stood on its head. Some of them were very large and required considerable strength to dislodge from their firm hold in the soil. Eliza was peeping through the venetian blind in the kitchen at him, he knew, and he was afraid the master was doing the same from the front parlour. The thought of his doing so had nerved Charley for the work; but after an hour's pulling he felt himself growing weak and his head bewildered. The next in the row was a monstrous, large cabbage. Charley laid his chest on its head and, dropping to the ground on his knees, he folded his arms around its great stalk, and then lost consciousness.

How long he lay in that state he knew not, but remembers falling into a dream. He was at Hoskin's husking match. The house was finely lit up with tallow dips. He knew every one at the gathering, and was surrounded by several fine young girls who paid him great attention. One of the number was Emily, and she looked especially handsome to him that evening. Her eyes sparkled and her words pleased everybody, and when she laughed, it seemed catching, for the rest were sure to laugh too. They were talking over something that had happened at Seagrist's husking the week before, when two young fellows had quarrelled about a girl. Emily, looking right at him, said, "Surely, there's girls enough for…" A voice saying, "Charles! Charles! get up, what are you doing here?" accompanied by a slap of the palm of the hand on his back, quickly awoke him. He was in a supplicating attitude, if not in a supplicating humour.

"You've been sleeping this half hour. This is what comes of attending husking matches," said his master.

Charley was greatly confused and stammered out:

"What—what a big—er—um—head of cabbage this is, the biggest I ever saw in my life."

"Yes," was the sarcastic reply, "you seem to have mistaken it for a bed."

"Oh, Master," exclaimed Charley, "I was so sleepy."

"Well, get these cabbages up. You may sleep tomorrow all you like, you sleepy head."

Charley was glad his master had omitted the word "cabbage" in his designation. It was, however, a heavy disappointment to him that his master broke in upon his dream and prevented Emily from finishing her sentence. "Poor Emily, I'll see her," said he to himself, "and see what she was going to say when I was in my great nap." He learned from Eliza afterwards that she saw him drop across the big cabbage, and that she became uneasy for fear the master would see him asleep. She was afraid to go out herself, because that would attract attention. And so she kept passing between the old fireplace and the window while she was iron-ing, during the half hour he lay dreaming of Hoskin's husking and of Emily.

On the same day, Jim Dingley, who had been hired from his master for that purpose, came to pull corn on Ridgely's plantation. He came a little late, and was seen climbing over the fence into the cornfield at its farthest corner. Nothing more was seen of him until sunset, when he was seen going toward home. During the day Ridgely inquired for him, and said that it was strange that his friend Hamilton would disappoint him. In the evening, the two slave owners met at Hamilton's place and, after the usual greetings, the former said, "Why didn't you send Jim over?"

"I did," said Hamilton.

"Did you? Well, I didn't see anything of him, and I looked for him in the cornfield."

Jim was summoned into the presence of his master.

"Jim, I thought I sent you to Mr. Ridgely's to work in his cornfield?"

"Yes, Master," said Jim. "I was in Master Ridgely's cornfield all day."

"I didn't see you," said Ridgely, somewhat astonished. "What were you doing Jim?"

"Sleeping, Master. You see I'd been at Master Wicker's husking match all night, and was kind of tired, and getting over the corner of the fence in the corner of the cornfield yonder, I fell lengthwise in the corner, my head resting on a corner hill. So I thought I would rest just a minute. All I remember was the rustling of the breeze among the tassels and leaves of the corn stalks. When I woke up, I didn't know whether the sun was rising or setting, I thought it was better for me to go home. I was very sorry, Master, but I only meant to rest a minute, just a minute." At this, both slave owners broke out into a loud laugh at the length of Jim's

minute sleep "in the cornfield." Both agreed that, in view of his explanation and eloquent defence, he ought to be forgiven.

"But, then," said Mr. Hamilton, "to let it pass would make the nigger
disobedient."

So Jim was ordered to strip to the waist, when Mrs. Hamilton, who
was old Major Badgley's daughter, learning what was being done,
stopped it. She detested whipping at best and, when she heard the
circumstances of the case, she told her husband he ought to be ashamed
of himself. Thus Jim escaped. He was, however, never afterward known
to fall asleep again in "the corner of the cornfield."

20

❦

Wonderful Meetings

S LAVE HOLDERS were very much opposed to religious meetings being held by slaves. To assist them in their opposition, they obtained various legislative enactments, of which the following may be given as a sample:

"A slave shall not attend any preaching in the night-time, although conducted by a white minister, without a written permission from his owner, overseer, or master, or the agent of one of them.

"No slaves, free Negroes, or Mulattoes, shall preach or exhort, or hold any meeting, either in the day or night; and no slave, free Negro, or Mulatto, shall attend any assembly held, or pretended to be held, for religious purposes, or other instruction, conducted by any slave, free Negro, or Mulatto preacher."[1]

The latter enactment was a prohibition and was difficult to enforce. As a compromise, they would allow a meeting to be held with the overseer or young master present to control the proceedings, his duty being to prevent excitement. As soon as any ebullition of feeling was exhibited, he would order the speaker to "go slow," as he did not want his slaves to become excited. This espionage and supervision was not acceptable to the slaves themselves, and hence their wonderful secret meetings which were all the more numerously attended, and all the more intense, on account of being forbidden. Occasionally they were discovered, raided and routed. A watch night service, which Charley attended, was in this way broken up. They would dance, drink, whoop and make a great racket till near morning at a husking, without fear of disturbance; but when it came to holding a religious meeting, the slave holders felt it necessary to draw the line just there, and suppress it. And when it was found impossible to do that, the next best thing was to control it.

The restrictions, however, were in time gradually relaxed. Religious meetings, after a few years, became common and revivals broke out among the slaves in all directions. There were some wonderful meetings in those days, in which melodious singing was a prominent feature. They had inherited soft, sweet voices, and with these voices exquisitely blending, they poured forth their souls in their own native lore, in rapid flights of rapturous melody, as they worshipped the Creator of the universe, in accordance with the feelings and dictates of their untutored natures.

How they would ring the changes as they sang their favourite pieces:

There's a meeting here tonight

View the land way over Jordan
I'm rolling, rolling, rolling through an unfriendly world

Brighter are the heavenly glories

Hear them bells, don't you hear them bells?
They are ringing out the glory of the Lamb

Sweet by-and-by
Oh, my sweet by-an-by;
    Eh! Eh!
I am going to leave
For to put on the starry crown

Keep inching along, inching along
Master Jesus coming by-an-by
Inch by inch I sought the Lord
Inch by inch he saves my soul

REFRAIN

Keep inching along, inching along

I ain't got time to stop and talk
    Keep in the middle of the road
Because the road is rough and it's hard to walk

Keep in the middle of the road
Turn your back on this world of sin
Knock at the door and they will let you in
Now, you will never get such a chance again
So keep in the middle of the road

CHORUS

Then, children, keep in the middle of the road
Then, children, keep in the middle of the road
Don't you look to the right, don't you look to the left
But keep in the middle of the road.

The men would sing at their work in the fields, and the women would sing at their work in the houses. With nothing in this life that they could call their own, they were ravished with the thought of becoming entitled to a wonderful inheritance in the next. In this, they had neither houses nor lands; in the next, they were to enjoy some of the "many mansions" in the skies. In this, they were treated as chattels whose bodies were owned by others, and the existence of whose very souls was denied; in the next, they would enjoy heaven's treasures as an inheritance by an heirship of the Creator and a joint heirship with the Saviour of mankind. Frequently, in the transport of ecstatic hope, with an eye of faith they would catch a glimpse of the mountain tops of Beulah Land, gorgeously tinted with the reflected rays of the rising Sun of Righteousness, and shout "Hallelujah! the Lord God Omnipotent reign," and he will deliver those who put their trust in Him, by "binding up the broken-hearted, proclaiming liberty to the captives, and by opening of the prison to them that are bound."

A great revival broke out at Gregory's house, at Middle River Neck, conducted by two freemen preachers, named Jerry Williams and Joe Wilson. The former was a fine singer and the latter a wonderful preacher, who, by his fervid eloquence, had almost unlimited control over his audience and could make them weep or laugh at pleasure. The house, a large one, was seated with rough boards and had a raised platform at one end. Overhead, one half the board ceiling had been taken out and the remaining half, opposite the platform, did service as a gallery, in all making a seating capacity for about five hundred persons. The house had, in fact, been converted into a temporary church. There was a narrow aisle up the middle of the building, on one side of which sat the men and boys and on the other, the women and girls. On the platform on a certain night, when the meetings created the greatest interest, were the two preachers named and three large slaves who lived in the vicinity. Every inch of available space was occupied. Here were men and women of all ages and all shades, from the light yellow tinge up to the full black. There was also a large number of young people, but not one in all the crowd through whose veins did not course African blood. Enthusiasm and religious fervour were everywhere apparent. Williams had not proceeded far in this discourse, when the responses, "Amen!" "Bless the Lord!" "Hallelujah!" "Glory!" and others, rolled up in great volume as he discoursed on the beauties and happiness of heaven. He pictured the city of the King Eternal, with its walls of twelve foundations of precious stones, and "streets of pure gold," "gates of pearl," "a pure river of water of life" and "the tree of life" whose leaves are "for the healing of the nations," and closed with an impassioned appeal to his hearers to secure the rest and rewards of the heavenly city.

One of the three mentioned then stood up, and sang, with great compass of voice:

> He rose, he rose and burst the bands of death
> And went to heaven in a cloud.

As soon as he had finished, the other two stood up with him and each one, with outstretched arm, placed the right hand on the left shoulder, and left hand on the right shoulder of the man next him, thus forming a circle of three. The man who had just sung began to improvise words and music. All three kept circling round in a sort of dance, and then crashed in with a tremendous chorus:

> The Lord our King, He's on our side
> He will help us all our foes override
> We will shout old Satan down to hell
> And bid his kingdom fare-ye-well.

Suddenly a great enthusiasm broke out all over the audience and, as soon as they caught the words, they joined in the refrain. It seemed as if electrical fervour took possession of the entire assembly, and everyone was not only singing, but keeping time in some way with the dance and melody of the three men on the platform. This was done by tapping the floor with their feet, slapping their hands together and rapping on the wall with their knuckles. Old men tapped the floor with their canes. Bodies swaying to and fro, arms gesticulating, faces fairly shining with happiness—shouting, occasional rippling laughter, and not a few throwing their bodies in such a manner as to endanger their lives by falling off the gallery. All went to make it a most animated scene, and the most memorable meeting that had ever been known in the vicinity up to that time. In the midst of this excitement Joe Wilson sprang to his feet and announced his text, "What shall it profit a man if he gain the whole world and lose his own soul, or what shall a man give in exchange for his soul?"

The three dancers immediately dropped, exhausted, into their seats and the standing audience became seated, and the wild, weird commotion became hushed in a comparatively short space of time, considering the high tension up to which it had been wound. Soon all were listening to this eloquent man. And as he talked of the rich and his temporary enjoyment, of his riches turned into ashes, of the fleetness and uncertainty of life; of the poor man, and the pleasure of an endless life, they settled into rapt attention. He naturally glided to the subject of the great Judgement Day, which he proceeded to portray with pathos and power. The long and high tension of his audience now began to tell, and one female after another fell in a swoon, and was quickly carried out and tenderly cared for. His closing application was an eloquent appeal to be ready against that great day. The congregation, led by Jerry Williams, then sang with great spirit:

> We'll walk about Jerusalem
> When we arrive at home
> My brother I'm going over
> I really do believe
> Go sound the jubilee.

This was repeated many times, with a change of the word "brother," to suit the different relationships of a family. The meeting, which was kept up till very late, was known among the slaves of Middle River Neck for years after as "the wonderful meeting." Soon after, revivals broke out in various sections of that part of the country, and hundreds were converted.

21

∾

A Camp Meeting

THE VERY next summer, after the wonderful meetings at Gregory's log house, great preparations were made for an African camp meeting. It was talked of far and near, and was to be held in Dr. Jamieson's beautiful grove in the month of August. When the time arrived, upon the first Sunday, there was a vast crowd in attendance, among whom was a slight sprinkling of white people. Canvas tents and temporary shelters surrounded the rough, pine board seats placed among the trees for the people. Opposite the entrance to the grounds was the preachers' stand, from which hung a long tin horn; and a little to the right of the entrance was a remarkably well patronized refreshment stand. The latter stood directly opposite the prayer meeting tent. In front of the preachers' stand was a platform for the singers and an extensive cedar pole railing, still lower upon the ground, for the seekers of religion. On the stand were the following notables: Dan Coker[1], a slave by trade, and owned by Edward Lloyd* in whose slave quarters the celebrated Fred Douglass[2] was born; Nathan Lyon and Joe Young. The last named was sometimes, curiously enough, designated old Young, but was more generally known as "The Man of Thunder in the Woods." He was a freedman and a full cousin of the well-known lay preacher Thomas Miller of Owen Sound, Ontario.[3]

There were besides, Nancy Smith, the great woman preacher,[4] and several others of more or less celebrity. As Charley entered the grounds,

*Since the above was put in type, the following paragraph has appeared in public print: "Just before Fred. Douglass sailed for his post as Minister to Hayti, he was called upon by Lieut. Edward Lloyd, of Maryland, whose great-grandfather owned Douglass and his mother when they were slaves."

115

Joe Young stood with his back against a tree, and a crowd about him listening to him as he fairly made the woods ring with his singing:

> I'm travelling on the heavenly road, Children, come along,
> I've left the one that is so broad, Children, etc.
> The way is rough, and narrow too, Children, etc.
> But I've shod with the Gospel shoe, Children, etc.
>
> This sinful heart won't ache anymore, Children, etc.
> I'm shouting louder than before, Children, etc.
> I'll keep shouting till I die, Children, etc.
> On Canaan's land I've fixed my eye, Children, etc.
>
> It's no use a hangin' back, Children, etc.
> You better join me on this track, Children, etc.
> Then hurry up, or you'll be too late, Children, etc.
> They're going to shut the golden gate, Children, etc.

Joe had been heard in the morning prayer meeting a mile and a quarter from the campground. The sound of his voice had travelled that distance along the silvery stream that threaded its way through the lovely grove of the campground. Directly, Elder Joyce, who was as black as ebony and wore a large pair of spectacles, took the meeting in charge. He began by "tooting" the long horn, and calling out to the vast crowd to be seated. "The forepart of the congregation, at least," said he, "must sit down, so the hind part can see the forepart, for the hind part can't see the forepart, if the forepart persists in standing before the hind part, to the utter exclusion of the hind part by the forepart." They sat down, and he proceeded to give some of his own personal experience, as follows:

"I've been in the ministry," said he, looking over his spectacles, "nigh going on twenty year, and I've buried over a hundred people, but I'd a heap sooner married a hundred couples, specially if the bridegroom planks down the money for my marrying fee, as he ought to for joining him to his female bride. What's the reason they're willing to pay so little for the job? Lot's of them would afterwards give a heap more to be unmarried. I once married a big man and a little woman together. In a week he came back to me and said, 'Parson Joyce, see here,' and I said, 'Well, sir, what's the matter?' and he said, 'A great deal's the matter—I want you to take that wench off'n my hands.' 'Oh brother,' said I, 'I can't, for the law only allows me to marry, but not to unmarry.' 'Is that so?' said he, as he left me in great disappointment."

The Elder concluded with an urgent appeal for a good collection to defray expenses. The singing and preaching of the morning service were both good. Dan Coker preached. He was, however, occasionally disturbed by a racket at the refreshment stand. A mild expostulation from the Elder generally had the desired effect, although it must be admitted, he was not as prompt as he should have been, owing, it was said, to his "harbouring a feeling of animosity agin the preacher for outpreacherin' him." Dan's subject was "The wages of sin and the power of the devil."

"Your sins," said he, "are sure to find you out. The wages paid by the devil is poor, and don't pay. When he gets you into his power, he makes you toe the mark every time. In the end he'll use you mean, and by and by he'll tyrannize over you forever and ever, if he gets the chance. The devil's true character is seen in that portion of the Scriptures which says, 'The devil as roaring lion walketh about, seeking whom he may devour.' "

"That's so," exclaimed Preacher Lyon.

"Today I want to tell you about the devil, that old serpent the dragon. The wolf gets the stray sheep. Come into the sheepfold," said he, pointing to the cedar pole railing, "and be safe from the devil's power and wicked wiles, for he's an unremittigated deceiver."

Just then another racket occurred at the refreshment stand, and the Elder shouted at the top of his voice, "Will Brother Johnson keep the bar a little more quiet over there? The police will please see that the noise is not repetitioned."

"A great cry and little wool, said the devil, as he caught a pig. That's about the way of it at the refreshment stand," said Dan, complainingly.

"Was that pig caught under a gate?" shouted a black man with a white head, who sat far back in the crowd; at which everybody laughed.

"The devil makes great promises, but he doesn't keep them worth a cent, and disappoints every time, and his followers will turn out to be fools in the long run," continued Dan, as soon as the hubbub had subsided. "The Lord," said he, "pays the best of wages, both here and in the great hereafter." He then proceeded to illustrate "the contrast 'twixt the two kinds of wages," and to warn his hearers against Satan's seductive power, making many uncomplimentary references to his Satanic majesty throughout his discourse.

After singing and taking up the collection, the vast audience was dismissed for dinner. There was great expectation as the afternoon service, as, besides Nathan Lyon, Nancy Smith, the great freedwoman preacher, was to speak. Nancy's personal history was well known. She had been a slave in Maryland, but was now a freedwoman of Philadelphia. Nancy once took a notion to return to eastern shore Maryland, as she said, "to tell what the Lord had done for her." When about to return home, she was interviewed by a member of her church, who said to her, "Wait, Sister Nancy, till next week, and I'll call a farewell meeting for you. Since you've got to be such a great preacher, the people will be glad to hear you preach." She consented to wait and her kind friend made all the necessary arrangements for the "farewell meeting," and at the same time notified the authorities of the breach of the law committed by Nancy in remaining in the place longer than the permitted ten days. At her meeting she was, in consequence, arrested, and was only released on bail being secured for her after much trouble. Her old master became her surety and paid the expenses, and the scheming church member pocketed half the fees.

Elder Joyce opened the afternoon service with the usual "toot" on the long horn, and an appeal to the singers on the platform to "do their very best," as "good singing always helped the collections." "The crying devil of the day," said he, "is bumptious. The bumptious man is the man who plants himself right agin everything other people do or say. He wants his own way always, like a spoiled child, knows everything, and what he don't know ain't worth knowing. And there are lots of bumptious sinners here on the campground this afternoon. The great cure for this sin is sanctified gumption. It removes bumptiousness, and helps a man to rejoice mid the troublesomeness of this present wicked world."

The Elder stopped just in time, as his dusky audience began to be restless. Then followed some excellent singing, and a practical and telling discourse by Nathan Lyon, which, however, was considerably marred by a row among some roughs at the far end of the campground.

As soon as Nathan had finished, the Elder introduced Sister Nancy Smith. On rising to her feet, Nancy pulled her bonnet off and threw it on the platform, and announced her text to be "I am the way." "Children," said she, "we're all fellow travellers to the eternal world. When your going to a strange part of the country, you remember to enquire about it 'fore you go. You don't fail to learn all you can about the place your going to for the first time. Just so you ought to learn all about the heavenly country before you cross the river of Jordan. If you don't, how can you ever reach the promised land? You ask me how you ought to learn. The Bible is declared to be 'a lamp to our feet, and a light to our pathway.'

The preparation must be got here; and if by chance you get to the heavenly land without learning the proper way, and without this preparation you wouldn't feel at home there, and you would want to come back. There is a way that leads to death, it's the way of disobedience, and there is a way that leads to life everlasting, and it's the way of obedience. Enmity towards the Lord must be slain by the sword of the Spirit. The tomahawk of war agin the Lord must be buried, and you must follow the still small voice of His teaching. Then you'll know the way, and can walk in it, and be a bright and shining light to others. Different historics and commentators," she continued, "say that the book of Revelations is a sealed book, but in this present disposition it is not so; for it has pleased the Lord to make his will known in these last days to be children of men, by the power of His own word instead of by prophecies, dreams and visions, as afore time."

Occasionally, in her discourse she grew excited and her voice went up to a scream. Her imagination found full play, as she gave description of "the separation of the sheep from the goats," and of the regions of the lost, which was as realistic as Dante's *Inferno* itself.

"The Lord," said she, in conclusion, "is no respecter of persons. It's no matter about the complexion of the face. It's the complexion of the soul that will count then. Every man for himself, and every woman for herself, in that last great day."

"Amen," shouted Elder Joyce.

The effect of these discourses upon that vast assemblage was very marked, and when the invitation was given by the Elder not to be "backward in coming forward," the cedar pole railing was filled from end to end.

In the evening, the fire stands were lit up and as the shades of evening fell upon the leafy temple, and the crackling fires threw their unsteady light in every direction over the sable crowd, the effect was odd and weird. The Elder, in opening, as usual referred to the collection and reminded his hearers that "the contribution box wasn't helped a bit by the loudest kind of amens." The collection was then taken up and, after some congregational singing, Joe Young stood up, and announced his text: "Men love darkness rather than light, because their deeds are evil."

He referred to the beautiful grove in which they then worshipped. It would be all dark but for the platform fires. Light was contrasted with darkness. Man's heart was by nature dark, "deceitful above all things and desperately wicked." The Sun of Righteousness had risen, the Gospel was lighting up "the dark places of the earth," still so "full of the habitations of cruelty."

"But," said he, "there is a city which has no need of the sun to light it. There is a land free from the scourge of sin, and where all is bright, peaceful and happy. There is a place where man can enjoy the society of angels and the pure and good of all ages."

He closed with a powerful exhortation for his hearers to turn in with the overtures of mercy, and enjoy the liberty of the Gospel and the rich rewards of an endless life. "And when you cross the river of Jordan," he continued, "you'll find yourselves on the fair banks of deliverance:"

> Far from a world of grief and sin,
> With God eternally shut in.

His hearers, who were greatly moved by his powerful address, were more than pleased when he announced that he would sing another piece. All were completely captivated by his rich baritone voice, which filled the leafy temple in which they worshipped as he sang:

> Oh! how I long to reach that heavenly shore,
> And meet old Peter standing in the door,
>   And dip in the golden sea.
> He'll ask me to sit in his ivory pew,
> To look and listen to the music new,
>   And dip in the golden sea;
> To drive with his ebony coach and snow white steed,
> Enjoy the glories of the saved indeed,
>   And dip in the golden sea.
> I'll wear a crown and float in the air,
> I'm awaiting, waiting, to go up there,
>   And dip in the golden sea.

Great was the crowd of seekers at the close of this meeting. Many were loosed from the bonds of sin and entered into the liberty proclaimed in the Gospel to the captive.

The next morning at nine o'clock, the whole camp assembled for a grand fellowship meeting. This was conducted by the last speaker of the previous evening, "The Man of Thunder in the Woods," who, after a short, earnest address, a reference to his personal experience, and a quoting of the passage, "Ye are My witnesses, saith the Lord," threw the meeting open. Testimonies and singing followed in quick succession, and were accompanied with hearty outbursts of responsive remarks. When the excitement and noise were on a rapid increase, an exceedingly large woman, whose avoirdupois was probably not less than three hundred pounds, rose on her feet and, with uplifted arm, shouted in a high key, "Hooray for King Jesus!" With that she glided back into her seat, at which the whole meeting rose and cheered, as if to give vent to their fervour.

A white sister named Duke, who occasionally spoke at religious gatherings, felt grieved at such proceedings Immediately, she stepped forward to the railing and inveighed as strongly as she dare, without giving offence, against noise and confusion at religious services.

"It was quite unnecessary to get excited and shout so loud," she went on to say. "God was not deaf that He could not hear. People who made the most fuss did not always do the most work. The power that split the tree into splinters was the noiseless lightning, not the belching thunder. The steamboat made a deafening noise as she blew off steam, and yet wheels revolved not, nor did she move an inch." Giving these and other illustrations to press her subject home, she wound up by quoting the passage, "Let all things be done decently and in order," and by saying nothing was to be gained by noise and confusion.

A cold chill had, in consequence, struck the meeting and the suspense was painful. A black man with a head large compared to his diminutive body, of keen eye and nervous temperament, who was called "Happy Hunchy," or "The India Rubber Man," and who sat within the railing, and had been pretty demonstrative up to the commencement of the remonstrance, rose and said:

"Good sister Duke likes the quiet road to the heavenly land, but was there no noise when the priests blew on the crooked rams' horns, as they went round and round the walls of Jericho." While he spoke his arms fairly whirled about his head, and his body swayed back and forth till his head at times nearly touched the ground. "Was there no noise, no confusion," he demanded, "when the big blast of the horns made the great walls of the city fall down flat." Suiting action to word, he turned a complete and neat somersault before the people, and proceeded with his address as if nothing unusual had occurred. "Sister Duke says the Lord isn't deaf. Well no, nor was He deaf when 'Joshua said unto the people, Shout! and all the people gave a great shout'? Nor when they 'shouted aloud for joy.'"

121

Here he shouted "Hallelujah!" and was quickly followed by the meeting with a chorus of hallelujahs, in the midst of which he turned another summersault. It was now evident that Happy Hunchy was having one of his good times, and that he had the meeting with him in full swing. From the constant action of his limbs and body, it was quite apparent why he was called "The India Rubber Man." Suddenly he straightened up, and sang in a clear, musical voice:

When Israel comes to Jericho,
    I must cross to see my Lord.
Begin to shout, sing and blow,
    I must cross to see my Lord.
Jordan's waves I must cross,
    I hope to cross and not get lost.

CHORUS

Give way, Jordan,
Give way, Jordan,
Give way, Jordan,
I must cross to see my Lord.

As his voice rose so did his arm, until the highest note was reached when the hand and fingers extended to the utmost and, pointing upward, quivered with the intense emotion of the singer.

By this time, as may be readily supposed, every vestige of the chill had disappeared. His listeners had caught his inspiration, and were demonstrating it with tremendous enthusiasm.

"Sister Duke," he continued, "wants work without noise. Doesn't the busy bumblebee make a noise as it gathers honey from the clover field? Bim-im-im, says the working bee, but the drones are as silent as the grape. Sister Duke's content with the little drops of honey that fall by the way of peace and quiet; but give me the bustle of the busy bee and the big honey in the honeycomb. Hi! ho-oo-o!" he shouted in a prolonged and powerful tone, then over he went again. "The lightning kills," he went on to say, "but the thunder clears the air and brings the needed rain. The Lord promised to open the windows of heaven and pour out a blessing. Sister Duke's satisfied with the droppings, I want the big shower and the storm." Then he turned another somersault, amid a shower of amens and hallelujahs from the meeting. "Sister Duke is afeared of confronting the fine people with exciting noise in religion; but what about confronting the King of Kings and Lord of Lords by unbroken silence? Some people is stiff in the back, stiff in the joints, and stiff in the neck, and treat the Creator like a stranger. Stillness shows death—action, life. Better wear out than rust out. Give me the commotion of life." At which he revolved like a ball before the astonished hearers. "Sister Duke says, the more noise, the less speed on the boat. Hi! ho-oo-o! crowd on the steam. The more steam, the faster the vessel will go, and the sooner she'll get safe into the haven of rest. Crowd on the steam; crowd on the steam, brethren and sisters. It's a noisy world at best, but there's more noise and worse in the next if you get to the wrong one." Here over he went again, making the sixth revolution, adding, as he came on his feet, "We're going to sail through the stormy sea of this life straight up to the land of the blest, and leave this vexatious world clear out of sight." As he dropped into his seat, the amens and hallelujahs, and other exclamations, broke out afresh over the campground, in the midst of which some one struck up:

> We'll stand the storm, it won't be long,
> We'll anchor by-and-by.

Then came:

> Steal away, Jesus.[5]

The hallowing influence of this slave hymn subdued every heart. A sacred awe fell upon the worshippers as they felt the saving presence of Him of whom they sang in their very midst. A touching prayer from Nathan Lyon brought this wonderful meeting to a close.

In all, about 250 persons openly professed conversion as the result of the services of this great camp meeting, held in Dr. Jamieson's grove.

22

⌒

Turning Over a New Leaf

AT TWENTY-FOUR years of age, Charley had unfortunately become much addicted to drinking, and was, as we have seen, passionately fond of cockfighting, the headquarters for which were still at the Bull's Head. At Easter, a number of young fellows at Lower River Neck made up a purse of fifty dollars, against one of the same amount put up at Middle River Neck, for a great match. A couple of hundred assembled to witness the fight. Great interest was felt on account of the number of birds entered for the contest and the largeness of the stakes. There was a heavy slaughter among the birds that day, and conscience, upbraiding Charley, seemed to say, "Ain't it a shame for you to put steel gaffs on to kill them birds." Just then, Harry Bowey, who was on the opposite side in the match, came to him and said:

"The devil's given you the greatest luck I've ever seen in my life. I'll never fight against your side again, but I'll join your side."

"Join my side," said Charley, "that's curious, for I'll never put a spur on a heel again."

"Sure! How you talk," said Harry.

'You'll see," replied Charley.

Before the fight came off, Charley had gone over to old La Pere's, who claimed to know something of the "black art."

"They tell me," said Charley to him, "that Harry Bowey is a conjuror and, as we're going to fight gamecocks, I want you to help me beat him."

He said he would, and instructed Charley to go to the Roman Catholic Church and get a bottle of holy water, and sprinkle it on the floor of the cockpit. This, he said, would break his power. "Tell the caretaker," said he, "you assemble with the Bennett people."

Charley went to the church, and being questioned by the caretaker, answered as directed. The caretaker was satisfied and told him to do as he did, and then took him to the marble pool, crossed himself and bowed. Charley filled his bottle and hastened away to the cockpit, which he sprinkled well with the holy water. As soon as Charley's bird killed his opponent, his heart smote him because he obtained the victory by such deception. He determined to quit the business forever, and left the company at once, taking his bird with him. His share of the money won in his pocket only seemed to increase his misery.

A couple of weeks before this main [event], good old Eli Hawkins, a black preacher, had taken him to task on account of his reckless manner of life. "Such a course," said he, "leads down to the place of everlasting torment. You will be called before the bar of God on the day of judgement, to answer for the deeds done in the body." His earnest words troubled Charley. They rang in his ears while he stood in the cockpit, watching the varying success of the fighting birds, and just then he was convicted. He felt he had a soul to save, and it might be lost, and he became deeply troubled in spirit and concluded to leave the cockpit forever. He now lost his natural sprightliness and his spirit of joking left him. To others he was dull and forbidding, while he was conscious only of his lost condition, and withdrew from his companions. In this frame of mind Charley visited the preacher who had so faithfully warned him as to his headlong career, and asked him to read a chapter in the Bible to him.

"Child," said the preacher, "I can't read the Bible."

"Can't read?" said Charley. "Then how do you manage to preach?"

"Well, you see," said Brother Hawkins, his face lighting up with a smile, "my wife Isanthe reads to me, and I expound and explain to the people."

As Isanthe was away from home, no chapter was read, but, in its stead, Charley received a goodly portion of advice.

At the following Whitsuntide,[1] a great horse race was advertised to be held at the city of Baltimore, Charley concluded to go and see if he could not throw off this feeling which oppressed him night and day. A number of horses were speeding. Ridgely's "Lady Lightfoot," which had never been beaten, was among them. After a little speeding and a few false starts, they got away in the race. There was a large number of spectators, perhaps two thousand, or even more. General Sleeper was one of the managers. Contrary to all former experience, the race gave Charley no satisfaction. "If the ground were to sink," thought he, "what a lot of people would go to ruin. It would be bad for me, for I'd have to go with the rest." He then went to a tent where a black man was selling whiskey. There he bought a pint bottle and put it to his mouth, hoping to drown the strange feeling of misery that had taken such a deep hold of him; but to no purpose, for something seemed to say, "Quit that!" He threw the bottle and whiskey away and started for home. In due time he reached, but did not enter, the house. All night he walked the streets of the city. At this time he was chopping in Ridgely's woods, and next morning started back at his work. After being some weeks in distress, he went to see and talk with some old Methodist blacks about the way he felt. After explaining his sorrowful condition to them, they said to him, "You must fast and pray, and look to the Lord for help." To make sure work of it, he neither ate nor drank anything the next day, and the following is his version of what happened:

"When the horn blew, I didn't go for breakfast. I thought I would never be forgiven my sins, and would have to go down to perdition sure. I spent the noon-spell praying between two woodpiles. I said, 'O Lord, it appears how I must be lost, I've been so wicked.' At sundown I went again to my praying place and wrestled all night, with a great weight resting on my shoulders, but at break of day, a faint light strove with the darkness of my soul. Someone seemed to speak to me like the voice of a man saying, 'Come unto Me all ye that labour and are heavy laden, and I will give you rest.' Then I saw a Saviour able to save 'to the uttermost,' one 'who His ownself bare our sins in his own body on the tree,' and I said to Him, 'I believe Thou dost save even me.' All in a minute, the light got the mastery, my great sorrow left me, my load rolled off of my shoulders, joy filled my heart. I felt the Lord owned me for his child, and was so overcome, I would have fell to the ground, but for a sapling I caught hold of. Soon my strength returned, and I shouted my praises to the Lord, and would have shouted if there had been fifty cannon pointed at me. So loud did I shout in my joy, that they heard me at Hamilton's, a mile away. I kept on shouting till night. Just a short time before life seemed almost unbearable, but now I was saved and joyful. My Master encouraged me, I was happy all the day long; although my body was in slavery, my spirit was free in the Lord. And the first time I told in the meeting how the Lord had saved me, didn't they strike up and sing:

> Twas just about the break of day
> When Jesus washed my sins away.

"And that hymn just suited my experience, and was very precious to me then, and is very precious to me still."

23

⌘

Visiting Virginia

THE LAST summer that Charley was Ridgely's slave, two preachers, friends of his named Rattray and Ringo, of the Methodist Episcopal Church from the State of Delaware, attending a Church Conference at Washington, concluded to take a sail down the Potomac in a steamer, for the purpose of visiting the city of Alexandria. They had heard much of the beauty of the city and anticipated a more than usually pleasant day. On arrival, they were interviewed by a sharp-featured man who made himself very friendly. They talked freely with him of their Conference just ended, and of their respective charges at home. Besides this, their white neckcloths which were pretty liberally displayed, and their frequent references of the one to "my reverend Brother Ringo" and of the other to "my dear brother, Reverend Mister Rattray," precluded any possibility of mistaking their social position on the part of their new-found friend. After enumerating many points of interest in the city, the man wound up offering to take them to one or two of the city's chief attractions. They were both highly pleased at the deference thus shown them, and never felt prouder of their ministerial standing and Conference connection Accepting the proffered offer, they immediately started to see the city. They were conducted straight to a point which was daily the subject of much interest, but which had not been enumerated by the obliging Alexandrian. It was known as the Police Station. Their smooth-tongued guide, who proved to be a policeman in plain clothes, at once ushered the city visitors into the presence of the chief magistrate of the city.

"Here are two niggers," said the policeman, "I arrested at the steamboat wharf. They say they belong to the State of Delaware."

The magistrate was a large, rough-looking man, with a thin, squeaky voice; peering over his spectacles at the prisoners, he said:

"What you niggers doing here? Come to decoy other niggers, eh? You must know you're in Virginia, and Virginia law don't allow anything of that kind."

The preachers, who had quite overlooked Virginia law, which forbade freedmen from entering the State, were now greatly crestfallen. They both knew of many instances of blacks who had been arrested on suspicion of being runaways, and thrust into prison, and who, on being advertised, remaining unclaimed, were sent to the slave market of the city, and sold for the expenses of arrest and imprisonment—or, as it was generally termed, "sold for jail fees." They now fully realized the seriousness of their situation, and fairly quaked with fear at the thought of such a fate. Reverend Mr. Rattray was the first to crave a hearing, and rehearsed the story of their ministry, the recent Conference and the object of their visit.

"I was born and bred," said he in conclusion, "in the city of Washington, and now live in the State of Delaware. I had never seen your beautiful city and proposed the trip to my good friend, Brother Ringo."

The Reverend Mr. Ringo also stoutly disclaimed any object other than that of seeing "the beautiful city of Alexandria."

"I come," he declared, "expressly for that purpose."

The magistrate was, however, quite incredulous as to their every statement, and was about to deal out summary justice of an unjust nature; but on learning that Ringo was acquainted with a merchant in the city, postponed the hearing for half an hour, and sent for him. On his arrival the merchant at once recognized Ringo, and said from what he knew of him his statement could be relied on. Thereupon the magistrate eased up considerably, and after stating that the law must be obeyed, deemed it a sufficient vindication of the law in its majesty, to inflict a fine of $5 upon each prisoner, with costs which amounted to $2.50 each. They were thus fined in all in the sum of $15 and allowed to go. On being released, they went straight back to the steamboat which was being loaded with freight. Here they remained for five hours without anything to do or anything to eat. They had, of course, lost all desire to see the "beautiful" city they had heard so much about, and anxiously awaited the boat's departure. Never did hours go more slowly, and never did a day seem longer. They feared another arrest and detention, and hence were on the jagged edge of suspense through all that weary waiting. Rarely was a word spoken between them, so greatly were they dispirited.

At last the time for departure came. "Ding-a-ling-ling," rang the bell. The last freight was hurried on board. "Haul in the gangway, let go the bowline," shouted the captain. "Ding-a-ling-ling," rang the bell. "Puff, puff, puff, sis-s-sis," said the steam engine, as the paddle wheels began to move. While all this was going on, the two visitors got in a high state of excitement. "Cast off the stern line," finally sang out the captain, upon which the boat moved off from the wharf. When three feet away, Rattray, standing on deck, took off his hat and, waving it in the air, shouted to the crowd on the wharf: "Ah! farewell, farewell, farewell, Alexandria," making a complete circle in the air with his hat, with each word farewell pronounced in dramatic voice and with swaying body. The crowd gazed in wonder. "Ho!" he continued, "fair city of Alexandria, with your big-bellied, resumptious old squire. You may be full of rats from cellar to garret, and you may set your traps for all the rats you like, but you'll have a chance to catch this Rat-ray in your beautiful city that we came to visit and didn't see never more. So farewell, Alexandria, beautiful city, with your sweet-mouthed police, to you I say fare-ye-well for ever!"

As the boat moved away slowly and quietly, the crowd got the full benefit of Rattray's exulting performance. Catching its significance from a remark made aloud by someone on the wharf who knew of the arrest, they gave him a hearty cheer for a sendoff, the crowd on shore and the passengers on the boat both uniting in a loud and hearty laugh at the close.

On their way home their minds were greatly relieved to think they had escaped the meshes of Virginia law.

"All's well that ends well," said Ringo, "but our bitter experience today shows that curiosity must at times be suppressed or it leads to trouble. It's a strange circumstance of this life that the very occasion you expect to realize your highest wish brings disappointment. When you look for the fruits, there's nothing but ashes."

"That reminds me," said his companion, "of the great debatable question: 'Which affords man the most happiness, anticipation or participation?' With me that question was settled some years ago when travelling one day in the country on foot to my appointment. Passing through a field, I came across a hardy-looking yellow boy about seventeen years old, and I was surprised at the way he laughed. As I came up to him I heard, 'Te-he! he! he! ha! ha! ha!' And I said, 'What you laughing at boy?' and his answer was, 'Ho! ho! ho! ha! ha! ha!' My curiosity was aroused and I asked him again. Then he held up for a minute and pointed with a sharp-pointed stick up the side of the hill I was passing, and said, 'Do you see that donkey?' I looked first at his stick and saw it had a sharp steel prod on it, and then I looked at the donkey grazing a little up the hill. Then I said, 'Yes, but I see nothing to laugh at.' 'Don't you?' said he, and he laughed again. 'Well,' said he, 'if I was to give him a few prods with this stick about where his tail is joined to his body, wouldn't he kick?' He laughed again and kept on laughing. He couldn't help laughing, it tickled him so. The sounds of 'Ho! ho! ho! ha! ha! ha!' still fell on my ears, and was gradually dying away as I travelled on, when very suddenly I heard a scream. Then I turned and ran back and up the hillside, for I saw the boy lying in a heap and the donkey, with head down and heels up, kicking over him viciously. On the way, perhaps twenty feet from the scene, I picked up the prod, and with it I beat off the donkey. 'Poor child,' I said, as I picked him up, 'are you dead?' The first answer of the boy was a groan. After his breath came to him and he kind of straightened out like, he said, 'Plague that mean, treacherous, contemptible jackass. I'd no sooner touched him with the prod, than he up and hit me in the stomach, and sent the prod flying in the air; and after I fell, he kept on kicking as no donkey ever kicked afore. But for you he'd have killed me sure.' Then I said to him, 'I guess, boy, you wish now you hadn't laughed so much about tickling the donkey?' And would you believe it, he gave me the most surprising answer I ever heard in my life."

"What did he say?" said Ringo, as Rattray had unexpectedly stopped speaking.

"What did he say?" repeated Rattray in a mechanical way, as if his mind were elsewhere, and then he burst out laughing, as if he were enjoying the boy's fun previous to the mishap.

" 'Why,' said the boy, 'No, I don't. It's well I had my laugh first, or I couldn't have had it at all, for I can't laugh a bit now.' "

"Brother Rattray," said Ringo, "I see the prod—er—ah, I mean the point. You've more education than me, and you mean to apply that principle to our visit to Alexandria."

Then both these African brethren, forgetting, for the moment, their recent troubles and, as if to snuff the remembrance of them out forever, laughed a good, hearty, rollicking laugh.

"Our Alexandria experience," continued Ringo, "corroborates the great poet Alexander Pope, in his 'Essay on Man,' when he says:

Man never is but always to be blessed.

24

ℰℐ

Sold Again

IT WAS G.W. Rollins, a slave holder, who put Charley in the notion of running away from slavery. Said he: "There are not many bigger men than you here." This was quite true, for he then stood six feet two inches, turned the scales at two hundred and twenty-five pounds, and had prodigious strength, as shown at the close of this chapter.

"They told me you were a great worker. You ought to be free. Your master has made a heap of money out of you these last two years. He has made a thousand dollars out of the knees you have grubbed, and has put the money in the bank, so he told me himself. You are worthy of your freedom."

Charley, for two winters previous, had been grubbing knees for vessels[1] in Ridgely's woods. It was the strongest appreciation of his work he had ever heard from anyone, and he said:

"Yes, Master, I know I've worked hard, and I hope to get my freedom in a few years."

The words, "you are worthy of your freedom," were now deeply pondered. Until this conversation, he had had no idea of shortening his allotted term of slavery. He had hitherto striven to serve his several masters the best he could, and looked for nothing better that servitude in slavery, until he should reach the age of thirty-five years. This was to be to him the year of jubilee. Then, by virtue of the will of his old "Missus," the shackles would fall and he would stand a free man, amid bond and free. In an instant, he would pass from a chattel to be a man among men. Of this wondrous change he had many a daydream, and had his eye fixed upon the date as a rising star of hope. But now he chafed, and longed to break the chain which bound him.

By purchase, at seventeen years of age, he became chattel property and laboured long and well. In bush and field, at home and with the stranger for hire, the service had always been satisfactory to his master. Early in his slave service, he had won his master's confidence, became his trusty slave foreman, and held his position to the end. He was now, however, uneasy and discontented; and Ridgely, seeing this, concluded that, although a profitable slave, it would now be of interest to dispose of him. Hearing that W.H. Freeman, a leading lawyer of the city, wanted a man, he went to see him. Shortly after, both master and slave went to this lawyer's office. After a little conversation, the lawyer and Ridgely went into another room, leaving Charley alone. What took place between the two was afterwards revealed to the waiting slave, namely, that he had been sold. A Bill of Sale had been executed, the price had been paid, and Charley was the slave of Freeman the lawyer.

He subsequently learned from his new master that his age had been put down at twenty-six, and the price paid was five hundred dollars. Charley's actual age was twenty-eight. As he could not be held after attaining thirty-five, the reduction of age, of course, enhanced his price and the slave would, doubtless, be governed by the last Bill of Sale. Charley took little interest in the proceedings, as his burning desire for freedom crowded out all other thoughts; as he put it, "My heart and bones were full of freedom."

His new master had a stony farm of one hundred acres. It was covered with small hard heads which were to be picked up and thrown into fences. This was the first work Charley was put at, just as eleven years previous it was the first work he did on Ridgely's farm. It seemed monotonous. On the opening of spring, however, more congenial work was assigned to him. His master cultivated a market garden, in which he had a couple of hands—two Irishmen. One of these was a good worker and the other was a good talker. The talker would show Charley what to do, look on, and talk; the other would rather do any particular piece of work than be bothered showing how he wanted it done. There were now three hands in the garden, but only two workers, as the talker had concluded to substitute Charley's work for his, so that the lawyer was to a partial extent in the same position as old Colonel Biglow, who used to say, "When I had one boy, I had a boy; when I got two boys, I had only half a boy; and when I got three boys, I had no boy at all."

From the examples afforded by the two Irish gardeners, Charley concluded "that a lazy man was better than an industrious one to learn a trade from."

At this time, Charley's brother Sam, still owned by Dr. Buchanan, worked in a shot factory[2] in the city. One day, when visiting him, a trial of strength took place among some of the men in the factory. Charley outlifted them all. Taking six fifty-six pound weights in each hand, he straightened himself up with them, thus lifting three hundred and thirty-six pounds in each hand, or a total of six hundred and seventy-two pounds. And, hitherto, the great strength and activity with which he had been endowed were willingly placed at the service of the slave master, but now a change had come in the spirit of his dreams.

25

A Wedding

One day, months after Charley had last seen Emily's father, Mr. Freeman told him to hitch up his team, as he was going to drive over to a place in the country to attend a plantation sale.

"An old fellow," said he, "is going to be sold out, 'lock, stock and barrel,' by auction, and I am going over to see if I can pick up a few slaves for the farm."

"Who's going to be sold, master?" asked Charley.

"Oh, some old fellow named Caskey."

"Caskey!" Charley fairly shouted.

"Yes. Why, do you know him?"

"Yes, I know him, and some of his slaves, too."

Charley's great interest had betrayed him, and his master was soon able to elicit sufficient information to find where Charley's heart was. He also noticed that Charley had suddenly become absent minded and dull as to the orders he was leaving with him.

Freeman drove off, leaving Charley in a state of bewilderment, crushed with a disappointment as heavy as it was sudden and unexpected. "Without doubt," said he, "Emily will be sold away, and I'll never see her more." While brooding over his troubles, a faint ray of hope fell upon him, on account of very particular inquiries made by his master about Johnson. True, he might buy Johnson, but that would not bring Emily.

At nightfall the next evening, a heavy double wagon, loaded with household stuff and a slave family, was driven up to the house. Immediately after them, driven at a rapid pace, came Freeman. All was bustle. The slaves came flocking around. Hurried orders were given for unhitching both teams and for the disposition of the household stuff in the wagon. As yet the living freight had not moved.

"See here, Charley," said his master, "I've brought you some old acquaintances. Here are Johnson and his wife. You know Emily, don't you, and her brother Tom?"

Charley, whose heart was in his throat, rushed to them, saluted them warmly, and assisted them out of the wagon and conducted them into the house. His anxiety for freedom vanished and his joy knew no bounds. He was as happy as he had before been disconsolate. No one was more blithe and gay now than he. It soon got noised about that "Master had

Slave auction.

bought Charley's girl, with her parents." Charley was kept fully engaged through the day, and Emily, as well as her mother, had their household duties assigned to them and were both kept quite busy at the farm. The young pair, however, always managed to get an evening or two a week together, and became warmly attached to each other. Life now seemed dearer to Charley than ever before. Everything prospered on the farm that season. At its close, when farm operations had ceased, the men and women were put out to service. The Johnson family had made an arrangement for a share of earnings, with a view to purchasing the freedom of Mrs. Johnson. During the winter poor Johnson took sick and died, but Emily and Tom and their mother, all continued earning and saving, and finally their mother's freedom was purchased. This accomplished, she commenced housekeeping in the city, and took in washing and ironing.

Emily was still at service, and used to call at her mother's every Sunday afternoon. Charley generally made it convenient to call about the same time. Long before this, he had recounted to her his wonderful experience at Caskey's, and his subsequent efforts to see her.

The following summer he returned to work at the farm, but Emily remained at service. He, however, use to make it a point to see her, as occasion would permit. One pleasant early summer Sunday afternoon, sitting on a bench beneath a black walnut tree, in the little garden attached to her mother's house, the following dialogue occurred:

"Emily."

"What, Charley?"

"We've been acquainted a long time now, and some persons believe and say we're engaged. But you know we never talked about marrying. Emily, my gal, I want to talk about it today."

Emily's head dropped a little, but her eyes rested upon Charley, whom, she was conscious, had her undivided affection.

"I want to know, Emily, if you'll be mine."

"Charley, you know I've always been yours," said she, laughing.

"I know, Emily, I've had your love, and you've had mine. We've spent a happy time together this last half year. Now, I want you to marry me."

"Charley," she said, naively.

"Yes, I mean what I say," said he.

"But what will Master Freeman say?" she interposed.

"Oh, he understands it all first rate. I know his mind about it," said Charley, "and it's all right. So then it's settled?"

"Well!" was the only reply, in a low, soft tone. This was sealed with a kiss and Charley felt a new joy spring up in his heart. It was a supreme moment for both. They were happy and, after a hearty goodbye, they parted, Charley first promising to be back at a certain time, to ascertain what arrangements could be made for the wedding. He at once told his master, and Emily told her mother. Preparations were immediately set on foot for the coming event. Freeman himself contributed to the wedding supper. The invitations were sent out and two weeks of hard work by Emily, her mother and Tom followed. The happy hour at length arrived, and a host of friends, including all the hands from Freeman's farm, were gathered on the auspicious occasion. The Rev. Benjamin Franklin Rattray, minister, with whom the reader is already acquainted, officiated; but, as to the rest, Charley must give the account in his own words:

"When the proper time came, we stood on the floor midst our friends. The minister soon pronounced Emily and me one, and introduced us to the company as Mr. and Mrs. Chance. This is the first time I was ever called Mr. Chance, and I had lived 'bout twenty-nine years then, and it made me feel very grand, but I took care to get the first kiss from Emily on that important occasion. She was then about twenty, was dressed elegant, and looked the prettiest yellow gal I ever saw in my life. There was a general kissing and handshaking all round. Everybody appeared happy. The table was set out in great style and was loaded with provisions. It was, indeed, a great feast. I reckon there was more than fifty dollars spent over the affair. I suppose it was foolish, but it was a wonderful wedding.

"My friend Debbs was among the rest, and told me his experience on the same line. 'You know,' said he, 'I've been paying my distresses to Lucinda. I have a good ear for music, and I first won her in the serenade singing and picking my old banjo. The first time I went to see her after the husking, I'd very bad luck. I stood under her bedroom window, and was playing and singing my very best:

> Hey oh! hi oh! my sweet Cindah,
> Up! up! gently with your windah;
> For you, my love, I've come from far
> To sing and touch my sweet guitar;
> I have no wave of trouble, love,
> No, not the slightest bubble, love;
>   Hey oh! hi oh!—

" 'Here, all of a sudden, old Caskey hoisted the window and flung a bucket of sour butter milk upon me. It took all the starch out of my brand new collar and shirt bosom, and spoiled my clothes. But Caskey allowed he didn't know 'twas me. The master that bought Caskey's plantation bought Lucinda and she's there yet, so it's come out all right, and we're going to get married next week.' At his urgent request I had to lend him two dollars to buy some more clothes for his wedding suit. I couldn't help thinking he was easily suited, and that the bucket of buttermilk was almost as bad as the vicious dog Cap."

26

The Star of Freedom

AFTER A year and a half, Charley broached the matter of buying his freedom to his master, who said he would consent to any arrangement for that purpose, and fixed his price at $350. This was only fifty dollars a year for the remaining years, and was less than the rate at which he had been purchased. But Charley had no money, and set about thinking how he could manage. He knew a man named Barton who kept a livery stable, and he went to him and unfolded his plan. Charley wished him to become his surety to Lawyer Freeman, and he would work for him until he paid up the whole amount. Barton apparently fell in with the plan, and already Charley began to feel as if he stood upon the threshold of emancipation. But he was doomed to an early disappointment; for this greedy man, seeing that Lawyer Freeman was willing to part with Charley at so low a figure, went to him and secretly bought Charley, obtaining from him the usual bill of sale. Now, instead of being human chattel of an honourable man, Charley became the human chattel of a dishonourable man. When he learned the trick which Barton had played on him, the old ardour returned, and the desire to be free at once became a passion. In his extremity he went to good old Quaker Theophilus Tyson, and told him his trouble. Mr. Tyson said, "If Barton will let you work in my medicine factory, I will pay you twenty-five dollars per month," adding, "As you will have to work at preparing arsenic, it will be necessary for you to take salts, or castor oil, twice a week, otherwise you will get sick."

"I am willing," said Charley, "to take salts, castor oil and arsenic, the last, of course, to be in small doses, if only I can get shed of this vile man who's just bought me."

He went to Barton and reminded him of the arrangement he had made with him, and then explained his chance to make plenty of money with Quaker Tyson to buy his freedom but this devil-man laughed in his face, seemed to enjoy his discomfiture and refused the offer, saying: "You'll get over your pet in a little while."

Charley looked at him a moment, and then a terrible wish came to strike him to the earth. He could gratify his revenge easily, as he would be nothing in his hands. "For the Lord, it was a terrible temptation," added Charley, "and might have sent me down with the lost. But I turned and left him with his words 'You'll get over your pet in a little while,' ringing in my ears."

Old Jacob Davidson, hearing of Charley's distress, offered Barton a good price for him, but he refused to part with him, saying he required "just such a man for his stables." Charley returned to Lawyer Freeman and explained to him the arrangement he had made with Barton, and how he had deceived him.

"Barton told me," said Freeman, "you said you were not satisfied with me, and that you wanted him to buy you, so I let you go."

"Oh, what a falsehood!"

"I am very sorry," replied Mr. Freeman, "but it's past recall now."

The discovery of this man's perfidy only increased his weight of woe. Freeman was a man of integrity and a kind master. The contrast between him and Barton was very marked. Duplicity and heartlessness in this transaction stamped the latter with infamy. Life under such a mastership he could not, and would not, endure. Escape, henceforth, became his silent watch-thought. "Barton has fooled me," said he, "but there's a weak link in the chain he's forged for me, and I'll break it and fool him yet." Eight months rolled away before he got his plans sufficiently matured to put them into execution.

Charley had twice passed into different hands by will, had been sold thrice; and, counting Executor Howard as one, had had seven different masters in slave land. He had now made up his mind to make a tremendous effort to burst the shackles of ownership, achieve his freedom and be his own master for the rest of his life. He was now thirty years of age, and owing to Ridgely's trick, had seven years of service before him.

The result of his musings on the subject was the formation of a plan for his and his wife's escape. His sister Fanny had now become a woman, was free, married, and lived in the city of New York. She had written home that Emily could get $8 a month as a family servant, if she could be sent to that city. Charley had told his wife that he did not intend to be a slave much longer, and that his scheme was for her to take flight on board some vessel bound for that city, when he was away in the country, and thus would be supposed to know nothing about it. Once there she could go into service at good wages, until he could join her. He had not gone far in the relation of his plans when she in great impatience, said:

"What do you want of liberty? Why ain't you satisfied to live where we are—among our friends? I'll do nothing of the sort. I'm not willing to risk being kidnapped, if you are."

She then proceeded to find fault with him for thinking of such a thing. In vain he recalled to her the shameful way he had been deceived by Barton, and told her that his heart was set on obtaining their freedom. She stoutly refused, and he saw at once that he had endangered his whole scheme, and became afraid she would tell his master, and begged of her to say nothing to any one about it. He begged in vain, for she at once told her mother and brother and, but for their interference, would, in all probability, have told his master, and that would, doubtless, have been followed by another sale. He felt there was no time to be lost, and that he must escape alone, and at once. He had been sold and transferred until he was sick and tired of it; and now the act of this last master, the man Barton, had aroused him, and he resolved to risk flight at all hazards. He confided his purpose to a couple of trusty friends, who feared the undertaking and advised him not to run away.

"What if you are overtaken?" said one of them.

"What if I am?" he said; "I tell you they'll not bring me back alive."

"Oh!" said his friend, laughing, "it's only white people who commit suicide; Negroes never do."

Charley also went to see his Quaker friend, Jacob Davidson, and had a long talk with him on the subject. During the next two days his whereabouts was known to but very few. One of those visited by him was his good mother. He told her all that had happened between him and Barton, and that he could think of nothing now but escape from slavery.

"Barton," said he, "will hold me no longer."

"But Emily," said his mother, in an excited tone. "Are you going to leave Emily?"

He, of course, told her of his effort to have her go first, and the danger which came to him in consequence. He hoped she would yet follow him. Seeing his intense feeling on the subject, and realizing that she was about to lose him, she sprang to her feet, and threw her arms around his neck. Weeping and kissing him passionately, she said:

"Charley, must you go? Cornelius is lost these fourteen years. Fanny is far, far away, and I'll never see her again. You going too; what'll I do?" and she burst out crying.

Charley tried to console her as best he could and, after a little, she became somewhat pacified; and as he talked to her of the blessings of freedom, and his absorbing ambition to be his own master, she at length became reconciled. He talked over all his plans with her, and at the close, in the last farewell, she said: "God bless you, my son, and bring you out to the land of freedom." Thus they parted forever in his life.

27

The Escape

A T THE end of the second day, now Wednesday night, Charley, as arranged, returned to Quaker Davidson, who said to him, "I have not seen thy master since, but I see he has advertised thee in the papers, and has offered a reward of $50 for thy capture. Thee should stay no longer. Has thee seen thy mother, and is she willing?"

"Yes," said Charley, "I've seen her, and she's now willing for me to go. I've bid her, and all I wish to see, goodbye, and now I'm ready to start."

As he possessed no worldly goods, his affairs were easily arranged. He had served many masters faithfully and well, but their presents to him had been small indeed; and now, fully realizing the fact, he could not refrain from saying to Mr. Davidson, "Ridgely, in all my years of toil for him, never gave me a tuppenny bit." His whole fortune, in fact, consisted of a good suit of clothes, which he then had on, an overcoat, hanging on his left arm, a cane in his right hand, a bright silk handkerchief, and a few bits of silver in his pockets. He was now eager to undertake the difficult journey which lay between him and freedom. The good old Quaker[1] talked freely as to what course he was to take, until Charley at length stood up to leave. The Quaker also rose, and smiled approvingly upon him, and said, "May the blessing of heaven rest upon thee, and prosper thy journey." The two shook hands, and Charley weighed the slave anchor and glided from the Quaker's presence into the deep shades of night, and struck out for the haven of freedom. This was the point to which he had looked forward with such eager interest. This was the realization of his daydreams. His whole soul had been absorbed with this great idea of freedom. Now that the time had come, and he was actually travelling, with his back on slavery and his face toward freedom, his whole soul was, by a sudden impulse, thrilled with delight. It was a moment of supreme happiness. The star of freedom had appeared above the horizon, and he fairly bounded along. He would have shouted aloud, if prudence would have permitted it, "I'm bound for the land of freedom." His great anxiety was to reach Pennsylvania, a free state. He expected pursuit, and well knew the consequence if taken. It was quite late when he parted from good Quaker Davidson, and the streets of Baltimore were almost deserted. By daylight he had covered fully twenty miles, and then came a lovely autumn morning, with a glorious sunrise. The eastern horizon was fringed with long strips of gold-lined clouds. There had been a heavy dew, and the sun's level rays glistened upon the spears of grass at his feet. Overhead the sky wore a soft leaden hue; the air was balmy, and tarrying birds awoke to their morning melodies in the now leafless trees that skirted the road he travelled. All nature seemed to beat in unison with his own happy heart. He had no fear; not a single cloud of doubt arose to hide the goal of his ambition from his mind. He was on the way to freedom, and that was all the happiness he could then contain.

Presently he overtook a black woman, the first person he had seen since he left the outskirts of Baltimore city the evening before. Then, as he heard a footstep on the sidewalk, his heart beat quicker for an instant; now he felt free to speak, and learned from the woman that she was employed as cook at Young's tavern, close by. She invited him to go there, and said Mr. Young was a kind man, who would give him some breakfast. He thanked her, told her nothing of his business, pushed on all day, and in the evening reached his Uncle Harry's place at Long Green. His uncle worked with Geddis, a market-gardener, and did his marketing. He found him with a wagon loaded and ready for market. His uncle was greatly surprised at seeing him and, when he told him he was running away, he said, "I'm sorry! What'll I say to Aunt Peggy (Charley's mother) when I see her?"

"Oh, she knows I'm off. But tell her, if I never more see her in this world, I'll try and meet her in heaven."

He asked him to stay overnight and the following day, and intimated he could start the following night; but Charley, fearing such delay, declined, and said he must push on; he even refused to have anything to eat. The fact is he could not eat, and felt no need of food or rest. When he told his uncle he was going the short way to Columbia, he said, "Child, you can't go up that way. It's just forty miles by the road to the border of Pennsylvania, and there stands Burt Husband's tavern. No slave ever got past that place in daylight without being took up. His place is right on the line 'twixt Maryland and Pennsylvania. His stable's in Pennsylvania, and his tavern's in Maryland."

"What did you say his name is?" asked Charley.

"Burt Husband," he replied.

"Burt Husband! I must get past that place somehow," said Charley.

"Even then you're not safe," said his uncle, " 'til you go eleven miles and cross the Susquehanna River." They shook hands and parted, and Charley went on walking the whole night long, as rapidly as if it had been his first night's walk.

At daylight he came in sight of what he knew by his uncle's description to be Burt Husband's tavern. Ordinary prudence said, conceal yourself and rest through this day, and pass this place of danger under cover of night, and he debated the question in his mind. He was unknown to everyone as far as he knew. He might by chance be discovered, even in a hiding place. There, straight before him, within a short distance and in full view, lay the great free State of Pennsylvania. He was a slave still. Yonder, although still in danger of capture, he would be a free man. Here a chattel, there recognized as a human being. It was the same country, had the same government, the same president, and yet there was this great difference. Suddenly an impulse seized him, and it seemed at all hazards he must push on, and on he went. It was still early, and he thought, perhaps, there would be no one about; but to his surprise, he found several men on the verandah of the hotel, and could hear them speaking. Listening closely, found they were talking about him.

"Look here," said one, with an oath, "there's a strapping big nigger coming up."

"He is well-dressed, too," said a second.

Charley passed without showing that he saw them, but before he got out of reach of the sound of their voices, he heard one of them say, "I'll go and question that nigger a little." He had not proceeded far when he saw a man come out of the hotel, mount a big gray horse and bear down on him. As soon as he came up alongside, the man said:

"Where are you from?"

"Limestone Bottom," said Charley, meaning the lime kilns.

"Where are you going?"

"Little York."

"Looking for work?"

"Yes, I want to get something to do pretty soon."

"You're just my man; I want a man to thrash out my rye. I've a thousand bushels, and it's wanted away for the distillery."

"Perhaps it's too wet," was suggested.

"No, it's fine and dry," said the man.

"What will you give a bushel?"

"A fippenny bit a bushel, and you can make money at it."

"Where d'you live?"

"My place is just on the other side of that strip of bush, about a mile from here. My house and barn's hid by them trees," pointing in their direction. "You can take a short cut across, and I'll ride around by the road," he said, pointing toward the hotel.

"Do you mean for me to go cross that field?"

"Yes."

"Is there any water 'twixt this and your place?"

"No."

"Well, don't be long before you come," said Charley, knowing very well the stranger was only bent on mischief, and then started across the field in the direction pointed out to him. As the horseman turned to ride off, Charley cast his eye over his shoulder and caught a glimpse of a chuckling expression on his face, which to him meant, "We'll bag him at the barn."

After walking a little distance, he turned to take another look at this man who was so anxious to have his rye thrashed. He had gone back to the hotel, and was in the act of taking a glass of liquor, probably gin, from the attendant, which was quickly tossed down his throat. Soon after Charley gained the strip of woods, and could see a house on the other side of it. He was now out of view, both of the road and the hotel. Fortunately, the belt of timber which appeared to consist mostly of black oak and hickory, ran in the direction of the road he wished to travel and, under cover of these trees, he went as rapidly as possible in a direction at right angles to his course across the fields, in hopes that it would afford him a probable means of escape. He soon reached a crossroad, which fortunately led to the road he had left; and he pushed rapidly along until he thought his pursuers had time to gather and follow. Then, taking advantage of a thickly wooded ravine, he entered and selected a spot behind a big oak log, where the dry leaves were several inches thick. He covered himself with these leaves, and had not been long in his hiding place when he heard the distant clatter of horses' hoofs. Nearer and nearer they came, the sound becoming painfully distinct, and soon he could hear the voices of the riders. Directly he rose from his leafy hiding place, and had the intense satisfaction of seeing the troop of seven slave hunters gallop past him on their steeds with a single bloodhound, all enshrouded in a cloud of dust. He had been holding his breath, but now breathed more easily. The rascals had gone; but he knew not how soon they might return.

Feeling that he was safe for the present at least, he returned to his leafy couch and, after a little, fell into a deep sleep, from which he did not waken until near sundown. And in his sleep, after a long rest, he commenced to dream of his pursuers. He was fleeing before them. Everything that would impede his progress—coats, vest, shoes and hat—had all been cast away, and on and on he sped with the swiftness of a deer. He could hear the clatter of the horses' hoofs, and hear the voices of the riders, and became painfully conscious they were gaining on him. Contact with the brush had torn his pants and shirt into tatters He had run a long distance when he was startled with a view of the horsemen coming down the hill in hot pursuit, and heard the foremost of them, with the whip extended, shouting back to the others, "There he is, among the reeds. We have him. The dog's almost on him." Every muscle and nerve were strained to the utmost, and he felt he could not hold out much longer. The voice caused him to look over his shoulder for the bloodhound, and when he caught sight of him just at his heels, he screamed with fright and—awoke. And when awake, glad he was that it was a dream. Part, indeed, was real; and the rest might yet be, although he hoped to elude his pursuers. He was thankful it was no worse, and gave a great sigh of relief to find that he was still beside the oak log, and that neither horsemen nor bloodhound were to be seen.

When it grew darker, he started again, listening cautiously for the sound of the returning slave hunters, but it was all silent and dark. He had not proceeded far until he came to a point where there was a second slightly diverging road. Here he got down on his hands and knees and felt for the hoof tracks of the horses and, after a little effort, was able to decide as to which road his pursuers had taken, and made out pretty well, too, by the tracks that they had returned. His sleep had been too deep to hear them. He concluded the road the horsemen had taken in pursuit was the one he should take, and did so. He walked briskly until after midnight, and concluded to turn in, as the sailors say, for the rest of the night.

The night was exceedingly dark, but he succeeded in getting a couple of rails which he threw over a picket fence, got over himself, and placed them in an inclined position, stretched himself on his temporary bedstead, and was soon soundly asleep. He awakened before daybreak

The slave hunt.

and, just at the first gleam of light, came to the conclusion that he had got into a stumpy field. He was used to chopping and clearing land, but could not account for the number of stumps in the field. He thought they must clear land differently in Pennsylvania from what they did in Maryland. His eyes rested on one of these stubs not more than a couple of rods from him. "What's that? Surely not here? Why, that's marble, a marble pillar. Why in the world has it been put among these stumps? What! There's another and another! More and more still! The Lord have mercy on me! I'm in a graveyard!" he exclaimed; and he felt, or thought he felt, the rails shake beneath him, and the fence, against which one end of the rails rested, moving. His eyes just then fell on the other end of his temporary bedstead, and he found it was supported by a grave mound. He at once sprang up in a half-dazed condition and, as the mists had lifted and the gray dawn had become clearer, he looked over the ghostly scene in bewilderment. He had slept in the city of the dead. At the same time he heard a dull noise of "tum! tum! tum!" like a still-pump, and saw a flash of light, as if reflected from some neighbouring window. Here lay before him a cemetery of considerable extent, full of marble slabs and pillars, the latter being what he supposed to be high stumps. It looked old and neglected and the very heart of ghostland.

For the first time since leaving Baltimore, he felt faint and weak. The excitement of his escape bore him up no longer. With great difficulty he was able to get over the fence and crawl a short distance, and was then obliged to rest. He had eaten nothing since he left Baltimore on Wednesday night, and it was now Saturday morning. He must now have food, or die from exhaustion. He looked around to see if there was a house where he could get something to eat. There was a large stone house close by the cemetery, but it was dilapidated and evidently without occupants. On the other side of the road, in a valley, was a still-house. He knew from what Quaker Davidson told him before starting that he must be near the Susquehanna River. Away to the right and before him, he saw a mountain, but no house. He got up, and dragged himself wearily along down to the still-house, found it in ruins, and then started for the river, but did not go far until he came to a little house, which had been hidden from his view by a clump of trees. This he gladly entered, and found a little Dutch woman and some small children. He quickly told his story of distress and great need of something to eat. After first telling him about her husband, who was a chicken huckster and who had already gone to market, the little woman set about getting some breakfast.

"I was soon seated at the table," Charley relates, "and had spread before me hot corn-cake, cold pork and molasses, and a mug of coffee. It was the most delicious meal I ever tasted in my life; and more than once I'd eat pork and beans, corn beef and cabbage, and possum, and sweet potato, but this beat them all. It was my first meal out of slavery, and I suppose that accounts for it."

The little Dutch woman asked him where he stayed overnight, and when he told her, she opened her eyes wide in surprise, saying: "Why, the big stone house is haunted, and so is the still-house." She then gave the history of the haunted house and the still-house. Lights were seen and sounds heard there at nights. Both houses had been built, when Pennsylvania was a slave state, by a wealthy Virginian who owned five hundred acres of land and kept a great number of slaves. He was a cruel man and had, at different times, killed no less than four of his slaves. No one had lived in the house since he left, and could not, for it was haunted. Charley thought it was well he had not heard her story when he awoke and found himself among gravestones, beneath the shadow of that great haunted house, as it would probably have finished him. The chatty, kind-hearted little woman said if her husband had been home he would have assisted him. While at breakfast, for he lingered at the table for a long time, the little woman drew water from the pump, and then he knew the noise he had heard at break of day. Her husband's early lantern, doubtless, accounted for the glimmer of light reflected from the window of the deserted house, and his turning heavily on his rail bedstead would account for the shaking of the fence.

He was not absolutely safe until he got across the river. He, however, concluded not to go over that day, but to climb the mountain which overhung the river near the village of Wrightsville [Pennsylvania], and there rest through the day. While walking in that direction, he saw a gentleman with a white hat on, resting, with folded arms, on his gate; fearing to pass him, Charley changed his course for the mountain. He, however, subsequently learned that the gentleman he avoided was no other than James Mufflin, a noted abolitionist, who would doubtless have befriended him. Charley went up the mountainside and, like Moses on Mount Pisgah,[2] feasted his eyes on the promised land. He looked over the Susquehanna River at the city of Columbia, whose tall church spires glistened in the sun, and whose streets he soon hoped to walk without fear or molestation. He saw, too, from his commanding position, a large area of country stretched out enchantingly before him, and his hopes

The final goal.

grew with the wondrous view in borderland. But while thus resting in body, and feasting in heart and intellect, as his eyes swept over nature's panorama, they fell upon a long procession on the road he had so recently travelled. A closer inspection showed the procession to be headed by a hearse drawn by two black horses. It was a funeral wending its way to the cemetery where he had just had such a terrible night's experience.

While he was thus congratulating himself on the threshold of a new life of liberty, someone had lain his down and had closed his earthly career, and his high hopes sank low as he communed aloud with himself, saying: "How strange life is! After all, it comes down to this in the end. Whether he be black or white, rich or poor, bond or free, to every man the gravestone is the final goal."

28

∽

Over the River

WHILE RESTING on the mountain, and enjoying its refreshing air and inspiring prospect, Charley kept several houses, situated on the same side of the river along its bank, well under view, to ascertain if any of them contained people of his own colour. He saw that one of them did and in the evening he visited it, and found a tall yellow woman its occupant. He told his story, and said he wanted to know about the people in the city on the other side of the river, and inquired as to his safety there.

"I knew," said she, "the minute I clapped my eyes on you, that you was a refugee, and was getting away. Where you from, and how'd you work your way so far?"

After getting a brief reply, she continued: "A committee engaged John—he's my man—to assist refugees, but you must be very careful and don't tell him too much about your business, as he isn't true, and takes money from both sides."

This woman's account of her husband reminded Charley of a conversation he heard in Maryland, at a great camp meeting.

"One of the brethren," said his informant, "went to a Baptist meeting, and he big Baptist then; next he went to the Methodist meeting, and out shout them all, but he took good care to eat hearty with both denominations."

John was willing to accept favours both from the friends and the pursuers of the slave.

The tall yellow woman asked Charley if he would not like a shave. On his admitting he would, she took a razor and went at his face like a professional barber, and gave him a very good shave. On her husband's return very shortly afterwards, she announced him as a refugee, whereupon, without waiting for more, John threw his arms around Charley's neck and kissed him with great fervour several times, and expressed much joy at seeing him. It was now plain to see why his wife had suggested a smooth face. Charley remained with them that night and over Sunday. He had a comfortable bed and plenty to eat, and began to feel pretty well again. On the Sabbath morning, however, he was not a little surprised to see the tall woman wash her face with the dishcloth and wipe it with the linen drying towel. As there was a fine roast turkey for the Sunday dinner, Charley asked John how he came to have such good fortune.

"That turkey," said John, "has been roosting on my fence for several nights, and last night I seized him for the rent of the fence. Brother Chance, which part will I help you to?"

Charley felt a twinge of conscience and said, "I'll take a little piece of the breast. But, friend John," said Charley, "I suppose you're a member of the church?"

"Why, Brother Chance, do you suppose I'd let a bird of any kind stand 'tween me and the Lord? But to tell you the truth, sir, I ain't no member now."

"How's that?" said Charley.

"Well—er—ah—I used to attend the church in Columbia. Let me give you this second joint, it's the best of the whole turkey. More stuffing? A little gravy? Manda is about the best cook in these parts."

"I wish she wouldn't wash her face with the dishcloth," thought Charley; and just then he remembered he had the day before noticed that, when knitting, she used the point of her knitting needle to tickle her scalp a moment before she had thrust it into the pot to try if the potatoes were done.

"Well, as I was saying, the first year I attended church, I subscribed ten dollars to the minister's salary, and the people all called me Brother Watkins. The second year, I give five dollars, and they call me Mister Watkins. In the next year business was poor and Manda was sick, and I give nothing. Well, sir, after that, they call me old Watkins, and so I left the church. But every man ought to be a professor of religion, that's only right and natural."

The conversation then turned upon domestic matters and, on Charley's inquiring as to whether he had children, John said:

"Oh, yes, we've five children, but I've sought 'em all out in Columbia, Lancaster and Philadelphia."

On noticing a fiddle hanging on the wall of the cabin, Charley asked John if he played on it.

"I play, and used to dance, too, but me and the old woman ain't never going to dance anymore."

"How's that?" asked Charley.

"Well, you see," John went on to say, "when Manda and me experienced religion at the camp meeting, we quit dancing."

"But you hain't quit going to dances yourself," chimed in Manda.

"You know I only go to play the fiddle for the dancers," rejoined John, "and if I don't go, some other fellow will, for without music, who could dance? Beside that, I need the money, and I often save them from having a poor player and worse music."

Charley learned from John, who, it will be seen, was a talker as well as a fiddler, much of the condition of the black people on the other side of the river, as well as of the city of Columbia itself.

On Monday morning it was arranged that the two men should go over to the city, and visit John's brother-in-law, Chris Dickson.

"John," said Manda, "you must take the best of care of your new brother," as if she wished to strengthen his good intention.

"Yes'm," obsequiously replied John.

Just as they were about to start, he, however, hesitatingly said:

"My brother, er-ah-you needn't take that coat over with you. Very likely they have advertised you in that coat. Just leave it here, till you get settled at work, and I'll bring it to you. It's a nice overcoat."

The coat was left, and they started, taking the bridge, which was a mile and a quarter long. At the outset, a toll, a fippenny bit, was demanded. John had no money. He was in the habit, he said, of getting over free himself. The gatekeeper was firm; they could not get through without a fippenny bit. What little money Charley possessed, he had already given to the little Dutch woman for his breakfast, and to John's wife for keeping him while he rested. Seeing the dilemma, Charley pulled out his silk handkerchief, and told the gatekeeper to keep that until he returned. They were then allowed to pass over. Before they got over the bridge, John said in a confidential tone, "Don't say nothing to Dickson about the coat you've left at my place."

The moment they reached the other side of the bridge, and Charley stepped on the ground, he shouted, "John," in such a loud, sharp voice as to quite frighten his slippery guide. "John, I'm free; free at last," he added, in the same high key, as John stared at him; then, facing in the direction of Barton's livery stable, swung his hat high in the air and shouted at the top of his voice, "Goodbye, Barton; goodbye, slavery, forever."

"Certainly," said John, "you're a slave no more, but you spoke so sudden like, you frightened me. You're boiling with excitement; you ought to suppress yourself, till we get over to Dickson's."

"John," said Charley, "I can't wait; I feel powerful good 'cause I own myself, and I feel as I must holler or bust." And he shouted again, "Hurrah! I'm free; I'm a beast of burden no more; at last I'm a man!"

At Dickson's the new freedman, now exhilarated and almost startled with the thought of his new found manhood, was heartily congratulated on his escape from slavery, and warmly welcomed to freedom. On Tuesday morning, Charley went out into the country, looking for work. After walking ten miles, he came to Lancaster City, passed through it, and about two miles farther on came to a stone tavern, kept by Dick Wilson. It was a holiday and there were thirty or forty black men and boys assembled, pitching quoits, and amusing themselves in various ways. As he passed along he heard a man say, "Look, William Henson, there's your brother." Charley had called himself James Brown since leaving Baltimore, so he concluded it was a case of mistaken identity. He noticed a man, who apparently came out of the crowd, following him, and thinking some trick was intended, he grew angry, and determined to fight if necessary, but had no desire to get into a row. Then he heard someone call, "Hi, stranger!" but he hurried on, thinking the safest course was to get away from the crowd as soon as possible. When well away from them, he entered a house where blacks lived, and inquired for work. At the same time a yellow-skinned man came to the door, and he was asked if he knew of any work. He said he knew a man named Levi Akitt, a Dutchman, a couple miles farther down the road, who wanted a man to chop. Charley went to Levi's and applied for this chopping.

"You got axe?" said Levi.

"No, I haven't," said Charley.

"No axe? You carry off my axe? It's good and sharp."

Charley assured the Dutchman he would not do that, and bargained to cut his wood for twenty-five cents per cord, with board. On wet days he was to feed his cattle. He worked with him for three weeks, and then wanted to send a letter to Quaker Davidson, and to see about his coat, which John was to bring over to Dickson's. He walked into Columbia and called for his coat, but it had not been sent. He complained to Aaron

Hicks, a Quaker, about it, who declared that the committee should know how John had acted. A middle-aged black man, named Napoleon, with heavy voice, big head and short bowed legs which made him appear to waddle rather than walk, volunteered to go with him for his coat.

"We wondered where John got that fine coat," said Charley's companion. "He's been wearing it these three weeks. If I'd been you, I'd have taken that coat along with me."

The two men crossed the river in a boat, went up the bank and rapped at John's door. When the door opened, John appeared and growled:

"Why, child, what're you doing here?"

Charley replied, "I came for my coat."

"You fooling about here yet?" said John, evasively. "The white folks'll get you yet, sure."

"Give me my coat," again demanded Charley.

"I supposed you'd have been in New York before now," continued John. "Don't stay here, for if they catch you, they'll tie you up and cut you all to pieces."

"See here!" shouted Napoleon. "Give this man his coat, er-ah we'll take you to Squire Buttonwoodtree or Squire Cherrytree, and give you the very mischief, and get you suspended from your office. D'you hear?"

Under this terrible threat, given in a thundering tone, John reluctantly handed the coat over, saying, "Child, I forgot it. Don't be angry."

The two men returned to Quaker Hicks with the coat. Hicks on the same day, at Charley's request, wrote to Jacob Davidson of his safe arrival at Columbia. Charley remained at his house over night, and next morning started to go back to the Dutchman's place, to cut hickory at twenty-five cents a cord. On the road, however, near Lancaster, he was suddenly taken ill, and entered a house where a black family lived. They were very kind to him and allowed him to lie down. Their name, as he afterwards learned, was Johnston. Johnston generally came home drunk, and his wife was uneasy lest he would make a racket and disturb the sick man. As soon as he learned there was a stranger in the house, he shouted, "Give me the light," and went into the room where he was.

"Where you from?"

"Baltimore," said Charley.

"Baltimore? I come from Baltimore myself. Dr. Littlejohn used to own me, but I ran away from him."

Johnston sent for a Quaker, and when the Quaker came, he sent for a doctor. Charley continued very sick. On New Year's Day there was a quilt-

ing bee at Sam Bixby's close by, and at some one's suggestion the whole
party came down to see the sick refugee at Johnston's. Charley was too
sick to notice much, but there was a man among them who looked closely
at him.

After Charley got better, he obtained a job at chopping cordwood, at
forty cents per cord and board, and splitting black walnut rails, at five
shillings per hundred. He was a good chopper and, like Lincoln many
years after, had few equals as a rail splitter. Shortly after his sickness, while
working in the woods, a man came to him and said, as he stood upon
the tree he had just fallen:

"You're a heap better then you were last time I saw you."

"Yes, I'm better," said Charley to his visitor.

"I saw you," he went on to say, "when you were laying sick at Johnston's. I was there with the quilting bee from Bixby's, but you didn't notice
anything taking place, so I didn't speak to you."

"I was very low then," replied Charley, "but, thank the Lord, I'm pretty
well again."

"I saw you before that time," continued the visitor, "more than a month
before. Do you remember hearing a man calling, 'Hi! stranger'?"

"Yes, well I do," said Charley, "and was very vexed, because I supposed
those holiday people wanted to make a little fun out of me."

"Lord sakes! No, I wanted to see you, for I took you to be my brother."

"That's right. One Father in heaven is father of us all. We're his poor
children, and of course we're all brothers according to the scriptures."

"I don't mean like that there; I mean that your father was my father
and your mother was my mother."

"Hey! Guess you're mistaken. What's my name?" asked Charley.

"Don't know your first name, but my father's name was Chance."
"Chance?" Charley fairly shouted, as he repeated the name, and let go
the handle of the axe he had been leaning upon.

"And my mother's name was Peggy Chance," continued the stranger.

"What, be you Cornelius, been given up for dead so long?"

"I'm Cornelius."

"And I'm Charley," each said, as they sprang into each others arms.

"Is mother living yet? Brothers and sisters, are they all alive?" inquired
Cornelius, hastily.

"All living except poor Peter. Poor Peter is no more. And we all thought
you were dead too. Why, it's fourteen years since you were given up for
lost," said Charley.

"Yes, it's a long time," said Cornelius; "and I often wanted to let you all know where I was, but dare not."

"What happened to you, Cornelius?" asked Charley, after explaining Peter's illness and death.

"That name sounds queer to me. I changed my name to William Henson. That's my name now," said Cornelius, before answering. After a little he cleared up the mystery of his loss, and explained how he came to leave home so suddenly.

"I was going," said he, "for Master Maynard, the bootblack, with seven pairs of polished shoes to deliver to their owners, when I met a Dutchman on the road with a pair of mules and a covered wagon. You know I was always fond of mules. That Dutchman said to me 'See here, boy, you like to go with me to Pennsylvania and be free, and work for yourself?' I said I would. He asked me what my name was, and I told him it was Cornelius. But he called me William Henson, after an uncle of his own, and I've being going by that name ever since. He then stowed me in his wagon and brought me right through here. Now I'm married, and I've been living on a rented farm near here. Let's go over to my place and see my little home." They started immediately, as suggested, and William continued: "On the holiday didn't you hear a fellow call out, 'William Henson, there goes your brother'?"

"I did hear that," said Charley, "but didn't know what it meant. I knew my name wasn't Henson. I called myself James Brown, and I was very vexed, and thought I might have to fight before I got through the crowd. I wasn't going to let anyone run the rig on me, if I was a refugee."

"Well," said William, "the young fellow that called said to me, 'If that stranger ain't your brother, I'm a ninny.' 'My brother,' said I, 'why what do you mean?' 'I mean,' said he, 'that he looks just like you.' At hearing this, I followed you; but, as you didn't answer me and I hadn't seen your face, I thought it was perhaps only his fancy, and left off following you. When I saw you sick in bed at Sam Johnston's, I couldn't see any family likeness, and so I came to the bush today to find out about it. Now it's about time you told me how in the world you came here, and how you got away; but see, we're at my little home. This is Mary. Mary, here's my brother Charley, all the way from the city of Baltimore. He's been here a month, and I've only just done found him out."

Charley had a warm welcome from Mary and her four little boys. Her house was neat as a pin, and the family appeared to be living comfortably. After supper, Charley told them the story of his escape and all about those left behind in Maryland. Here he had a comfortable resting place with his newly found, long lost brother. A lost brother restored and a new home found, in his newly acquired freedom, gave him a twofold joy. As may be supposed, until each obtained a full history of the other, their conversations were of an animated nature.

"So they all thought I was dead, when I left home," said William, next morning.

Mary's boys.

"Yes, indeed," replied Charley, there was a great excitement when you didn't come home. Mother sent up to Maynard, the bootblack, and he said the last he saw of you was when you started in the morning to take the boots to his customers. Every one of them was visited, but you hadn't got there with the boots, and they were angry enough about it. Some of them had to send out and buy more boots. All day we searched the city over for you. We thought poor mother would've gone crazy. She accused Missis of selling you down to Georgia. The Missis denied it and felt very bad because she was accused that way. Mother never got right over the shock. When I was coming away, she spoke about you as her lost boy."

This touched the listener, who now saw more clearly than ever before the deep wound he had inflicted by his flight, and he shed tears as he thought of his mother's wonderful love for him.

On Charley's asking, "Hadn't the Dutchman a good deal of trouble getting your through?" he said, "Not much, as he explained to those seeing me, and they were very few, that he'd taken me down to see the city of Baltimore and was then taking me back to my people. A tavern keeper wanted him to sell me, saying he could get $250 for me and, if the Dutchman would divide the money, he would help him fix it. 'I will not do such a thing,' said the Dutchman. 'I promised to bring him back to his peoples, and I will do it. I must take that little nigger back to his peoples.'"

As Cornelius had taken the name of Henson, Charley thought he might as well do so too, so he called himself James Brown no longer, but James Henson; and that is the way Charley Chance became James Henson.

As Charley, after crossing the river thus laid aside his slave name of Charley Chance and renamed himself James Henson, he will hereafter, in this narrative, be designated by the latter name. His slave name was put off like an old suit of clothes; and the new one, a free name, as a new suit, was put on and was, from henceforth, to be worn in its place. In a physical, as well as a spiritual sense, he could say, and rejoice as he said it, "Old things are passed away, behold all things are become new." He soon became known to the people as Bill Henson's brother. As he remained here month after month, he heard a great deal about Philadelphia and longed to visit that great city. At the end of a year this desire culminated in a tramp of seventy-two miles, terminating in that City of Brotherly Love. Here he soon found work and became acquainted with a great many freedmen, many of whom he found making money in various pursuits. The children of some of these freedmen dressed in what appeared to him to be a very extravagant style. He had seen nothing like it in Maryland. For a child there to call a parent anything but "daddy" or "mammy," or a grandparent, "granddaddy" or "granny," would have been deemed the height of presumption and impudence. In this city, however, the youngsters, he found, were putting on airs and imitating the white folks both in language and dress.

"On the street," said he, "I met young men as black as myself, wearing a dickey, high linen collar, long cuffs, cheap rings and nice clothes. These upstarts would sneer at newcomers, and call them 'men of the field nigger class.'" A new acquaintance, who had just bought a watch and chain, on

This version of Mother Bethel African Methodist Episcopal Church
in Philadelphia was a familiar site to Jim Henson.

meeting him in the street pulled out his watch, and said, "Look here, I'll give you five minutes to reach the next corner of the street," pointing toward it with a ringed finger.

Henson visited little Bethel Church[1] the first Sabbath morning after reaching the city, and here, as at Jacob's Bethel, the place seemed signally close to the spirit world. Here his weary spirit rested and was greatly refreshed by his Lord's presence. Here, too, his way was opened and work for his hands readily obtained, as the little church was eminently practical in its methods. It was presided over by a lay coloured preacher, named Tom Workman, who, like St. Paul, laboured with his hands as well as in the Church. He was an earnest, consistent man. Through the week he wielded the whitewash brush within, and his bucksaw and axe without the houses of the good people of the city who gave him employment. On Sabbath he was regularly in his pulpit and preached the Word of Life to his hearers. His singing ability was of great service to him in his work among his people. White people, too, gladly heard him sing spiritual melodies, of which he seemed to have an inexhaustible store. After his morning discourse, which was a short one, he proceeded to make some announcements.

"Brethren," said he, "I've learned this morning that Brother Henson, who's lately escaped from slavery, has come to the city, and is here this morning. Who knows where the brother can get board and work?"

Up went a hand. "I can find him a home at Sister Hut's, and work from the corporation."

"That's right, Brother Tompkins, you'll look after this new brother. Last week," he went on to say, "in visiting, I found that several persons required help. Sister White is sick. She irons laundry Fridays and Saturdays, and she's afeared of losing her place. Who'll take Sister White's place?"

"I'll take it on Friday," said a stout girl. "And I'll take it on Saturday," said another.

"Widow Cook is out of work, and nearly out of fuel and food," said the minister.

"I can spare a little coal," said Brother Clemens.

"And I'll take it over to her with my wheelbarrow," said a chunky boy, called Wash, after the father of his country.

"I think I can give some provisions for her," said Mary Potter.

"The next case," said he, "you know about yourselves. It's Brother Hannibal Ruff, who fell off the scaffold when carrying the hod of brick, and broke his leg and ribs and hurt his head. His wife is all worn out sitting up with him. I want seven persons to sit up with him through each night of next week." Seven quickly volunteered and their names were taken down. "Now," said the speaker, "I come to my last case, and it's the hardest of all. Poor Simon Eaton's taken to drinking again. You all know what a hard drinker he was, and how he came into the church and walked in the right way for a long time. Now he's falling in the old snare. Brother Perkins, you've fought the same battle with the demon drink and you came out victorious. I want you to go and see poor Simon." Brother Perkins bowed an assent twice. "Show him the way of your deliverance. You know the way out of the pit." Then he lifted his hands and said, "Let us pray for Simon." Earnestly he petitioned the throne of heavenly grace for Simon's rescue from his "upsetting" sin, as he termed it, eliciting a hearty responsive "Amen" from Brother Perkins.

For many years after the good, dark-visaged lay preacher was permitted to remain in charge of his flock, meeting the wants of his people, and exemplifying to the world, as far as the light shone from little Bethel Church, a practical Christianity.

29

Stephen Girard

I N 1830, the first summer after his arrival in Philadelphia, Henson, along with ten other black men, went out about four miles from the city to the Girard farm to mow hay. Henson was appointed speaker and, addressing a gentleman near the fine house of the farm, said:

"Be you Mister Girard?"

"No," said the person addressed, pointing to a field, "that is Mr. Girard, with the high Leghorn hat on, with his men."

The crowd went toward him, Henson advancing as they came near him. Stephen Girard[1] was busy at work and did not notice them coming. As Henson saw him that morning, he was a thickset man of swarthy countenance, quick in his movements, dressed—as he had always been from time immemorial when on the farm—in linen drill pants and coat and a pair of strong shoes, his head covered with the memorable long-worn high Leghorn hat. Altogether he had anything but the appearance of an old sea captain, as he really was.

"Mr. Girard," said the spokesman, whose language had already greatly improved, "we've heard that you wanted men to cut hay."

"What's that you say? Do you want me?" said Mr. Girard, in a strong French accent and with a shrug of his shoulders.

"We're looking for work, and heard you had some hay to cut," said Henson.

"Well, yes. I've twenty-eight acres. How many men you've got?"

"Ten."

"Very well. I shall give you one dollar and a quarter an acre. You see those men in that far field down toward Schuylkill Point. Tell 'em I sent you to cut the hay."

This was not extra pay, as some of his meadow was exceedingly heavy. Once this job finished, the ten men left, but Henson remained, the only coloured man in his employ, at half a dollar a day, including Sundays, wet or dry—the same wages that Girard paid all his men. Meals and lodging were furnished in the culinary portion of the house.

Girard had a bank in the city, vessels at sea and this large farm close to the city and south of it, where the Schuylkill (Hidden Creek) falls into the Delaware. Although so wealthy, and carrying on so much business, he gave a considerable share of his time to his farm where he delighted to work in summer. He had seven barns with stone foundations, a dairy, along with a slaughterhouse and storehouses, making a village of buildings. He employed thirty men about the farm and carried on extensive trade in provisions and supplies.

He fattened cattle and killed them. The stone foundations under the barns were used for the storage of his beef, pork and other supplies in connection with his shipping trade, to the value, it was said, of a hundred thousand dollars. His milk-house had a floor of blue and white marble. Every Wednesday morning Henson had to pump water for Charity to wash off this floor. Charity was an exceedingly plain, full-black woman, whom Mr. Girard drove up from the house to the dairy every other morning, with his old gray horse, then twenty years old, named Dick, and his grasshopper gig, almost as old. Charity wore her hair tied in knots, which, with her coarse feature, gave her a decidedly ugly appearance. One day, as Henson pumped water for her, he ventured to say to her, "Madam, are you married?" She replied with an emphatic "No," and added, "All the men worth having are already married." At which Henson quoted the old adage, "There's as good fish in the sea as ever was caught," without creating the slightest apparent waver in her belief.

Many a morning Henson opened the gate wide to let Dick and his gig, Steve and his dairymaid, pass through. "Get up, Dick," Mr. Girard would say as he touched his favourite horse with the whip, and off they started toward the dairy.

In an upper room in the great Girard College at Philadelphia, there stands a stuffed gray horse, clad in an old harness and hitched to a gig, which has been shown to thousands of visitors as a curiosity.[2] This is the horse and rig that Philadelphia's benefactor drove through her streets, and back and forth between city and farm for so many years. It is Dick and his harness and the grasshopper gig, the selfsame for which Henson used to open the farm gate wide when Old Steve and his dark dairymaid passed through.

A number of his men were raw Irishmen who continually broke one of Mr. Girard's rules. "Mister Girard allowed each man two 'jiggins' a day, but these men weren't satisfied with the allowance. When occasionally they would get drunk, they were quarrelsome and, as there were seven of them and Henson was obliged to be among them, he remembered his former experience with the seven men from the Emerald Isle, and was not without occasional bodily fear. A number of Girard's men were French, and when these imbibed, they became excitable and talkative and much of their talked appeared to consist of "la! la! la!"

The hay season had been catching weather, and Mr. Girard had had his hay cut and stored very green. One warm, muggy morning, one of the barns was enveloped in a sort of mist.

"Look at the mist 'bout the barn," said Henson to Tom Burns, the Girard Bank night watchman, as they chanced to meet not very far from the barn.

"I've been looking at it for some time," said Tom, "and I don't know what to make of it."

"Why, the hay is heating," said Henson.

"I believe you're right; that's just what it is," said Tom, as he walked away.

The next morning smoke was rising from all parts of the great roof, and the two men again met near the same place.

"Do you see that?" said Henson, pointing to the smoking roof.

"I do; it shows you were right yesterday. Do you think it will do any harm?"

"Harm!" shouted Henson. "If that hay isn't got out before two o'clock this afternoon, the whole barn will be on fire; and if that goes, all goes."

"Whew!" said Tom. "I'll run and tell Mr. Girard." And away he went. Mr. Girard was soon on the spot and concluded to put all hands to work, and bundle all the green hay out. Inside was as hot as an oven. The men, stripped to their waist, worked away till all the overgreen hay was put out. And thus his property was saved. As this, along with the stock in the storehouse underneath, meant a very large saving, Mr. Girard was thankful for his escape from loss. He said to Henson, "I'll remember you for this," waving his hand toward the barns.

During the troubles in Haiti, on the isle of San Domingo, Girard plied a trade with a little vessel, in cigars—which he then manufactured—and in oranges and other commodities, between that city and Philadelphia. During the excitement of the times, many people gave him their silver, gold and other valuables to take with him for safekeeping. In this way he became the custodian of great wealth, some of which, on account of the death of the owners in the subsequent massacres, forever remained unclaimed. At the close of his mortal career, he willed the magnificent sum of six million dollars to build and endow the college which bears his name at Philadelphia, stipulating that no clergyman should be allowed to enter the threshold of the building—a stipulation still rigidly adhered to by the trustees of the college.

The next year, on Henson's return from the county of Lancaster, where he went to visit his brother, he learned from Tom Burns that Mr. Girard was very sick and likely to die. "Go and see him," said he. "I'm sure he will do something for you; he said he would remember you for saving his barns."

Henson, acting on this suggestion, went out to the farm on Christmas Day, but, seeing a great many passing to and fro from his residence and that the house appeared to be full of people, his heart failed him. And he passed the house. Stephen Girard died the next day. Charity was left a brick house in the city and sixty dollars a quarter during life; but in all the provisions of his great will, Henson, who had saved so much of his property for him, was not remembered.[3]

30

Flight to New Jersey

ONE AFTERNOON in early winter in Philadelphia, three years after Henson's escape from slavery, as he was assisting in loading a vessel with wheat for Liverpool, he discovered his old tricky master, Barton, watching his movements. Neither one addressed the other. Barton soon after disappeared, doubtless for his proofs, as the Fugitive [Slave] Law[1] was still in force. Henson, after considering the matter, decided on flight to New Jersey. He thought, as he says, "cunning was just then better than strength." On asking the skipper for a release, the latter said, "I guess your too big and fat to carry wheat," little divining the true cause of his request, and paid him his wages.

Preparations were then made for a hasty departure. The Delaware, now partly frozen over, had to be crossed. This was effected by a small boat, which, where it could be used, was rowed in open water, and then drawn upon the ice by men having creepers on their boots. He went to the locality, now called Medford, in New Jersey, and thus made good his escape from Barton.

At this place he found that the people spoke of the days of the week by number, as first, second, third, etc., instead of by name. Here he spent the winter in the bush, burning charcoal and chopping cordwood which consisted of pine, chestnut and black oak. In the spring he had some diversion with his fellow labourers, in 'coon and 'possum hunting. One day he had his fortune told for a penny-bit by a shrivelled-up, sharp-featured, mulatto woman. She had but one tooth in front, and that was a long one, and seemed to split her words in two, as they were spoken. It consisted of a story of love, money, friends and a fuss out of all of which he was to come out victorious, to which was added, "You'll lend much and borrow little." In the early summer he obtained an offer to burn charcoal near Philadelphia and, as he now thought that all danger was past, he returned for that purpose.

Here he soon after met a man from Baltimore who told him of Emily's death. The news was a terrible blow, for although he knew she clung to her slave home and its associations, he had hoped by some means to get her away from slave land. It was the first news he had had about her, and it was bad indeed. He had not communicated with her, as he feared Barton might in that way ascertain his whereabouts and capture him. The sad news of her death brought back vividly to his mind her many good qualities and their pleasant life together. He never, he was sure, could find another Emily, and he greatly mourned her death. At the same time, too, he learned, as he expected would be the case, that she had given birth to a child a short time after he left; that her master had permitted her to go out to service to try and earn her freedom; that this had not been accomplished and that she had returned to his house to die, leaving behind her little daughter. She, as he long afterward learned, lived until a young woman, and then followed her mother.

During the next four years he spent his time alternately in the city of Philadelphia and in the State of New Jersey. He preferred living in the city, but earned most in New Jersey; and, besides, he had made the acquaintance of Kate Truitt, a woman who pleased him well, and who, after a time, he married. After his marriage he remained in New Jersey and worked as a farmhand. A man named Broderick, in whose hay field he worked, had a great mover as leader, a man named Hal who was also something of a bully. Henson was assigned the fourth place, and cut leisurely.

"Ain't you going to mow faster?" said Hal. "You keep the whole of them men behind you back."

At this Henson pulled up a little, but still not sufficiently to please the leader, who shortly after shouted back to him: "Jim, I believe you are poorly this morning. Can't you make that scythe travel faster than that. Perhaps it's too heavy for you."

This sally raised a laugh at Henson's expense, but he appeared not to hear it at all, and kept about the same pace as before. All the men in the field were strangers to him, but he had made up his mind to teach their leader a lesson. He waited for more of his banter, but took care to lose no ground. The day was cloudy and comfortable, and the smell of the new mown hay nerved Henson for his contemplated task. As they neared the other side of the field, and as Hal finished his swath and rested on his scythe, he said:

"Jim, a big fellow like you ought to be ashamed of yourself; you better take your place after the little man at the end."

"I expect you are a great mower," said Henson.

"Yes, the king of mowers in these parts," said Hal, proudly in reply, as he struck out a new swath.

Henson thought the time had come for action, and quickly he gained on the man next ahead, until he came close up and then exchanged place with him. Hal, seeing this laughed loud and long. Henson pushed on until he came up to the next man, and exchanged with him. Hal saw then that his man was bent on giving him a trial, and said: "You disrespectful nigger, that's your game; then come along, and I'll travel you around till you are sick."

Henson put on a spurt. So did Hal, but in vain, for before he got across the field he was overtaken by Henson, who found him pretty well fagged out. It was now Henson's turn.

"I believe," said he, "you're poorly this morning. Can't you make that scythe travel faster; perhaps it's too heavy for you."

Hal could not spare breath enough to answer, but exerted his whole strength and pushed on. Henson, still crowding him, chased him till he could go no farther.

**The Hensons worked for a number of summers at Cape May,
one of the leading resorts in the United States.**

"You had better take your place after the little man at the end," said Henson, as a crusher.

At this Hal wanted to fight, but finding himself without breath or strength, he concluded that he might possible fail here too, so he changed his manner and said: "I know you were a good mower, but it's the custom here to run a little on strangers."

"Well," said Henson, "I suppose you have had running enough now?"

From this time on Hal was agreeable enough, and Henson's rapid mowing became the boast of the field hands.

In the huckleberry season, Henson and his wife picked large quantities of these berries for the Philadelphia market, and obtained four dollars per bushel for them; still, it took a good deal of 'hustling in the huckleberry patch' to make good wages. As the rich marl deposits of the locality now began to be utilized as a fertilizer, he picked no more huckleberries. Now he had constant employment in pits, at wages varying from a dollar to a dollar and a quarter per day. It was hard work, the marl being thrown up from scaffold to scaffold until the surface was reached. After a few years he concluded to remove to Philadelphia. In spring he whitewashed, in harvest he worked in the fields, and later he threshed grain with his flail. He and his wife, in the bathing season, for many years worked at Cape May and Miller's Island, and earned money there freely. Henson, although working hard, was comfortable and contented. Three daughters had been entrusted to them; and so they would doubtless have continued happily together, but, unfortunately for them, there came a change in slave law which put him and thousands like him, who were escaped slaves, in great peril.

31

The Underground Railroad[1]

RALPH SHAW conceived the idea of going south and rescuing a slave or two, and was furnished with money for that purpose. Like many others, he was fond of risks. His friends hardly expected to see him back, but in the course of a couple of months he returned to Philadelphia with two brown-skinned women—mother and daughter. These women were in the field alone, pulling the grass from the young cotton, when found by Shaw, and were persuaded to come with him. Stark, their owner, was a great cotton grower, and annually took prizes for his fine cotton. The stories the women told of their own experiences elicited profound sympathy, and created intense interest. A public anti-slavery meeting was announced to be held in a large Baptist church of the city, at which the rescued women were to appear. They were placed on the platform, and surprised the large audience, in which Henson sat as an attentive listener, in the relation of their experience of slave life in Georgia.

Said the mother: "I never saw a piece of white bread, or sat on a chair in my life, till I come here. I lived on corn cake and herrings. The cake we baked and the herrings we cooked in the ashes. A quart of corn and two herrings was the daily allowance for each woman. We was often tired, and if we slept too late in the morning to get this meal ready, at the sound of the bullwhip we was marched off with nothing to eat." Her talk showed that slavery was indeed the "sum of all villainies." The younger woman spoke of a tragic incident of which she had been an eyewitness. "My master," she said, "had a dreadful temper. Once, when a young slave named Ned was getting him a pitcher of water, he fell and broke the pitcher. Master had him stripped and whipped, and then cut off his head

170

with a sword, and threw it into the fire. I screamed, and he hit me with a hoe." His wife, on finding that young Ned had been killed, berated him for the loss. She said Ned was her property, as he very well knew, and had been given to her by her father. He admitted this, and then, to console her, gave a reply which, of itself, showed the terrible nature of the system: "There is to be a drove next week from Cuba," said he, and you shall have your choice of the lot in Ned's place."

Ralph was on the platform, and spoke of the risk he ran in getting these women away. He had obtained them near Augusta. Said he: "If you will furnish me with money, I will go again. My brother is at the same business, and they now have him in prison. They will probably torture him to death, but the work of rescue must go on. The underground railroad extends farther south and in more directions than is generally supposed." He then gave them a sketch of slave life in Georgia, as he saw it, and closed by saying:

> And shall the slave, beneath our eye,
>   Clank o'er our fields his hateful chain;
> And toss his fettered arms on high,
>   And groan for Freedom's gift in vain?

This underground railroad, it may be added, was organized assistance given runaway slaves, in the way of money, conveyances, shelter, disguises by changed clothing, men often wearing women's clothing, and women men's, and in various other methods. On some lines there were regular stopping places, where rest, refreshments, clothing and means were provided. Even the stopping places, to maintain secrecy, were frequently changed. All the work on these lines, however, seemed like a drop in the bucket, and made but a slight impression on the great slave life of the country; yet it served as a strong protest against the whole iniquitous system.

At the close of Ralph's address, the chairman introduced Mrs. Steele, a philanthropist of the city, whom he designated a skilful underground railroader, who had recently diminished the number of slaves in New Orleans and increased the number of freemen in Philadelphia, by one. Mrs. Steele then proceeded to explain what the chairman's statement meant. Her story was a short one. While visiting relatives in New Orleans, she became acquainted with a slave lad named Rift who was owned by a rich merchant of the city. Rift had occasion to visit the house at which she was a guest, and would on these visits amuse himself by talking to and playing toss-up-high with her little two-year-old-boy. The child became greatly attached to Rift, who was a fine featured and good mannered lad. On one of these visits, a sudden desire seized the child's mother to set the slave lad free. She had not the means to purchase him and, after a little reflection, resolved on the following ingenious plan. Taking advantage of the child's fondness for the lad, she concluded to make him a nurse. She obtained Rift's personal history, enlisted his sympathies, and then broached the subject of his escape to freedom. He readily assented to her proposal and eagerly adopted her plan, which, in short, was that he should dress as a girl and act as nurse for the child, on her coming trip home to Philadelphia. Suitable clothing was obtained and worn a few times, to accustom the child to the new order of things. Finally the day for her departure came, and driven in a carriage to the wharf, she stepped on board the steamer, attended by a fine looking young person, whom she called Aunt Jen. Aunt Jen, who was appropriately dressed as a lady's nurse, carried the child in his arms. So complete was the disguise that, although Rift was well-known by persons on the wharf at the time, he passed in unsuspected by anybody. Throughout the trip he successfully played the nurse, and in due time safely arrived at Philadelphia.

"Perhaps, Mr. Chairman, you will now," said Mrs. Steele, "allow me to introduce to the audience Aunt Jen." Then from behind a screen on the platform lightly stepped Aunt Jen, clothed just as he was when he embarked at New Orleans for liberty, looking ever inch a nurse. Amid the applause and laughter of the audience Rift gracefully bowed his acknowledgment and retired. A liberal subscription in the good cause followed. The meeting produced a profound impression and greatly strengthened the abolition movement. The agitation had produced a marked effect in Maryland and other slave breeding states. As the subject became more and more ventilated and knowledge of it increased, the conscience of many a slave holder was touched and, as a matter of duty, he denied himself the privilege of holding his fellow man in bondage, as the law allowed.

Thus the number of slaves made free increased from year to year. Some of the churches of the south had gone so far as to hold that their members could no longer own slaves and retain their membership. Greater interest also began to be taken in the freedman. In Philadelphia, and other cities of free states, schools and churches were opened for their use, and thus the condition of the race began to improve. But all this aroused the keenest antipathy of the pro-slavery men, who did not hesitate to designate every true well-wisher of the African a shabby sheep, nor to treat the abolitionist as if he had forfeited his standing in society.

Chief Justice Taney ruled that "Negroes had no rights which the white man was bound to respect." The average Southerner, looking only at the requirements of King Cotton and the money value of the black person, boldly denied that he was a man, and hence could read the Declaration of Independence without a blush. The individual in the South who now had the courage to avow his convictions against an institution held to be providential, was marked for rough usage. They did not hesitate to imprison for the offence of teaching slave children to read. Vigorous efforts were made to smother every vestige of anti-slavery conscience. But it could not be smothered; and manumissions were no longer confined to wills, when testators had no further use for their slaves, nor to cases where owners resorted to this method of ridding themselves of the burden of supporting aged and infirm slaves. "The Nigger Question," as it was called, grew till it became the great agitation of the nation, and pointed to a coming crisis.

32

A Discussion on Freedom

WHEN HENSON lived with Job Venables, the hub-maker, the railroad between Baltimore and Wilmington [Delaware] was completed, being the first railway constructed in that part of the country. To have had a ride on the train was considered something worth talking about. Wilmington was to have a great political meeting, and Venables concluded to have a ride on the train and attend the meeting. The subject of slavery had become a burning question. It had got into Congress, into the churches; was talked about in taverns, in shops and in the streets, resulting in pretty general irritation. The abolition party was divided, some being in favour of the colonization of freedmen on the coast of Africa. Others were in favour of gathering them into the free states. The slave states hated the free blacks, and wanted none of them within their borders.

When Job Venables returned home he was full of the slave subject. He had returned by boat, and was in company with a Baptist minister who was a slave holder.

At the glassworks store it was quite a common thing to have a discussion in the evening, in which Henson occasionally joined and thereby greatly improved his pronunciation and command of language. There would sometimes be an audience of from thirty to forty persons. Henson called at the store the evening after Venables' return, to get a little tobacco, and found his employer relating what the Baptist minister had said on the slavery question. This minister, who was a very rich man and owned fifty slaves, had said if it were not a sin, he would give his slaves their freedom. But he held they were like children, and it would be wrong to send them adrift, and expect them to make a living for themselves. They knew nothing about it. "Why," said he, "a nigger is like a hog in a corn field. He will eat some, but he will waste a good deal more than he eats." The minister, he went on to say, was dressed in the best of broadcloth, and had told him he was paying $1,000 a year to keep two of his sons at college. When he had finished speaking, Henson wishing to overhaul the minister's views, delivered himself as follows: " Mr. Venables," said he, "do you think the parson was a Christian? Did he say slaves couldn't work and make a living, except under a master? Did he say slaves didn't know the good of freedom?"

Job Venables replied in the affirmative to all these questions.

"How can a man," continued Henson, "be a Christian who holds his brother in bondage? Who made a living for the reverent gentleman and his family, and who earned his fine broadcloth suit, and the $1,000 a year to educate his sons at college; who but his slaves? And if they can do it for him and his family, they can do it for themselves, if only they get the chance. The slave has the same mother-wit as his master. God gave it to him, and nothing on earth can take it from him. If a slave has sense enough to work for another he can work for himself by the same sense. This Baptist minister may be a rich man, but he is a poor Christian." At this point the crowd in the store gave Henson a little cheer, and all gathered closer around him. Others outside, hearing a discussion going on, came in, so that there were now perhaps fifty or sixty people present.

Job Venables, at the close of the cheer, was quite aroused and without giving Henson an opportunity to enter upon the third point, opened out again. He considered there was but one way to dispose of the black population, and that was to take them all back to Africa. It was their own country and native home and the proper place for them to live; and colonization, he thought, was the only way of disposing of the vexed question.

"Mr. Venables," asked Henson, "what is a man's native country?"

"Why, of course, the country he is born in," he quickly answered.

"His birthplace fixes his native country?" said Henson.

"Yes, certainly," replied his employer.

"A great many of the white people of this country," continued Henson, "come from Europe. Their children have been born here and hence are native born. Are these children of European parents born here better adapted to live in Europe because their fathers and mothers have come from Europe? No more should slave children born here be considered native still of Africa. These slave children born here are natives of this country, and have a right to live here and to live in freedom. They are American citizens, of—er, ah—African extraction."

At this point Henson was honoured by a lively cheer from the crowd, which encouraged him to make an other venture, so he said: "Mr. Venables, you say the reverent gentleman said, 'the slaves wouldn't know the good of freedom.' It's true he hasn't had much opportunity to learn about it, but, once free, you don't find him wishing to return to slavery. The beast of the field and the birds of the air alike prize their freedom." At which another cheer was accorded him. Henson then asked leave to explain what he meant, by relating a recent occurrence at this master's own house. Job Venables had three granddaughters, all sprightly girls who had recently come to live with him. These girls took a lively interest in a fine mockingbird in a cage, which hung in the dining room. "Grandpa," said the youngest, "I let Dickey out of his cage a little while yesterday, and he seemed to enjoy it greatly."

"Did you?" said Grandpa. "I guess that is the first time he has ever been out since I got him, now over two years ago, and he was then a very young bird, just in feather."

"Indeed," said the eldest girl, "I think the poor thing should be let out awhile everyday."

"Oh," rejoined grandpa, "I don't think he cares very much about being out."

"He would like it all right, if he could get out into the garden," chimed in Emma, the remaining girl.

"Yes, miss," said Henson, "it's freedom he wants."

"Freedom!" replied Venables, in an elevated voice. "What does he know about freedom? He has always been well taken care of and knows of nothing better. He enjoys cage life. I do not think he would go away even if you let him loose in the garden; I am sure we do more for him than he could ever do for himself, and we give him everything he wants."

"Except his freedom," interjected Henson.

"Freedom!" said Job Venables, in a still louder tone, looking straight at Henson, "is to him a meaningless term. He knows nothing and cares less about it. He is as happy as a king all day without it."

As Henson saw his employer was getting warmed up, he hesitated to speak again, but Emma, who had suggested the enjoyment of the garden for Dickey, said: "Well, we'll let him out in the dining room again." Suiting the action to her words, she rose from her seat and opened the door of the cage.

176

Job Venables and the other two granddaughters were sitting in front of the cage, watching their little favourite. Henson had come in from the garden with an iron-headed rake in his hand, and was standing in the doorway between the dining room and kitchen, asking for instructions about his work, when the conversation sprung up. As he entered, he found the old gent reading a newspaper, the eldest girl reading a magazine, the youngest doing some embroidery and Emma was in the act of feeding Dickey. Having become interested in the conversation, and now actually drawn into what he considered an important argument, he lingered to see what Dickey would do with his cage door open. He did not keep them waiting long. He first hopped from one perch to another, and then into his ring, then to the floor of his cage, and from that flew straight to the window and lit on its crossbar.

"I knew he would like to be in the garden this morning," said Emma.

"Very well," said Grandpa, "open the window and let him enjoy it."

"May I?" said Emma. And while she was thinking whether her grandpa really meant her to do it or not, he arose from his armchair and, slipping to the window, touched a spring and swung one half of the French window wide open.

Dickey, after rubbing his bill two or three times on the glass, hopped from the crossbar and quietly glided out and lit on the flowering shrub.

"He'll come when I call him," declared Grandpa. Just then the bird darted to the ground, in a flower bed. "I told you he would not go away," he continued, somewhat triumphantly; but after a moment the bird darted off to the shade of a fruit tree, higher and farther away than the shrub on which he first alighted. Up to this time, all were standing at the window eagerly watching him. Then the girls began to fear they might lose him; so they went out into the garden and commenced calling "Dickey! Dickey! poor Dickey, come here." They were quickly followed by their grandpa, and by Henson, at some little distance behind. Away went the bird to the orchard, on the other side of the garden fence. Then there was a little rush by everyone, through the little gate at the lower end of the garden, to find him.

Dickey was soon located in the leafy top of a cherry tree. All formed a circle around the tree, watching what he would do next. Fear and hope alternately predominated as he sat, apparently in no hurry to leave his temporary resting place. Emma ran for the box of birdseed to coax him with it. All were helpless now, and everything depended on the bird's own action. Grandpa's doctrine was about to be literally fulfilled, or shattered and cast to the four winds. Directly Emma came running up with the box of birdseed in her hand and, as she did so, Dickey soared away over their heads to the topmost twig of an exceedingly high chestnut tree that stood at one side of the little orchard. All eyes were steadily fixed upon him now. It might be the last look.

"Dickey! Dickey! shall we never hear your sweet voice again," said one of the girls. "See, he is moving," said another. Then the bird gave a couple of chirps, followed by a few low, sweet notes, as if tuning his pipes. Soon he threw himself into it heartily and poured forth the grandest song they had ever heard. Never had he warbled such mellifluous notes, even when in his very best form, and many a time he had charmed his audience. His listeners were now fairly carried beyond themselves. All eyes were moistened and every heart seemed brought into harmony with the rapturous song of the bird. Their feelings, influenced by the wonderful song, had been first subdued, then raised to a higher and holier plane, where innocence and purity reigned supreme, causing them for the moment to be oblivious to evil and emptied of selfishness and, as if by magic, drawn into touch with all that is good and grand in nature.

At the close of his song, Dickey mounted high in the air and winged himself away in a southerly direction. But not a shadow of regret now rested in the mind of anyone present. And after the song ended no word was spoken but one, and that was the word "freedom"—spoken, or rather whispered, by Grandpa, as Dickey rose from his seat on the top of the tree and soared away to true liberty. The girls and their grandpa returned in silence to the house, and Charley to his work in the garden. The household had sustained a loss, but Dickey had achieved an infinite gain, and so they were content.

"Gentlemen," continued Henson, "if that bird knew enough to enjoy freedom, and to prefer it to the fairest form of imprisonment, who can say a human being can't appreciate the natural freedom which the great Creator himself intended for all his creatures? His freedom's as sweet to him as your own's to you, and can you blame him if, like Dickey, when he soared from the top of the tall chestnut tree, he, too, tries to escape from the condition of a slave to that of a free man?"

A tremendous cheer now burst from the crowd. Hats flew up; some pounded on the counter, and they shouted until they were hoarse. Directly a big armchair was handed in and Henson, against his will, was thrust into it and borne out of the store by strong, willing arms, and up the street to his master's house, followed by a procession of men and boys, the people on the street and in the houses wondering what it all meant. At the house Job Venables made a short speech to the crowd, the purport of which was that if all the coloured men were like Henson, the slave question would soon be settled. "After what we have heard tonight," said he, "I am bound to extend to him the right hand of fellowship, acknowledge the rights of his race, whose cause he so eloquently pleads, and confess him a brother—yes, gentlemen, a brother—in ebony." At this sally of wit the whole crowd cheered lustily and separated, leaving Henson the uncrowned freedman champion of Medford.

33

John Brown

WHILE LIVING in Philadelphia, Henson took a run up to Lancaster to see his brother William (Cornelius), whom he found in a great fever to emigrate to the North Elba settlement, in the county of Essex, in the State of New York. Garret Smith had been through Pennsylvania, as an immigration agent, talking up this black settlement project. The two brothers, after going down to Philadelphia, went to New York City where they saw Dr. McEwan Smith, a gentleman from the West Indies, in the matter. Passing through Albany and Troy to Whitehall, and up Lake Champlain fifty-two miles, then eight miles west to Pleasant Valley, and again twenty-four miles, according to Henson's recollection of the distances, they reached North Elba. This was the home of John Brown, of subsequent Harper's Ferry fame.[1] Mr. Brown was farming and was interested in this scheme of establishing a large black settlement in that locality. By means of directions obtained in New York, they visited him and then learned that it was only blacks who were born in the Sate of New York who could get land free. Any black person could, however, purchase at the low price of one dollar and a half per acre. No white man could purchase at any price. The country was high, some sixteen hundred feet above Lake Champlain. On their arrival there came a fall of snow, and as it was only the month of September, the visitors thought it a strange country.

John Brown warmly welcomed them and had them stay with him overnight. During the evening Mr. Brown gave them many incidents of his life. He had been an extensive drover, handling at times as many as a thousand head of cattle and ten thousand sheep. He took a lively interest in the welfare of the blacks of the country, was an uncompromising abolitionist and a man of large soul as well as large body.

During their conversation the question of slavery came up. "While droving," said he, "in the South, I frequently had occasion to notice that a large plantation with several hundred Negroes was ruled over by two or three, or perhaps four or five, whites. Often acts of fierce cruelty and prolonged tyranny were practised by the handful of whites, and were meekly borne by the hundreds of blacks. I often wondered at this—a few holding as many hundreds in subjection. Indeed, it seems strange to me that all slavedom does not rise in the might of its numbers and strike a terrible blow for freedom, achieve it or die in the attempt. They could rise and destroy their masters in a day, and strike for freedom."

"Mister Brown," said Henson, "you're a drover, and you've often seen a drove of cattle and the driver urging them along. Where were the strong cattle, but in the front, and where the weak, but behind? How did the drovers urge that drove on faster when the cattle were tired? Did they ride in among them and shoot one of the drove? Oh, no; but they cracked the big whip and shouted, and the drove feared that whip and rushed along. It's the fear of the lash, the crack of the bullwhip, Mister Brown, that keeps them in subjection. The gun brings desperation, but the lash fetches fear. If you shot one of your cattle and they smelled blood, you could do nothing with the rest of the herd. It's just the same with slavery."

"There is a great deal of truth in what you say," said Mr. Brown, "and I never thought of the matter in that light."

"Poor fellow," Henson digressed to say his amanuensis; "I suppose 'twas such thoughts working in his mind as he then expressed to me, that led to the Harper's Ferry trouble and caused him to be hung [sic] at Charleston, West Virginia, on the second day of December, 1859. Little did I think, when I was talking with him about slavery, that he would come to such an end, or that I would so often hear the boys on the streets singing:

John Brown's body lies a moulderin' in the ground.

A carpenter bought the lumber that made his scaffold, and built a porch with it, and I heard it's just been taken to Washington and turned into a scaffold again, as a curiosity. Awh! What a curious world this is, to be sure."

"The country here," said Henson, when talking with John Brown at his home, "is romantic, and you've the finest Irish potatoes I've ever seen, and the woods are beautiful; but, oh, to think of winter in September."

Mr. Brown laughed, and said the flurry of snow which they then had would soon be gone. Henson was inclined to take up land and settle, but his brother William was not pleased with the country and would not entertain the idea, so both brothers returned to their homes.

34

✐

The Fugitive Slave Law

THE FUGITIVE Slave law, passed on the 18th of September 1850, which was shortly after [Millard] Fillmore became President of the United States, through the death of President Taylor, produced a panic among escaped slaves living throughout the free states. Hitherto, as in the case of an estray in the present time, the owner had been required to prove property and pay charges before he could take his chattel away. Under the Fugitive Slave Act, however, the slenderest evidence was sufficient to secure the arrest and possession of the escaped slave, who was now to be tried in the state and place of his owner. The numerous arrests which immediately followed, and the mode of recovery, irritated and aroused the people of the north. The act soon became odious and disturbances followed. At Boston, in 1851, a mob rescued a fugitive slave[1] when under arrest, and hastened him off to Canada. President Fillmore, in consequence, issued a proclamation, in which he announced "his determination to enforce the law promptly and thoroughly."

Philadelphia, too, had its scene of disturbance from the same cause. A slave owner, from the eastern shore of Maryland, claimed his escaped slave under the new law. His slave, Julius Caesar, had been gone for years. No matter—the Fugitive Slave Law gave the right to retake, and he determined to spare no expense in his recovery. The people of the city were determined that the escaped slave should not return to slavery. During the progress of the trial, the slave owner struck Caesar a terrible blow as he passed through the corridor of the courthouse, and felled him to the floor. The excitement got to a fever heat, and immense crowds assembled in and about the courthouse. The judgement of the court was that he was to be delivered to his slave master. As he passed down the steps of the courthouse in the charge

183

of two policemen, the mob rescued him and threw him over a high fence into a yard, where a number of men stood ready to hustle him away. He was immediately taken to Dr. Byers' office, where his clothes were changed. On Sixth Street there was an open riot, at which the Riot Act was read. The police soon learned that some cabs had just left the office of Dr. Byers, a man known to be a strong abolitionist. Those cabs had taken different directions. One of them went rapidly down Walnut Street toward the wharf. "There goes the nigger!" shouted some slavery sympathizer. And immediately several of the police and a considerable crowd pursued in hot haste and surrounded the cab at the wharf to make sure of their victim. The driver stepped down, opened the door and bowed out the occupant, an aged, well-known superannuated minister. The feeling of surprise and disappointment was great. A few persons raised a cheer at the expense of the pursuers. The latter returned as quickly as possible to Dr. Byers' office, which they searched thoroughly.

While this pursuit was going on a no less exciting chase, by other members of the police, was given the second cab, whose horses went galloping south down Sixth Street. The cab was chased a mile and, when overtaken by the police, who had taken other cabs, it was soon surrounded and its occupant demanded. The driver, a Hibernian, sprang to his carriage door, and told them to see for themselves whether he had a runaway slave or not. They looked in, and there sat a contented look-ing little old Quaker lady, in a nice drab gown and bonnet. Greatly chagrined, they beat a hasty retreat, arriving at the courthouse just in time to meet the crowd returning from Walnut Street wharf. A third cabdriver drove slowly through the crowds along Sixth Street and, all unsuspected by them, bore Caesar, the escaping slave, away to safe quar-ters. The rapidly travelling cabs had been successfully used to attract attention, and thus allowed the prisoner to escape.

Mr. Purvis mounted a table on the street and addressed the crowd, and hectored the police by accusing them of slackness in allowing their man to escape; who, he said, "was doubtless then on his way to Canada."

The following day the city newspapers stated that if blacks interfered with the police, the latter had the power to shoot them. This statement was read to Henson at the coal yard, where he was working.

Then came days of trouble when the man of colour, who had escaped from slaveland, often by suffering hardships and incurring great risk—had, as he supposed, achieved freedom and safety among freedmen—suddenly found that he was in danger of immediate arrest and of being carried back to the land of the lash and torture. Then escaped slaves, everywhere, eagerly counselled with one another, with their freed brethren and with abolitionists. The outlook was dark; commotion and fear had displaced fancied security and contentment, for it had thus been discovered that even in the free states, all were not free. There was nothing left but to escape, but where? Great fear fell upon them. They looked over the land and saw her bristling liberty poles, her great flag, her glistening church spires, her advanced civilization and boasted freedom, and were painfully conscious that all these could not, or would not, protect them, or save them from the hands of their pursuers. Where there was a chance of making anything by it, blacks were thrust into jail and advertised, so that their former masters might come and claim their lost property. This became so general that there would have been despair indeed if, in that trying time, a star of hope in the distant north had not shone out bright and clear. It was light from a far-off land, where the slave master was powerless and unknown. Hence the watchword passed along the lines in every direction: "Ho for Canada! No safety out of Canada!"

Henson had escaped from slavery in Maryland to Pennsylvania, and again from a pursuing slave master in Pennsylvania to New Jersey. Now, a third escape was necessary. And on learning that he was without protection even in any free state, he, too, concluded on flight from the United States to Canada. He wished, however, to see his old friend Abel Stephens first. "I'm going to Canada," said he to him.

"The President is a rascal and thee's a fool," was the strong language used by the Quaker in reply.

"Why am I foolish?" inquired Henson.

"Wait a little, my man, and we'll get the law changed," said Abel, in an encouraging tone.

"Law changed?" queried Henson. "Long before that I'd be carried away to Maryland, and sold down south."

"We won't let them do that. Besides, thee couldn't live in Canada a single winter. The cold is intense and the snow deep. Why, I've heard that milk vendors there in the cold season carry their milk around in sticks, and deliver milk icicles to their customers."

"It may not be as comfortable in climate there as here," said Henson, "but I prefer snow and frost to the crack of the slave whip."

"Well, if thee must go," said good old Abel, finally, "may God bless thee in thy journey and in thy new home."

35

✌️

A Second Declaration of Independence

THE FUGITIVE Slave Law caused very great irritation and, seven years after its introduction, the remarkable decision of the Supreme Court in the Dred Scott Case,[1] that a slave was not a citizen of the United States and was a slave though brought into a free state by his master, opened the eyes of the people of the free states to the importance of having this great slavery question settled. When the thirteen United States framed a constitution for themselves they numbered but three million souls; now, in 1851, the population had risen to twenty million, and the slave population numbered over three million, or as many as the thirteen original states did at the outset. The South had become powerful and very tenacious and sensitive on this great question. The difficulty of effecting an abolition of the slave traffic had immeasurably increased. True, as far back as 1808 importation from Africa had been declared piracy.[2] In the meantime, however, territories were being admitted into the union as slave states and the domestic slave trade was making gigantic strides. Thus the institution rapidly extended, until Lincoln's second election, in 1864,[3] when the slave population was estimated at over four million.

The slave states of the South, seeing their pet institution in danger, began the secession movement. They involved the whole country in the throes of a civil war, in which a solid North was arrayed against a solid South, and which were thus rent asunder, temporarily, by the slavery question—a question which could easily have been settled when the Declaration of Independence first declared liberty to be the inalienable right of man. Now, when the nation had grown to forty million, the question brooked no delay, but had to be settled at once, and forever, by the sword, rifle and cannon—and was settled at the great sacrifice of thousands of human lives and millions of money.

The last words written by Mrs. Stowe, in *Uncle Tom's Cabin*,[4] now appear prophetic. They are as follows: "Not surer is the eternal law by which the millstone sinks in the ocean than that stronger law by which injustice and cruelty shall bring on nations the wrath of Almighty God."

During the Great Agitation, and prior to his public career, Mr. W.H. Seward, at a public meeting in Auburn, enunciated the aphorism: "The irrepressible contest is upon us; we must be all free or all slaves." This sentiment was caught up by the press of the North and hurled as a battering ram against the great pro-slavery wall of the South until it wavered and fell. And as it fell, the nation caught sight of a banner floating over its ruin, which, as soon as the smoke of the battlefield cleared a little, was found to bear the following proclamation of emancipation:

"I do order and declare that all persons are, and henceforward shall be, free. Upon this act I invoke the considerate judgement of mankind and the gracious favour of Almighty God."

(Signed) *A. LINCOLN.*

January 1st, 1863.

By the rattle of rifles, boom of cannon, bursting of bombs, tread of cavalry, tramp of armies, slash of weapons, burning of buildings, destruction of property and slaughter of thousands of human beings in this greatest of civil wars, under this second Proclamation of Independence four million, enthralled in the most extensive and worst system of slavery which the world ever saw, came up from bondage. Suddenly they were thrust into freedom and were changed from chattels to citizens of the great American republic. Noble Lincoln! Grand proclamation, and wonderful deliverance of downtrodden people!

There stood in the Art Gallery, at the Centennial Exhibition in Philadelphia in 1876, a bronze slave, with a broken shackle in one hand, and in the other hand a scroll, on which was inscribed this celebrated proclamation of freedom by President Lincoln. Visitors, as they looked upon that bronze statue with its inscribed proclamation and broken shackles, wondered that so gigantic a traffic in human flesh could have flourished at so recent a period in a civilized, great and prosperous country.

36

Off for Canada

HAVING CONCLUDED to leave a free state that was not altogether free, Henson began to prepare for the journey. He found there were many others all around him of the same mind with himself, and in the course of a few days seven families had arranged to travel together with teams and wagons. In two or three instances these were purchased for the trip, and for use in Canada. Some, however, were already owners of fine teams of horses. The wagons were covered over like the prairie schooners of the North West, forming a sort of travelling house. When they all got together they made quite a caravan, as shown in the accompanying view of them as they make their first halt after starting for dinner.

Henson's wife had relatives in Lockport, in the State of New York, and that was the first point to be reached. As a little means had been saved up, the journey seemed no great undertaking and, in fact, was a sort of picnic all the way. On arrival there, the friends were easily found and were not a little surprised at their arrival. When Catherine told them how much money she and her husband used to make in a season at Cape May and Miller's Island, they expressed great surprise.

In due time Toronto was reached. Here employment was hard to obtain. Catherine made shirts at a York shilling apiece, and Henson had to resort to making split brooms and baskets for a living—the occupation of an Indian in the same place twenty years earlier. Worse yet, the children took the smallpox, of which the second one died. In the following spring Catherine returned to Lockport with the youngest girl, then about seven years old, leaving the eldest, who was fourteen years of age, to keep house for her father. The money saved up was now exhausted and, as soon as Henson could manage, it he started for Lockport. On his

Off for Canada.

way over he stayed a couple of days at the Falls of Niagara. From what he saw here he concluded there was an excellent opportunity for him to make a good living for his family at the Falls; or, as he puts it, "I saw there was a great living for us at the Falls." He informed his wife of the matter, but to his sorrow her views did not coincide with his. She had learned of the death of a rich uncle and expected to get a share of his property, so nothing would suit her but a return to their old home in New Jersey, where they still owned a house and three acres of land. Henson refused to run the risk of a return and was bound, as he said, to live in Canada.

Thus they parted. His wife and two daughters started back, and he was left alone at Lockport.

Here he remained about two years, when Chauncey Simons,[1] a black man, arrived from Canada, and told his friends a wonderful story. "The Queen", said he, "is making a present of fifty acres of land to every man, and gives him a chance to buy fifty acres more at one dollar and a half an acre when he is able to pay for it. It's just the place for a poor man," said he. In answer to Henson's inquiry as to the quality of the land, he stated that it was "as good as a crow ever flew over." It was also learned from Simons that the place where Her Majesty was pleased to manifest her generosity in this hitherto unheard of manner was in the Province of Upper Canada, in the county of Grey and township of Artemesia.[2] Simons created considerable excitement among the black people of Lockport over the Queen's free lands. Henson was one of the first to volunteer to return with him. He, however, got a note of warning from an Irishman (not one of the seven who beat him), who said "Sure and I've been beyond there myself and the free land's twenty mile from anywhere. It's all in woods. The people are all poor, and you'll starve there and get lost in the bush." He advised going to Michigan. Simons at once ridiculed the Irishman's story, and dispelled all fears by the flowing account he gave of the country; and as to going to Michigan, "Why," said Simons, "dogs shake there with fever and ague."

"The hills of Artemesia," said he, "are full of the best gravel for making roads. Its woods of fine building timber and full of pheasants, pigeons, fox, deer and black bear. Its pebbly streams swarm with speckled trout, the finest fish in the world. These and her little lakes are the home of the mink, marten, otter, beaver and wild duck. On their banks, cherries, nut and berries of many sorts grow wild. Its wild plum orchards, loaded in spring with the prettiest of white and pink blossoms, bear abundance of fruit. Its beaver meadows supply wild hay for the cattle. Its maple trees give sugar and its soil yield fine wheat and other grains and splendid vegetables. Thus are the wants of the settler well provided for. Right there is the great Cuckoo Valley,[3] stretching from the big Artemesia Falls[4] far away to the Blue Mountains and to the Georgian Bay, presenting scenery that must please all lovers of the picturesque, the grand and beautiful. My friends, it is a wonderful land. It's the finest country I ever clapped my eyes onto, and reminds me of what the paradise of our first parents must have been."

Simons' enthusiasm and eloquence were naturally rewarded, and in

Ontario and the states surrounding the lower Great Lakes.

due time he arrived with his band of black immigrants at the township of Artemesia. Henson here found a large colony of African people. There was a stretch of three miles on the Durham Road[5] which was all occupied by black families. Henson and his friend Simons hastened to the Crown Land Office, kept by Mr. George Snider, the Government's Agent, to get his fifty acres of land of the Queen's bounty, as so many hundred had received it before him. Alas, for his hopes of land proprietorship and a fine farm, for the agent informed him the last lot had been given away just two weeks before. This was a disappointment as unexpected as it was overwhelming. He had never once dreamed of any failure of the Queen's bounty in the township of Artemesia. Now he awoke to the hard fact, and far from home and without means, was thus suddenly thrown on his own resources. He was a good chopper and could handle a flail with any man, so there was nothing left but to look for work, which he was soon successful in finding. His friend Simons introduced him to Brother Oxsby, who, on learning about his great disappointment, grew sympathetic and talkative, and said, "This here brother has come among us, and we must treat him well and do what we can for him. I think I can give him some work for the first. See that stack of wheat? What will you thresh that wheat out for me for?"

"In Jersey," said Henson, "I used to get every ninth bushel. I reckon that wouldn't be too much?"

"No; I'm agreeable to that price," said Oxsby. A flail was soon fixed up and a floor laid beside the stack; off went his coat, and Henson went at his work cheerfully. He, however, had not threshed long until he discovered that the grain was remarkably light in the sheaf. He threshed away until night, and the yield was so surprisingly small that he began to suspect the capabilities of the township of Artemesia as a wheat growing section. Next morning he hesitated to lift the flail. He, however, had no other work and Brother Oxsby had spoken so kindly to him, he concluded to go on, although he well knew there would be very little pay for his labour. He had worked a couple of hours next morning, when he concluded to take a rest and have a chat with Mr. Oxsby's little daughter Becky, who had come out to see him thresh.

"Haven't your chickens been at this wheat, my little girl?" said Henson.

"Oh, no. We don't keep no chickens," was her immediate answer.

"Awh! I saw a pair of turkeys last night at the stable," was Henson's next effort.

"Oh yes, but we only just got them yesterday," said Becky.

"Well, then," he asked, "what in the world's been at this wheat?"

"Nothing," said the unsuspecting child, "only Daddy. He wanted to take a grist to the mill, so he trashed the sheaves, but didn't cut the bans."

"Awh! Awh! I see!" exclaimed Henson.

The secret was out; Brother Oxsby had found him a stranger, and had taken him in. Henson immediately stuck the handle of the flail in the stack and struck work. He had worked hard, obtained little wheat and much chaff. As the wheat would not measure two bushels, the ninth of this was not worth carrying away. He therefore made a present of it to his kind and sympathetic Brother Oxsby, at the same time, however, resolving very severely that he would look out better next time. Henson thereupon, after deliberating on the situation, remembered "It's not all gold that glitters," and came to the conclusion that he could be spared from the township. Having heard of Owen Sound, the county town, situated about thirty-three miles distant on the Georgian Bay, he bid an unregretful farewell to Artemesia, and arrived in that town on Saint Patrick's Day, 1854. His friend Simons went with him, and both obtained apartments in a cedar log house owned by the Rev. John Neelands on the west side of Poulett Street.[6]

Here one afternoon shortly after, as a black man came along the street, and was about to pass his doorway, exclamations of surprise, as follows, were quickly exchanged:

"What, Oh! can it be possible? Yes, sure as I live, here is my friend John Hall[7] that I saw so long, long ago in Kentucky."

"O Charley! you are here too! My heart's glad to meet you free. Mister—ah—Frost, the merchant, told me there was a large man coming here from Artemesia, but I never knew it was you."

It is believed that John "Daddy" Hall moved to Sydenham (later Owen Sound), sometime in the 1840s. He soon became a familiar figure. When well into his sixties, he became the town crier, bell ringer and night watchman. He died at the remarkable age of about 117 in 1900.

"How did you get clear from Haskill, way down in Kentucky, and come up so near the North Pole?" said Henson, as they entered the house and sat down.

"Well, after you left," Hall went on to explain, "some persons that your Master Ridgely spoke to took up my case. They knew me in Virginia, and knew I was brought from Canada, and a suit was entered in the courts to set me free. Fred Triplet (so named because of his trine birth, a freedman) told my master I was a British freeborn and was taken a prisoner of war in Canada, and how he knew, for he was in Virginia when I came there. He told him as how he ought to set me free."

" 'Set him free?' the master said, getting angry; while grass grows and water runs, and while the sun sets on yonder hill, I'll never free a slave.' "

"My case hung in the courts three years until, at last, my master got afeared he'd be beat, and concluded to send me down to New Orleans to be sold. Fortunate for me, he had a good son, who was very fond of me, and he gave me the secret. The same night, for I was to be shipped the next morning, I ran away and got to the Ohio River, twenty-five miles off, before they caught up to me. Billy Burns ran away with me. In the evening we tried to cross the river, but the ferryman wouldn't allow us, and began to whisper and talk suspicious-like in the crowd. We told him we were going to a village five or six miles further down, and then we walked away quick, going along down the bank of the river. After a little, we heard horses coming on the gallop and bloodhounds barking very hard. This made the cold chills creep down my back and my cheeks felt drawn queer. We ran and climbed to the top of a bushy tree. Soon they all went flying past force haste. We looked at each other and said, 'What will we do? All of a sudden Billy said, 'Let's take to the river.' "

"What! To try and swim across that great river?" I asked.

" 'Yes,' said Billy; 'we can do it. It's for our lives.' "

"I'm afraid," said I. "The night's dark; the river's wide and the water's cold."

" 'But we must,' said Billy, 'it's the only chance.' "

"Suppose we take the cramp or get exhausted, what then?"

" 'Well, I'd as soon be drowned as took. But come, Hall, we're both good swimmers, and we can reach the other shore,' said Billy, trying to encourage me like. At last, I concluded to swim the river or drown. We flung off our coats and plunged in. 'Twas a jump and a swim for life. 'Twas a long swim right ahead in the dark. We went slow. When we got about the middle, I said, 'Billy, I'm growing weak. I'll soon sink to rise no more.' "

" 'Hush!' said Billy; 'shut your mouth; stop that talk; turn over on your back and float. I'll put my hand under you to keep you up, and you'll rest.' After that we both rested a good many times. At last we reached the other side most dead, but safe. The next day we hid among the bushes and dried our clothes in the sun. We got two coats, and after a good rest we started for home. I walked twenty-three days till I came to Lake Erie, and crossing it in a schooner, got back to my old home at Amherstburg, just thirteen years after I'd been taken prisoner of war. When I left, John Wigle, Colonel Elliott, and some of the French had slaves, but there were no slaves when I came back. Lots of other changes had taken place. Most of my friends were dead and gone. My relations taken prisoner of war with me hadn't returned, and it was home for me no more. So I left, and in course of time came here."

"Well, well! What a great deliverance, to be sure," said Henson, as Hall closed his story. "I never expected to see you again when I left you at Haskill's, in Kentucky. In the Lord's mercy, we've both got a long way from our slave masters. At last our shackles are broken, and we're both our own masters now and for evermore. How thankful we should feel!"

"Well," said Hall, "so I do, and I always feel thankful to Billy too, for he saved me from going to the bottom of the Ohio River. Have you seen Mister Burns since you came?"

"Oh, yes," said Henson, "he helped Mister Simons and me put up our cook stove the day before yesterday. Well, well! Speak of the devil and you'll see him sure. Good morning, Mister Burns. I'm glad to see you. Take this chair, and I'll sit on the water pail bench." As soon as all three had shaken hands, Henson continued: "Mister Hall's just been telling me about your crossing the Ohio River when you were running away from slavery."

"Was he?" said the real Billy Burns, adding, "I often and often laugh to myself when I think of how we turned ourselves round and round to the sun on the bank of that great river to get our clothes dried, and about our hiding and peeking from the bushes, and the way we got them coats and hats the next day." At which Hall and Burns laughed heartily, while Henson wore a broad, appreciative and benignant [sic] smile. The two fairly revelled in the consciousness of an untrammelled liberty beneath a Canadian sky, as they have done many a time since, for all three still live in the same town. But that consciousness has been broadened and intensified by the fact that it has now no longer necessary to escape from slavery as they did, for a second Declaration of Independence, through the agency of a great civil war, has since restored the word "liberty" to

The British Methodist Episcopal Church, often referred to as "Little Zion," was established as an independent denomination on September 29, 1856 and served its congregation until 1911. This photograph was taken just before the frame church was demolished in 1993. Jim Henson was one of the church trustees.

its proper place in the first Declaration, and has broken the shackles of their race in the slave-holding South.

From the time of the meeting of the three escaped slaves just mentioned, down to the present, Henson has in the same place lived and laboured.

Personal as well as national history sometimes repeats itself. It is a year since the introductory chapter was written, and yet, near the spot in that chapter referred to, the writer, on looking out of an office window today—the hottest, so far this summer—saw, as he passed along on the opposite side of the same public thoroughfare, the same bent, broad figure. This man, now linked to two centuries and rapidly nearing the third—old man Henson, with his axe in one hand and his bucksaw in the other—using both to aid him in his locomotion—stopped and leaned his axe against one leg and his saw against the other, took off his hat, pulled out of his pocket a large red handkerchief and wiped the great drops of perspiration from his forehead, and then passed on with the crowd out of sight. This, too, is the last glimpse of him save one for the reader. It would be unfair to the man if, in conclusion, a peep were not given into the little brick church[8] on the bank of the Sydenham River, in which he worships from Sabbath to Sabbath, and of which he has long been a trustee. Here, in a recent fellowship meeting, he spoke as follows: "Brethren, the Lord has spared me many years. I've for a long time past put my trust in Him. He has been good to me, given me long life, good health and provided for my bodily wants. I'm very thankful for these great mercies to me. But, most of all, I praise Him because He set my captive soul at liberty, and still enables my poor heart to rejoice in His love. He has made me His child, and heir to His kingdom of grace here and to His kingdom of glory hereafter. The Holy Spirit is shed abroad in my heart, helping me to fight the good fight of faith. The devil sometimes hits me hard and wounds me sore. He often says, 'Do you expect to go to heaven?—kind of man you were in the early days—very wicked.' Then I remind him that Christ came to save the lost sheep, to save sinners, and I asked him if I'm not a sinner saved by grace? He quits bothering me then. Again, sometimes his agents try me. Only yesterday I met three white men on the street. One said to the others, 'Just see that old fella; he ought to be dead.' The others laughed loud. Then the powder flashed in the pan, and a feeling came up quick to say something ugly back, but I bridled my tongue. When my Master, the blessed saviour, was reviled, He reviled not again, so I said nothing. Brethren, this is the warfare within, the contest 'twixt good and evil. By God's grace, I expect to conquer every spiritual foe. The crown of life comes when the contest is over. I like Paul's experience about fighting the good fight, finishing his course, and the crown laid up. My work's about ended. I'm waiting for my Master to call, and when he calls I'll be forever with the Lord. Praise His holy name." Several hearty amens fell from the listening brethren as the old man took his seat.

Although thus resigned, the letters received during the past year have aroused recollections of former happy days at his Jersey home, and begotten a strong desire to see his distant friends. This had been the daydream of his life for many a year, but as age crept on and his opportunities lessened, the dream faded, until to the question, put by the writer, "How would you like to go and see them?" His quick answer came in the form of another question, "Ain't they all younger than I am, and won't I meet them in Heaven?" If life, however, be spared him, the invitation of

Major Truitt's daughter may yet be accepted, and his revived daydream soon realized by a visit *in propria persona* to "deah ole Jersey" and to the land of his childhood, early prime, and subsequent lifelong love—a land which now, happily, hears not the crack of the slave whip, sees not the whipping-house, and feels not the stigma of national inconsistency, as throughout that great slave land all slave shackles have been broken forever.

Epilogue

B ROKEN SHACKLES ends with Old Man Henson still working on the roads of Owen Sound. However, there doesn't appear to be any records of Henson in Owen Sound in the 1890s. In fact, there are few writings that tell of Henson returning home to his wife Kate and that this reunion may all be attributed to the famous watermelon photograph shown on the cover of this book.

In the book *From Quill to Ballpoint, 1591–1988,* the author, Dorothy Vick, mentions that the publication of *Broken Shackles* led to the reuniting of Henson and his wife in Philadelphia. But, a story in the July 1, 1927, Owen Sound *Daily Sun Times,* has the headline "Watermelon Means of Uniting Escaped Slave With His Wife" and carries a different version of the story. In this article, the newspaper contains these lines: "Taken with the photograph, he [Henson] set about to sell them among the friends in Owen Sound. By some means one got to a friend's house in Toronto, where the details of Henson's life were known. One day a preacher of the American Episcopal Church [coloured] was visiting at the Toronto home and in looking through the album came across [Henson's] picture with the watermelon. He became interested and learned the story."

The story continues with the American preacher making contact with Henson's wife and her family and initiating the correspondence from the United States. The writer adds that "Henson doubled his diligence and sold many of his photographs, until he had enough money to take him back to Maryland, where he was united with his wife, who was living with a granddaughter and thus his hopes and prayers were answered." The author of this article obviously had some of the information mixed up. For instance, Henson's wife was from New Jersey, not Maryland, and the letter in the first chapter of *Broken Shackles* indicates that she was not living with a granddaughter. However, the article certainly does suggest that the story of Jim Henson did not end in Owen Sound.

Any further information that would add to our understanding of the people, places and events mentioned in *Broken Shackles: Old Man Henson from Slavery to Freedom* would be received with appreciation.

Appendix

THE OLD DURHAM ROAD
PIONEER CEMETERY COMMITTEE

The Old Durham Road Pioneer Cemetery is located on Lot 21 Concession 1 North of the Durham Road, on the northeast corner of Grey Road #14 and the Durham Road. This is about 2.5 miles east of Priceville, Ontario, in present day Grey Highlands, formerly Township of Artemesia in Grey County. The Old Durham Road Pioneer Cemetery Committee is a voluntary group of citizens dedicated to the recognition of the contributions made by early pioneers of African descent. The Committee held its inaugural meeting in November 1989 and, in 1999, was formally incorporated under the umrella of the Ontario Historical Society.

The material that follows provides some background to the early history of these African settlers and work of the committee. A large number of the early settlers of the Old Durham Road were black. When Slavery was abolished in Upper Canada in 1793, it was not long before freed blacks and their descendants from the United States began coming across the border where life promised fewer hassles. Many others had come years earlier during the American Revolutionary war as part of the flood of United Empire Loyalist. A number of these pioneers of African descent made their way north up the Garafraxa Road to carve out new homes as early as the 1820s, in what is now the southern part of Grey County. In time, a growing black community was established in both Glenelg and Artemesia townships. Around the 1840s, as Scottish and Irish settlers moved into the area, they discovered the black settlers and regarded them as squatters. Some were driven out, and some went on to form another black community in Collingwood, Ontario.

The discovery of the four headstones at the Old Durham Road Cemetery in June, 1990, confirmed the presence of these early settlers. This is where they lived at least the last years of their lives, and this is where they rest. The markers found were for the following black settlers:

James Handy (1770–1863)
James Washington (1834–1856)

Founding meeting of the Old Durham Road Pioneer Cemetery Committee, November 1989. Left to right: Les MacKinnon, June MacLachlan, Clazien Catcher and Rev. Don Prince.

Christopher J. Simons (1835–1854), son of Chauncey and Mahatabele Simons, [his birth place according to the 1851 census was listed as Canada West]

Ellen Handy (1840–1856) [granddaughter of James Handy]

Although only four headstones have been reclaimed so far, we have reason to believe that this small cemetery plot contained the remains of possibly 50 to 60 black pioneers. The Pioneer Cemetery Committee is dedicated to:

reclaiming, transcribing and preserving grave stones; promoting research into all aspects of local black history; maintaining and beautifying the cemetery landscape.

The cemetery site has been surveyed and fenced, the acquisition of the burial site from the owner and its transfer to the township is completed. A display case for the fragmented headstones has been erected as a permanent setting on the site and a fund has been established to provide permanent care for the cemetery. The official recognition occurred in the fall of 1990.

The dedicated work of the Pioneer Cemetery Committee and its supporters culminated on the 13th of October, 1990, when Lt. Governor Lincoln Alexander visited the site of the "Almost Lost" Cemetery to unveil a memorial that honoured the early Black Pioneers of African descent.

Now, it is the committee's ongoing duty to arouse public awareness of, and pride in, this significant but little known aspect of our Community's past. "You must know the past to understand the present." As early as 1992, the long forgotten *Broken Shackles* came

Les MacKinnon, a member of the Pioneer Cemetery Committee, displays the four recovered grave markers.

The Durham Road Black Pioneer Cemetery site as it looked on the day of the dedication ceremony, October 13, 1990.

PHOTOGRAPH BY TED SHAW

Lieutenant Governor Lincoln Alexander unveils the inscribed boulder at the cemetery dedication ceremony.

to the committee's attention. Following many meetings and discussions, Peter Meyler who already was aware of the book through his research on Richard Pierpoint, accepted the challenge of being the editor of the proposed book. The republication of *Broken Shackles* is a totally new edition bearing the title, *Broken Shackles: Old Man Henson from Slavery to Freedom*, and is dedicated as a tribute to the early African settlers of this area of Grey County.

Old Durham Road Pioneer Cemetery Executive (Nov. 1999) and Book Committee:

Carolynn Wilson of Collingwood, President; Sylvia Wilson of Collingwood, Secretary; Peter Chepil of Markdale, Treasurer; Other members on the Book Committee: Pat Criddle of Collingwood; Les MacKinnon of Priceville, Howard Sheffield of Collingwood; Yvonne Wilson of Collingwood.

Notes

WHY REPUBLISH AN OLD BOOK

1 The quote attributed to Queen Elizabeth I is from *Capitalism and Slavery* by Eric Williams, (New York: Capricorn Books, 1966) 39.

EDITOR'S INTRODUCTION

1 T. Arthur Davidson, *A New History of the County of Grey.* (Owen Sound: The Grey County Historical Society, 1972) 314.

1. A LETTER FROM HOME

1 The town was Owen Sound, Ontario. Located on the southerly end of a sound whose name it bears, the town had originally been called Sydenham. The beginning of the community can be traced back to 1840. By 1888, at the time John Frost was writing this manuscript, Owen Sound was a major Great Lakes port, the railway had arrived in 1873 and arc street lights powered by a local small plant had just been in operation for one year.

2 The reference here to "dear old Jersey" would be to New Jersey, where some of Jim Henson's relatives lived.

3 The original text has the name as Milford. There is a town in northern New Jersey with that name, however the other place names referenced in the letter indicate that it should be Medford, a town across the state line from Philadelphia, Pennsylvania.

4 The original text used the name Cinnamon. The actual town in Burlington County, New Jersey, is Cinnaminson.

5 Source of these lines could not be located. Throughout the text there are many quotes, only some of which the editor was able to source. From this point on, only the identified quotes are annotated.

2. THE LONG, LONG AGO

1 The spelling of Croxall in the original text was Crocksell.

2 The original text spells the name as Baguirmi, however it is now more commonly spelled Bagirmi. It was one of three important states, the others being Kanem-Borno and Wadai, that now form part of Chad, Africa.

3 The river was spelled Shari in the original text, but the name is now commonly spelled Chari.

4 The original word in the text was "Arabs." This word was changed to "slavers." After reviewing the history of Bagirmi, it is highly unlikely that the slavers were Arabs. The reference to Arabs may just have been the prejudice of the day or there could be confusion between Muslim Africans and Arabs. It was felt that retaining the word Arabs in that context would give an incorrect impression of the history of Bagirmi.

5 Bagirmi, which itself dealt in slaves, was repeatedly raided in the 18th century by the neighbouring state of Wadai, even though both were Muslim kingdoms. It may have been one of these raids that led to the capture of Chandesia and her transport to North America.

6 A dhow is defined as a 19th century lateen-rigged Arab ship.

7 Richard Croxall's estate was described shortly after his death in 1795. The records show that the farm had 64 sheep, 143 hogs and pigs, 17 horses and colts and 66 cows, steers and bulls. John Marsh was the overseer of the farm and 31 slaves. The 1798 tax records show an estate of 957 acres which included property in addition to Garrison Forest. The property contained the main frame house which was 62 x 18 feet with a piazza of 62 x 8 feet, together with a stone milkhouse, a frame smokehouse, a poultry house, 2 slave quarters and 2 acres of ground. There were at least 12 more buildings on the remaining acreage.

3. STARS AND SCARS

1 Thomas Campbell, a Scottish poet born in Glasgow in 1777, was also recognized as a biographer and historian. He died in 1844. The "familiar lines" are from "Epigram to the United States of America." The work can be found in *The Complete Poetical Works of Thomas Campbell*. Edited with notes by J. Logie Roberston, Lincoln, New York: Oxford University Press, 1907.

4. "THE MISSIS"

1 Henson must have been confused about the actual timing of events in this case since Richard Croxall died in 1785. His wife, Catherine, was left the estate at that time. The date of her death is not known, but records indicate that James Croxall became the owner of Garrison Forest by the early nineteenth century.

5. A NEW MASTER

1 In the original text the name is spelled as Coughlin, however Charles Cockey was the purchaser of 454 3/4 acres of the estate after James Croxall died in 1809. The Garrison Forest estate, which was made up of 900 acres in total, was divided into three lots and offered for sale on December 7, 1809.

2 The original text uses the name Gwinne's Falls, but Owings Falls is found near Garrison Forest.

6. JOSH

1 The spelling was Willmore in the original text.

2 It appears that Josh was showing off by drinking a quart of milk, and got "stuck" when he was unable to hold any more inside.

3 Excerpt from "The Raven" written in 1845 by Edgar Allan Poe (born in Boston on January 19, 1809, died on October 7, 1849).

7. THE PICKET

1 The story that follows does not seem to match the overall timeline of events. Orrick Ridgely does, however, become Charley's master as explained in the following chapter, Chapter 8.

2 In the original text, the last name is given as Paul, however this man was John Hall, who later would become a resident of Owen Sound, Ontario.

8. THE RIDGELYS

1 The spelling was Ridgeley in the original text.

2 No specific reference to this enactment or to General Swan could be found.

3 This master may have been James Croxall Jr., since James Croxall Sr. had died in 1809 and Ridgely served as governor between 1816 and 1819, having been originally elected in 1815.

9. JOHN HALL

1 The name is Cutlett in the original text, but it is likely the officer was Captain Calmes Catlett from Frederick County, Virginia. He moved to Kentucky around 1817 so it may have been at this time that John Hall was sold to Haskill.

10. TRADE IN SLAVES

1 "This Missouri question has betrayed the secret of their souls"
—John Quincy Adams, February 24, 1820, Washington D.C.

Missouri's impending admission to the Union as a slave state was about to upset the careful balance of power between free and slave states. To maintain the status quo, the Missouri Compromise created the free state of Maine out of northern Massachusetts and set a dividing line between north and south that would act as a boundary between free and slave states. Missouri would be the only slave state allowed north of the line. The deal did not solve any problems it only delayed the Civil War (1860–1865). Information is taken from *Eyewitness to America,* edited by David Colbert, (New York: Pantheon 1977) 120.

The debate regarding which new states entering the Union would permit slavery led to the Missouri Compromise. In 1850, the compromise slavery solutions were laid before the U.S. senate.

2 The reference is to John C. Calhoun, a senator from South Carolina.

3 Possibly Austin Woodhawke, as an Austin Woodhawke, a slave trader appears later in this chapter.

4 On May 31, 1889, the South Fork Dam on the Conemaugh River gave way, releasing 20 million tons of water down the mountain valleys towards Johnstown (Pennsylvania). By the time the water had passed, 2,209 people were dead and more than 27,000 were homeless. From the *Toronto Star*, December 9, 2000, p.L31.

5 Taken from "The Witness" written in 1842 by Henry Wadsworth Longfellow (born in Portland, Maine in 1807, died 1882).

11. BIG BOB

1 Interestingly, no reference as to the meaning of "ironing off carriages" could be found.

2 Taken from "Our Countrymen in Chains" by John Greenleaf-Wittier (1807–1892), a contemporary of Longfellow.

12. AMUSEMENTS

1 Bonny-clabber is curdled milk or cottage cheese, a type of food according to the *American Heritage Dictionary*.

2 "Estray," was a word in common usage in the late 1880s. Estray when used in the context of slavery means stray, as defined in the *American Heritage Dictionary*.

3 The reference to the colour yellow would denote a lighter skin colour.

4 The 1996 *Oxford English Dictionary* states that the term "Sambo" is "slang, offensive. A black person. A person of mixed race." Joseph Boskin elaborates at great lengths upon the etymology of the term, tracing it through several lineages, pointing out specific African dialects where "Hausa Sam bo" translates to "name given the second son" or in mende and Vai dialect, where it is used as a term of derision . ("Via sam bo" equates with "to disgrace.") The earliest appearance of the name on an American document was upon the cargo roles of the ship *Margarett*, docked in St. Mary's, Maryland, in 1692. Thereafter, the name appears with increasing frequency, in plays, in runaway slave bills, in census toles. The growing association with comedy during the 1700s and early 1800s is exemplified in its association with music, lysrics, folk sayings and material artifacts. Information was researched by Rebecca Snyder, doctoral student of Syracuse University. For how the name made the leap in terms of symbolic connection and information on the term "Sambo" see: Joseph Baskin, *Sambo: The Rise and Demise of an American Jester*. New York, Oxford: Oxford University Press, 1986.

5 This last two lines are from the song "Oh! Susannah" written in 1848 by Stephen Foster. Born in 1826 in Lawrenceville, east of Pittsburgh, he died in 1864. No source reference could be found for the preceding songs identified in the text as part of serenading customs.

18. EMILY

1 Excerpt from song "The Swanee River" (Old Folks At Home) by Stephen Foster (1826–1864).

19. CORN HUSKING

1 Source of this song not known and the following songs not known.

20. WONDERFUL MEETINGS

1 No reference found for these statements of legislative enactments.

21. A CAMP MEETING

1 In the original text the surname is spelled Coco. However, this may be Daniel Coker who was a minister involved in the formation of the African Methodist Episcopal Church. He was born in Frederick County, Maryland, the son of an indentured English woman and an African slave. He changed his name to Daniel Coker after his escape from slavery.
2 Frederick C. Douglass was born around 1817 on the eastern shore of Maryland. After escaping slavery in 1838, he became one of the most eloquent leaders of the abolition movement. He was the U.S. ambassador to Haiti from 1889 to 1891. Douglass died in 1895.
3 Thomas Henry Miller was a trustee of the British Methodist Episcopal Church in Owen Sound and an acquaintance of Jim Henson. According to Ken Barker in "British Methodist Episcopal," a Church History column for the Owen Sound *Sun Times* [not dated], Thomas Miller was the first minister at the original British Methodist Episcopal Church.
4 It is not clear who Nancy Smith was, since no reference has been found for her. The most famous woman preacher at this time was Mrs. Jarena Lee. She was born around 1780 in Cape May, New Jersey to Free African American parents. She was the first woman allowed to preach by Richard Allen, the Bishop of the African Methodist Episcopal Church. This occurred in 1819 and she became a travelling minister, covering thousands of miles on foot.
5 These many African-American spirituals represent a musical legacy known around the world.

22. TURNING OVER A NEW LEAF

1 According to the *Canadian Oxford Dictionary*, Whitsuntide is the weekend or week including Pentecost, a Christian festival observed on the seventh Sunday after Easter, commemorating the descent of the Holy Spirit on the disciples.

24. SOLD AGAIN

1 Editor's Note: I was unable to find any definition of "grubbing knees for vessels." Any background information would be appreciated.
2 A shot factory is likely one that produces ammunition for muskets and cannons.

27. THE ESCAPE

1 Many members of the Quaker faith were involved in helping fugitive slaves. Among the leaders were Levi and Catherine Coffin. Levi Coffin was known as the "President" and his home as "Grand Central Station" of the Underground Railroad. For more information see *Underground Railroad*, produced by the Division of Publications National Park Service, U.S. Department of the Interior, Washington D.C.

2 According to a Bible published by Oxford University Press in 1912, Numbers 23:14 refers to Moses at the top of Pisgah in the Zophin fields (now in Jordan).

28. OVER THE RIVER

1 The church that Henson attended was likely Mother Bethel African Methodist Episcopal Church in Philadelphia. At this time, the structure was known as the roughcast church, the second one to be erected on the site. The property is now home to the fourth church which was completed in 1890. The lot is the oldest parcel of land that has been continuously owned by black people in the United States. It had been purchased by Richard Allen, one of the founders of the AME in 1787.

29. STEPHEN GIRARD

1 Stephen Girard was a native of France and is said to be America's first millionaire.
2 Stephen Girard's will, dated 1830, bequeathed $300,000 to the Commonwealth of Pennsylvania and $6,000,000 in cash and real estate to the City of Philadelphia. The bulk of his estate was to be used for the establishment of Girard College, a boarding school for "poor, white, male orphans." The school was opened in 1848. In 1968, the clause "poor, white, male orphans" was struck from the will by the Supreme Court of the United States. The gig (a light two-wheeled one-horse carriage) used by Stephen Girard is still on display in the college.
3 Stephen Girard died on December 26, 1831. He left lifetime incomes to a number of women in his will. One was his slave, Hannah, who was at his bedside when he died. She had served him for over 50 years. Hannah received her freedom as well as an annual income.

30. FLIGHT TO NEW JERSEY

1 The first Fugitive Slave Law passed by Congress in 1793 affirmed the Constitutional rights of slaveholders to their property. In 1850, the Fugitive Slave Law required escapees to be returned, and permitted the recapture and extradition of escaped slaves with the assistance of federal marshals.

31. THE UNDERGROUND RAILROAD

1 The Underground Railroad is the name given to the many ways that African-Americans took to escape slavery in the United States before the Civil War.

33. JOHN BROWN

1 John Brown, a fiery abolitionist, dedicated his life to the destruction of slavery. With 18 men, Brown unsuccessfully attacked the U.S. Arsenal at Harpers Ferry, Virginia (now West Virginia).

34. THE FUGITIVE SLAVE LAW

1 The rescued slave was Shadrach Minkins. He became the focal point of the battle between slave-holders and abolitionists with his arrest in Boston on February 15, 1851.

A group of black men freed Minkins and facilitated his escape to Canada. For more information see *Shadrach Minkins, From Fugitive Slave to Citizen* by Gary Collison.

35. A SECOND DECLARATION OF INDEPENDENCE

1 In 1846, a landmark legal case reached the U.S. Supreme Court. Dred Scott sued for his freedom. Taken into free territory by his owner, but returned to Missouri, a slave state, Scott argued that his earlier residency made him a free man. Ultimately, in 1857, the Supreme Court declared that Scott, as a bondsperson, was not recognized as a U.S. citizen under the Constitution. Therefore, Dred Scott was not eligible to sue in the courts.

2 In 1808, the United States abolished trade in slaves from Africa.

3 In 1863, Abraham Lincoln's Proclamation took effect, abolishing slavery in the Confederacy. The Union intensified their recruitment of blacks as soldiers in the Civil War.

4 Harriet Beecher Stowe's best-selling novel, *Uncle Tom's Cabin*, was published in the United States in 1852. The book, based on the memoirs of runaway slaves and abolitionist reports, focused national attention on slavery.

36. OFF FOR CANADA

1 In the original text, the name is spelled Simmons. However, a fragment of the gravestone of his son Christopher shows that the name was Simons. The burial site of Christopher Simons is the Old Durham Road Pioneer Cemetery in Artemesia township of Grey County. On October 13, 1990, this cemetery was officially recognized in a special ceremony involving the Hon. Lincoln Alexander, then the Lieutenant Governor of Ontario.

2 The Township of Artemesia is located in southeastern Grey County. Today, Artemesia township is part of the newly amalgamated Grey Highlands.

3 According to Les MacKinnon, this is a name believed to represent a portion of, or possibly all, of the Beaver Valley as it is known today.

4 Today, this is Eugenia Falls.

5 This stretch would have been that portion of today's Old Durham Road beginning, to the east, at its intersection with the Lake Wilcox Road and moving westward towards Priceville, Ontario.

6 Poulett Street (now known as 2nd Avenue) was the main street in Owen Sound.

7 John "Daddy" Hall lived in Owen Sound for his remaining years. He never gained title to his land even though he had been one of the earliest settlers in the town, arriving in the 1840s. Hall was reported to have had 5 wives over the years and at least 21 children. He died in April of 1900 and was said to be 117 years old. His youngest daughter and only remaining child, Elizabeth, died in April of 1951 at the age of 98.

8 This church would have been the British Methodist Episcopal Church known as Little Zion. The original structure no longer exists.

Bibliography

_____, *Underground Railroad*. Washington D.C.: National Park Service, U.S. Department of the Interior (not dated).

Baskin, Joseph, *Sambo: The Rise and Demise of an American Jester.* New York, Oxford: Oxford University Press, 1986.

Cathcart, Ruth, *How Firm a Foundation: Historic Houses of Grey County*. Wiarton: The Red House Press, 1996.

Colbert, David (ed.), *Eyewitness to America*. New York: Pantheon, 1977.

Collison, Gary, *Shadrach Minkins, From Fugitive Slave to Citizen*. Cambridge: Harvard University Press, 1997.

Davidson, T. Arthur, *A New History of the County of Grey*. Owen Sound: The Grey County Historical Society, 1972.

Meyler, David and Peter Meyler, *A Stolen Life: Searching for Richard Pierpoint.* Toronto: Natural Heritage Books, 1999.

Vick, Dorothy, *From Quill to Ballpoint 1591–1988*. Owen Sound: self-published, 1988.

White, Paul, *Owen Sound: The Port City*. Toronto: Natural Heritage Books, 2000.

Williams, Eric, *Capitalism and Slavery*. New York: Capricorn Books, 1966.

Illustration Credits

Black and white engravings:
> These illustrations, including the frontispiece, are taken from the original book published in 1889. Some of the artworks would appear to have the initials of the artist, others do not. Names of the artists are not known.

Archival photographs/visuals:
> John Frost (p. xv) and John "Daddy" Hall (p. 193) are courtesy of the County of Grey-Owen Sound Museum.
>
> The Atlantic Hotel and Beach front, Cape May, New Jersey (p.168). Courtesy of Pat Pennington Pocher Private Collection, Cape May.
>
> Bethel African Methodist Episcopal Church (p.160). Courtesy of this church in Philadelphia.

More contemporary photographs:
> Sheldon Place (p. xv): Photographer Ruth Cathcart
>
> Black Methodist Episcopal Church (Owen Sound) (p. 196). Courtesy Paula Niall Collection
>
> Old Durham Road Pioneer Cemetery Committee, inaugural meeting (p. 202). Photographer Sharon MacKinnon
>
> Les MacKinnon with the four tombstones (p. 203); Black Pioneer Cemetery at time of dedication (p. 203); Lt. Governor Lincoln Alexander unveiling inscribed boulder (p. 204). Photographer Ted Shaw.

Maps:
> Developed by Peter Meyler.

Front Cover:
> Jim "Old Man" Henson in his famous watermelon picture. Courtesy County of Grey-Owen Sound Museum.

Back Cover:
> Grave marker of James Handy, Old Durham Road Pioneer Cemetery. Photographer Ted Shaw.

Index

Abolition, 15

Abolitionists, 15

Act of Gradual Manumission, 15

Adams, John Quincy, 207

Africa, x, xvii, 8, 98, 174, 175, 186

African Methodist Episcopal Church, 209

Agabeg (Portuguese slaver), 8, 9

Akitt, Levi, 154

Albany (NY), 180

Alexander, Lincoln (Lt. Gov.), 202, 204, 211

Alexandria (VA), 127–130

Allen, Richard (Bishop), 209, 210

America, 10, 21

American Episcopal Church, 199

American Civil War, 195, 207, 210

American Revolution (American War of
   Independence), 10, 35, 201

Amherstburg (Upper Canada), 37, 195

Artemesia Falls, 190

Ashton, __Mrs. (Raymond), 78

Atlantic Ocean, 63, 64

Auburn (NY), 187

Augusta, (GA), 171

Back River, 34, 78

Back River Neck (MD), 47, 60, 76, 77

Badgley, Major, 109

Bagirmi (Africa), 8, 206

Bain, Jack, 86, 88, 90, 91

Bain, Sam, 86–92

Baltimore (MD), xvi, 8, 10, 23, 39, 41,
   46, 51, 57, 71, 125, 143, 148, 154, 157,
   159, 167, 174

Baptist Church, 49, 170

Barr, Harry, 58

Barton, __ Mr., 138–140, 154, 166, 167

Baskin, Joseph, 208

Beaver Valley (Grey County), 211

Bethel Church (see Mother Bethel
   African Methodist Episcopal Church)

Big Bob (Cassie's husband), 49–55

Biglow, Colonel, 132

Bird River, 34

Bixby, Sam, 156

Black, Bill, 80

Blue Mountains, 190

Boston (MA), 11, 183, 207, 210

Bowey, Harry, 124

British Methodist Episcopal Church
   (Owen Sound), 209, 211

Broken Shackles, x, xii, xiv, xvi, xviii, 199,
   200, 202

Broderick, __ (farmer), 169

Brown, John, 180–182, 210

Brown, Parson, 23–25

Brownsville (OH), 47

Buchanan, James (President), 20

Buchanan, George (Dr.), 21–22, 133

Buchanan, James (Colonel), 20–21

Buck, __ Mr., 40

Bull's Head Tavern, 60–62, 64, 68, 87, 124
Burlington County (NJ), 205
Burns, Billy, 194, 195
Burns, Tom, 164, 165
Bush River Neck (MD), 61
Bytown (Ottawa), xvi
Byers, __ Dr., 183

Caldicott's planation, 30
Calhoun, John C. (Senator), 45. 207
Campbell, Thomas, 14, 206
Canada, xvii 37, 41, 183–185, 188–190, 194, 210
Canahan, Christopher, 26
Canard River, 37
Cape May (NJ), 168, 188
Capitalism and Slavery, 205
Carroll, Charles, 14
Caskey, "Old" (plantation owner), 69–73, 94–99, 134, 136, 137
Cassie (Big Bob's wife), 49–55
Catcher, Clazien, 202
Catlett, Calmes, (Captain), 42, 207
Caesar, Julius, 183
Centerville (MD), 46
Centennial Exhibition (1876), 187
Chad (Africa), 206
Chance:
    Charley (Charles) (see also Jim Henson), xvi, xvii, 8, 10, 12, 14, 16, 17, 19–29, 34–44, 47, 56, 57, 61–65, 68–74, 77–79, 94–96, 98–100, 107, 108, 110, 115, 124, 125, 127, 131–145, 149, 151–159
    Cornelius (see also William Henson), 17, 141, 156, 157, 159
    Emily (Johnson) (Mrs. Charley), 96–100, 107, 108, 134, 135, 137, 139, 140, 167
    Fanny, 18, 19, 22, 139, 141
    Helen, 19
    Peggy, 8, 10, 11, 17–20, 22, 143, 156
    Pete, 19, 156, 157
    Phil, 19
    Polly (Poll), 19
    Sally, 19

Sam Jr., 19, 22, 133
Sam (Samuel) Sr., 8, 11, 12, 17, 19, 20
Susy, 19, 22
Tom, 18, 19
Chandesia (grandmother of Charley Chance), 8, 9, 206
Charity (Girard's servant), 163, 165
Charleston, (WV), 181
Chepil, Peter, 204
Chesapeake Bay, 56
Cinnaminson (NJ), 6, 205
Clemens, __ Brother, 161
Cobourg (ON), xv
Cockey, Charles, 26, 206
Coffin, Catherine, 209
Coffin, Levi, 209
Coker, Dan, 115, 117, 209
Colbert, David, 207
Collingwood (ON), 201, 204
Collison, David, 210
Columbia (PA), 143, 149, 152–155
Complete Works of Thomas Campbell, The, 206
Conemaugh River, 207
Confederacy, the, 211
Congress (U.S.), 13, 45, 174, 210
Cook, __Widow, 161
Craig, __, Mr. (photographer), 4
Criddle, Pat, 204
Croxall, xviii, 205
    Betsey, (Miss) (later Mrs. John Wilmore), 26, 29
    Catherine (Old Missus) (Mrs. Richard), 16, 17, 19–23, 25, 26, 39, 131, 158, 206
    James Jr., 26, 39, 207
    James Sr., 21–23, 25, 26, 206, 207
    Richard (Dick), 8, 11, 16, 23, 38, 74, 206
    Richard (Dick) (nephew), 21
Croxall plantation, 12, 20, 75
Cuba, 171
Cuckoo Valley, 190

Davidson, Jacob, 139, 140, 142, 143, 148, 154, 155
Davidson, T. Arthur, 205

Davis, __ Dr., 47
Debbs, Henry, 99, 100, 137
Declaration of Independence, 5, 13, 14, 173, 186, 195, 196
Dedrick, Nelson, 49–52
Delaware, 127, 128, 174
Delware River, 163, 166
Detroit River, 37, 42, 43 37, 42, 43
Dickson, Chris, 153, 154
Dilworth's spelling book, 39
Dingley, Jim, 108
Dorsey, __, Mrs. (Ridgely), 38
Douglass, Fred (Frederick), 115. 209
Dred Scott Case, 186
Duke, __ Sister, 121–123
Dunwaddy, __ Mr., 51, 53, 54
Dunwaddy, __ Mrs., 53, 54
Dunwaddy plantation, 53
Durham Road, 191, 201
Durham Road Pioneer Cemetery (Old), 201, 211

East, Joe, 85. 86, 90
Eastman, __ Mrs., 90
Eastman, Ted, 85–91
Eaton, Simon, 161
Elliott, Colonel, 195
Emancipation Act (New York), 15
Emancipation Day, 5
England, 10, 21, 42
Episcopal Church, 74
"Essay on Man", 130
Eugenia Falls (Grey County), 211
Eyewitness to America, 207

Falls of Niagara, 189
Ferguson, __ (grocer), 4
Fillmore, Millard (President), 183
Fleming County, 41
Flemingsburg (KY), 41
Foster, Stephen, 208
France, 15
Frederick County (MD), 209
Frederick County (VA), 207
Freeman, W.H., 132, 134, 136, 138, 139
Frogmore Landing (MD), 57
From Quill to Ballpoint, 1591–1988, 199

Frost: xiii
    John (Jr.), xvi–xviii
    John (Sr.), xiv, 193
    Mary, xiv
Fugitive Slave Law, xvii, 166, 183, 186, 210

Garafraxa Road, 201
Garrison Forest (plantation), 8, 206
Geddis, __(market gardener), 143
George III (King of England), 13
Georgia, 45, 49–51, 158, 170, 171
Georgian Bay, xi, xv, 5, 190, 193
Girard, Stephen, 162–165, 210
Girard Bank, 164
Girard College, 163, 210
Girard farm, 162
Great Britain, 5, 9, 11
Greenleaf-Whittier, John, 208
Grey County, x, xvi, 190, 201, 203, 211
Grey Highlands, 201, 211
Gulf of Guinea, 9

Hagerstown (MD), 49, 52
Haiti, 115, 164, 209
Hall, John "Daddy", xvi, 37, 41–44, 193–195, 207, 211
Hamilton, __, Mr., 108, 109, 126
Hamilton, __, Mrs. (Badgley), 109
Handy, Ellen, 202,
Handy, James, 201, 202
Happy Hunchy (The India Rubber Man), 121, 122
Harper's Ferry (VA), 180, 210
Hartford County (MD), 76
Haskill, __, (slave owner), 41, 42, 44, 194, 195, 207
Hawkins, Eli, 125
Hawkins, Isanthe, 125
Henson:
    Catherine (Kate) (Mrs. James), 5, 6
    Comfort, 5
    Jim (James) "Old Man" (formerly Charley Chance), xiii, xiv, xvi–xviii 3, 4, 6, 8. 20, 159, 160, 162–169, 174–182, 185, 188–196, 199, 200, 205, 209, 210

Kate (Catherine) (Truitt) (Mrs.
    James), 167, 188, 199
Mary (Mrs. William), 157, 158
Rose, 5
William (Bill) (formerly Cornelius
    Chance), 154, 157–159, 180, 182
Hickey, __, Lawyer, 83, 84
Hicks, Aaron, 155
Hidden Creek, 163
Howard, Cornelius, 26, 28, 139
Hunter, Dan, 81–83
Husband, Burt, 143, 144
Hut, __ Sister, 161

Jamieson, __, Dr., 115, 123
Jefferson, Thomas, 13
Johnson:
    Emily (see Emily Chance)
    __ Mr., 96, 134–136
    __ Mrs., 135
    Tom, 135, 136
Johnston, Sam, 155–157
Johnstown (PA), 48, 207
Josh (Josiah) (Charlie Chance's cousin),
    29–34, 207
Joyce, Elder, 116–119

Kanem-Borno (Africa), 206
Kentucky, 41–43, 194, 195, 207

Lake Erie, 195
Lake Champlain, 180
Lake Wilcox Road, 211
Lancaster (PA), 152, 154, 155, 180
Lancaster Country, 165
Lee, Jarena (Mrs.) 209
Leester, John, 75
Leester planation, 76
Lincoln, Abraham (President), 156, 186,
    187, 211
Littlejohn, __ Dr., 155
Lloyd, Edward (Lieut.), 115
Lockport (NY), 188, 190
Long Green (MD), 143
Longfellow, Henry Wadsworth, 208
Louis XIV (King of France), 15
Lower Canada, 15

Lower River Neck (MD), 124
Lucinda (Caskey's cook), 69, 72, 73,
    94–97, 99, 100, 137
Lyon, Nathan (Preacher), 115, 117, 118,
    123

MacKinnon, Les, 202–204, 211
MacLachlan, June, 203
Madison, James (President), 42
Mallory (slave owner), 81–84
Maine, 207
Margarett (slave ship), 208
Markdale (ON), 204
Marsh, John, 206
Maryland, xiii, xiv, xvi, 10, 11, 14, 18, 38,
    41, 45–47, 48, 51, 52, 56, 115, 118,
    144, 148, 151, 158, 159, 172, 183, 185,
    199, 200, 209
Massachusetts, 15, 207
Maynard, __ (bootblack), 157, 158
Medford (NJ), 5, 166, 205
Meyler, Peter, xviii, 203
Michigan, 190
Middle River, 34, 57, 58, 61, 124
Middle River Neck (MD), 39, 61, 112,
    114
Middobo (great-grandfather of Charley
    Chance), 8
Miller, Thomas Henry, 115, 209
Miller's Island, 169, 188
Minkins, Shadrach, 210
Missouri, 207, 210
Missouri Compromise Debate, 45, 207
Morgan, Dan, 42
Mother Bethel African Methodist Epis-
    copal Church (Philadelphia), 160,
    161, 210
Mufflin, James, 149

Napoleon (Charley's companion), 155
Neelands, John (Rev.), 193
New History of Grey County, A, xvi, 205
New Jersey, xiii, 5, 6, 166, 167, 185, 189,
    192, 198, 200, 205
New Orleans (LA), 45, 46, 171, 172,
    194
New York, 15, 180, 188

New York (NY), 139, 155, 180
Niagara Falls (ON), xiii, 43
Niagara River, 42
North, the, 186, 187
North Elba (NY), 180

Ohio, 44, 47
Ohio River, 41, 46, 194, 195
Old Durham Road Pioneer Cemetery
    Committee, xi, 201, 202, 204
"Old Missus" (see Catherine Croxall)
"Our Countrymen in Chains", 208
Owen Sound (ON), xiii–xvii, 115, 192,
    199, 200, 205, 207
Owen Sound *Daily Sun Times*, 199
Owens, Jack, 28, 35
Owings Falls (MD), 26, 41, 206
Owings Mills, 37
Oxsby, __ (farmer), 192
Oxsby, Becky, 192

Patapsco River, 33, 34
Peggy (see Peggy Chance)
Pennsylvania, xiii, 143, 144, 148, 149,
    157, 180, 185
Perkins, __ Brother, 161
Pete (Charlie Chance's cousin), 77, 78
Philadelphia (PA), 13, 15, 118, 152, 159,
    160, 162–167, 169–177, 180, 183, 187,
    199, 205, 210
Pierpoint, Richard, xiii, 203
Pickle, Ben, 76, 77
Pleasant Valley, 180
Poe, Edgar Allan, 207
Poll (sister to Peggy Chance), 10, 74, 79
Pope, Alexander, 130
Potomac River, 127
Potter, Mary, 161
Poulett Street (Owen Sound), 193, 211
Priceville (ON), 201, 211
Prince, Don (Rev.), 202
Providence (RI), 13
Purvis, __ Mr., 184

Quaker(s), 142, 155, 184, 185, 209
Quigley:
    Charles, 80
        Philip, 80
        Walter, 79, 80

Ramsay, Jake, 47
Rattray, Rev. Benjamin Franklin,
    127–130, 136
"Raven, The", 207
Raven, Thomas, 68
Raymond:
    Horseth, 77, 78
    __Mrs., 78
    Oscar, 77, 78
Raymond plantation, 77
Reed, __ (fishernan), 33
Rhynaker, George, 26
Ridgely:
    Charles (Governor), 38, 207
    David, 38
    Nicholas Orrick, 35, 38, 39, 41, 44, 68,
        69, 85, 94, 107, 108, 125, 127, 131,
        132, 139, 142, 194, 207
Ridgely's farm (planation), 56, 81, 108, 132
Rift (freed slave), 171, 172,
Ringo, Reverend, 127,–130
River Chari, 8, 206
River Niger, 8
River Nile, 8
Rollins, G.W., 131
Roman Catholic Church, 15
Ross, Joe (Mr.) (overseer), 23, 29
Ruff, Hannibal, 161
Russell, Peter, (Governor), 15
Rutledge's plantation, 99

Sambo: The Rise and Demise of an Amer-
    ican Jester, 208
Schuylkill Point (PA), 162
Scott, Dred, 210, 211
Seward, W.H., 189
Shadrach Minkins, From Fugitive Slave to
    Citizen, 210
Shaw, Ralph, 170, 171
Sheffield, Howard, 204
Sheldon Place (Owen Sound), xiii, xiv, xv
Shoal Creek (MD), 45
Shockley, Isaac, 5
Silverthorne, Lawrence, 45

Simons,
  Chauncey, 190, 193, 195, 202
  Christopher J., 202, 211
  Mahatabele, 202
Sleeper, General, 125
Smiley, Elijah, 47
Smith, McEwan (Dr.), 180
Smith, Garrett, 180
Smith, Nancy, 115, 118, 209
Snider, George, 191
Snyder, Rebecca, xviii, 208
South, the, 186, 187, 196
South Carolina, 45, 51, 53, 54, 207
South Fork Dam, 207
St. Mary's (MD), 208
Stansbury, John, 47
Steele, __ Mrs.,171, 172
Stephens, Abel, 185
Stoney Creek (ON), 42
Stowe, Harriet Beecher (Mrs.), xvi, 187,
  211
Supreme Court of the United States,
  186, 210, 211
Susquehanna River, 144, 148, 149
Swan, __ (General), 38
Sydenham (Owen Sound), xiv, xvi, 205
Sydenham River, 197
Syracuse University, xviii, 205

Taney, Chief Justice, 173
Taylor, Mary, xvi
Taylor, President, 183
Tecumseh (Native Chief), 42
Tompkins, __Brother, 161
Toronto (ON), 188, 199
Township of Artemesia, 190=193, 201, 211
Township of Glenelg, xiv, 201
Triplet, Fred, 194
Troy (NY), 180
Truitt:
  Kate (see Kate Henson)
  Julia, 6
  John, 6
  Major, 198
Tyson, Theophilius, 138, 139

Uncle Tom's Cabin, 187, 211
Uncle Harry (Charley's uncle), 143
Underground Railroad, xvii, 170
Underground Railroad, 209
Union, the (U.S.), 15, 45, 207, 211
United Empire Loyalists, 201
United States, 14, 15, 42, 168, 183, 185,
  186, 199, 201, 210, 211
Upper Canada, 15, 190, 201

Venables, Job, 174–177, 179
Vick, Dorothy, 199
Victoria College (Cobourg), xv
Virginia, 13, 51, 85, 128, 129, 194
Virginia Convention (1774), 13

Wadai (Africa), 206
War of 1812, 28, 35
Washington (DC), 37, 41, 42, 127, 128, 181
Washington, James, 201
Watkins, John, 151–155
Watkins, Manda, 152, 153
West Indies, 5, 180
White, Bell, 180
White, __Sister, 160
Whitehall (NY), 180
Wicker, Master, 108
Wigle, John, 195
Williams, Eric, 205
Williams, Jerry, 112–114
Wilmore, Mrs. John (see Betsy Croxall)
Wilmington (DE), 174
Wilson, Carolynn, 204
Wilson, Dick, 154
Wilson, Joe, 112, 114
Wilson, Sylvia, 204
Wilson, Yvonne, 204
Winchester (VA), 42
"Witness, The". 208
Woodhawke, Austin, 45–47, 207
Workman, Tom, 160
Worthington, Moses, 5
Wrightsville(PA) 5, 149

Young, Joe, 115, 116, 119
Young, __ Mr. (tavern owner), 143